GERMANS IN ILLINOIS

GERMANS IN

MIRANDA E. WILKERSON
AND HEATHER RICHMOND

Southern Illinois University Press
Carbondale

Southern Illinois University Press
www.siupress.com

Printed in the United States of America

22 21 20 19 4 3 2 1

Cover illustration: *background, top*, map showing percentage born in Germany living in Illinois, by county, 1870 (data from the 1870 U.S. census, "Selected Nativities by County," table VII); *background, bottom*, page from first-grade reader used in German American schools (from Witter's *Deutsch-Englische Schreib- und Lese-Fibel*, 1904, courtesy Max Kade Institute for German-American Studies at the University of Wisconsin–Madison); *foreground, top*, Weltin family in front of 1027 Hampshire, ca. 1910 (courtesy Historical Society of Quincy and Adams County); *foreground, bottom*, Siebel's Brewing Academy, circa 1902–4 (courtesy Chicago History Museum, ICHi-17537).

Library of Congress Cataloging-in-Publication Data
Names: Wilkerson, Miranda E., [date] author. | Richmond, Heather, [date] author.
Title: Germans in Illinois / Miranda E. Wilkerson and Heather Richmond.
Description: Carbondale, IL : Southern Illinois University Press, [2019] | Includes bibliographical references and index.
Identifiers: LCCN 2018043051 | ISBN 9780809337217 (pbk.) | ISBN 9780809337224 (e-book)
Subjects: LCSH: German Americans—Illinois—History. | German Americans—Illinois—Social conditions. | German Americans—Illinois—Cultural assimilation. | Germans—Illinois—History. | Immigrants—Illinois—History—19th century. | Illinois—Emigration and immigration—History—19th century. | Germany—Emigration and immigration—History—19th century.
Classification: LCC F550.G3 W55 2019 | DDC 977.3/00431—dc23
LC record available at https://lccn.loc.gov/2018043051

Printed on recycled paper. ♲

To Adah

CONTENTS

List of Figures ix

Acknowledgments xi

1. **Introduction** 1
   Sidebar / A Note about German Pronunciation 10
2. **Nineteenth-Century German Immigration and Settlement** 12
   Sidebar / Grays vs. Greens 19

   Side Stories
   A German State in the Upper Mississippi Valley 28
   Gustav Körner 29
3. **The Journey to Illinois** 33

   Side Stories
   Cornelius Schubert: Diary of a Journey 38
   1868 New York Immigration Commission Report on the *Leibnitz* 43
4. **Rural and Urban Living** 48

   Side Stories
   Observations of Industrial Working Conditions 63
   Chicago's Brewing Industry 72
5. **Nativism, Politics, and the Civil War** 75

   Side Stories
   Friedrich Hecker 86
   Lincoln, Liberty, and the Know Nothings 89
   The Haymarket Affair 91

6. Cultural and Institutional Life 95

Sidebar / Georg Bunsen 106

Side Story

On the Shift from German to English 111

7. World War I and Its Aftermath 114

Side Stories

Protecting English, Promoting Americanism: Better Speech Week 129

The Hanging of Robert Prager 131

8. Heritage and Linguistic Landscape Today 134

Side Story

German Effects on English in the Midwest 143

Notes 149

Select Annotated Bibliography 191

Index 205

FIGURES

1.1. German geographic distribution and population density, 1870 2
1.2. 1870 census page showing Michael, Franziska, Joseph Baetz from Bavaria 6
1.3. German Confederation, 1815 7
1.4. Political unification of Germany, 1866–71 7
2.1. German immigrants to the United States, 1845–99 14
2.2. Nineteenth-century sources of German emigration 15
2.3. Nineteenth-century migration routes and clusters within Illinois 24
2.4. Advertisement for brick homes in Chicago, 1883 27
2.5. Gustav Körner, 1836 30
3.1. Page from an immigrant guidebook to the English language 34
3.2. Water migration routes to Illinois in the nineteenth century 36
3.3. Overland migration routes to Illinois in the nineteenth century 36
4.1. Drawing of a farm in Adams County owned by Jacob Wagner 49
4.2. Percentage born in Germany living in Illinois, by county, 1870 55
4.3. German distribution and settlement in Chicago, 1840–1920 59
4.4. Tonk Manufacturing Company workers, 1893 62
5.1. Officers of the Eighty-Second Illinois in Atlanta, October 1864 79
5.2. Police confronting rioters at Turner Hall in July 1877 83
5.3. Friedrich Hecker, circa 1875 86
5.4. "Revenge" flyer, May 3, 1886 92
5.5. Circular advertising the Haymarket protest, May 4, 1886 93

6.1. First-grade reader showing *Fraktur*, *Kurrent*, and roman type 99

6.2. German *Turnverein* class, mid-1880s 103

6.3. Festival of the North American Turner Bund held in Wrights Grove in Chicago, 1869 105

6.4. Georg Bunsen 106

7.1. Children beside an anti-German sign in Edison Park, Chicago, 1917 122

7.2. German immigrants to the United States, 1900–1960 126

7.3. Watch Your Speech Pledge for Children 130

7.4. Robert Paul Prager 131

8.1. Historic German American house, Belleville, 2011 135

8.2. German ancestry in Illinois, by county, 2013 139

8.3. Top five countries of birth among Illnois' foreign-born, 1900 versus 2000 140

8.4. Languages other than English spoken at home in Illinois, 2015 141

8.5. German spoken at home in Illinois, by county, 2015 142

ACKNOWLEDGMENTS

This book couldn't have been written without the direct and indirect support of a great many people and institutions. First, we wish to thank all those who provided comments, criticism, and advice on the book at various stages of its preparation, though any mistakes in reporting, of course, remain entirely our own. Joseph Salmons set aside valuable time to read and answer questions pertaining to specific sections, while Jennifer Wilkerson readily commented on earlier bits and pieces. Particular appreciation, however, goes to the anonymous readers whose feedback and candor helped sharpen our thinking and writing throughout. We are also most grateful to the time and talents of Jeff Hancks, who solicited our earliest participation in this project and enthusiastically shares our interest in the state's diverse ethnic groups. Along similar lines, we would like to thank the helpful staff at SIU Press for making the publication of this book an enjoyable and rewarding experience, most especially Kristine Priddy, who never failed to be patient and kind in her role as acquisitions editor. Second, we owe a tremendous debt of gratitude to Mark Livengood, who created the maps and figures that enliven the narrative. Our gratitude furthermore belongs to Columbia College for making the writing of this book financially possible in the form of grants and other funding. Lastly, we thank our family, friends, and colleagues, who were there from the beginning and encouraged us to the very end.

Germans in Illinois

1

INTRODUCTION

While Germans have been a part of American history for generations, with early German settlement to the United States beginning as soon as the seventeenth century, this book focuses on the second half of the nineteenth century, as that is when the greatest influx of newcomers to Illinois from what we now call Germany took place. Aside from the French who had made homes in southwestern colonies such as Kaskaskia, Prairie du Roche, Fort de Chartres, and Cahokia, as well as Fort Crevecoeur (the future Peoria), the Illinois country experienced few outsiders throughout the eighteenth and early nineteenth centuries.[1] The region was known for cholera outbreaks, clashes with native tribes, slow population growth, and little else. A strong centralized government was lacking as well, and landownership presented its own set of challenges.[2] The only others to colonize the American Bottom as well as a region known as the Shawnee Hills during this period were migrants primarily from the southern United States, such as Kentucky, the Carolinas, and Tennessee. But suddenly, around 1830, that all changed. Migration, both foreign and domestic, began to pick up, and before long, a flood of people was pouring into Illinois, a flood that didn't ease until the early twentieth century.

German-speaking Europeans made up a significant portion of these nineteenth-century migrants. By 1850, there were approximately 35,000 Germans in the state out of a total population of 851,470 (about 4 percent of the population).[3] As German settlements grew, so, too, did the idea that Illinois was a promising place to live. Observers agree that the success of earlier immigrants was vital in bringing about the swell in numbers of those who came later. By 1860, the census reports that 1.301 million

Germans lived in the United States, with more than half living in the Upper Mississippi and Ohio Valleys, particularly in Ohio, Illinois, Wisconsin, and Missouri.[4] Illinois' German population now surpassed 130,000 (just over 7 percent of the total population). Centers of growth in the Midwest continued, and by 1890, 338,000 Germans lived in Illinois (just under 9 percent of the population).[5] Germans continued to comprise the largest single foreign-born group in the United States in 1910, with more than 2.5 million calling America home.[6] The vast majority—more than 85 percent, to be precise—lived in the Middle Atlantic region and in the Midwest.[7] These statistics represent German-born immigrants only; just think what that meant in terms of children and grandchildren born of German ancestry.

To understand why German immigration to Illinois exploded when it did, it helps to consider what was happening in both countries at the time. What was it about Germany that made people so eager to leave, and what was it about America, Illinois in particular, that was so appealing to newcomers? Historians often refer to reasons for why people emigrate, or leave a country, as "push" factors and those for why people immigrate, or come to live permanently

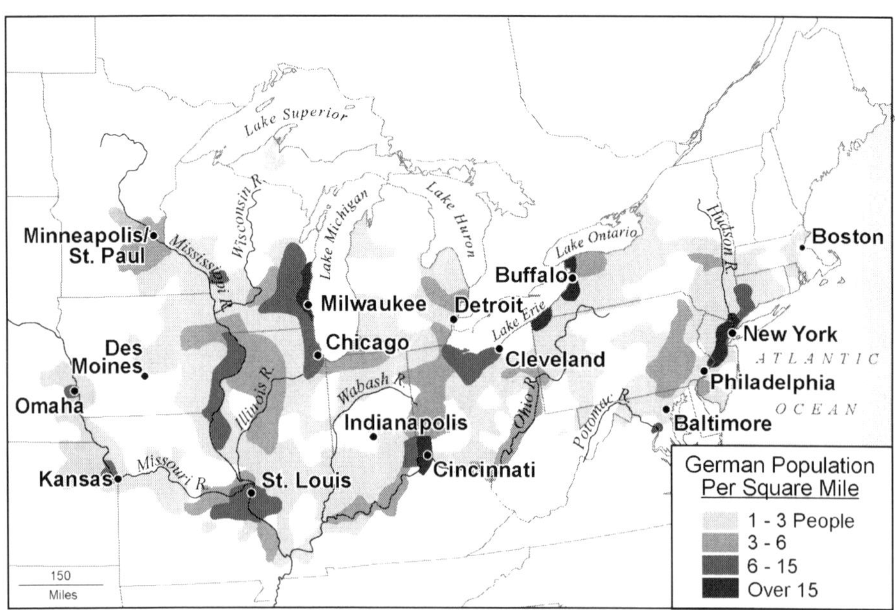

Fig. 1.1. German geographic distribution and population density in the Middle Atlantic and Midwest, 1870. Adapted from an 1872 U.S. census map drawn by A. de Witzleben and based on statistics from the 1870 U.S. census.

in another country, as "pull" factors. Both push and pull factors for immigration to the United States are explored in this book, and the timing of these factors was opportune. Along the way, we illustrate major waves in immigration, pointing to some well-known German communities in Illinois as well as answering some broad questions about everyday life in these communities. For example, what were some of the earliest actions German settlers took? In other words, what did they care about the most or hope to achieve in their adopted homeland? And, perhaps most importantly, how did those actions play out in public discourse and debate?

A group whose status in the nineteenth century has been likened to that of Latinos today, Germans made up the largest segment of non-English speakers in the United States at the time. They were diverse in many ways, and scholars have rightly drawn attention to the fact that their assimilation into mainstream American society was neither quick nor effortless. They strongly identified with German culture and commonly claimed that it was superior to Anglo-American culture.[8] Moreover, important institutions, such as religious congregations, schools, and the German press, enabled and supported the use of the German language for decades, with many immigrants and their descendants remaining monolingual years after mass migration had ended. This is, of course, at striking odds with what most people have come to believe about the Germans, which, in turn, has led to mistaken comparisons between earlier immigrant groups—touted as having acquired English almost immediately upon arrival—and contemporary ones, such as Spanish-speaking immigrants (who are, in fact, acquiring English at astonishing rates).

Despite all this, it may come as a surprise to learn that Germans constructed and even embraced American identities. In other words, being German was not incompatible with being American, particularly when it came to civic and political engagement.

The aim in making the above observations is to explain from the outset that the story of German settlement and assimilation is multifaceted and less absolute than "folk wisdom" would have you believe. Though some like to think of Germans today as "model" immigrants, they were not always revered as such in nineteenth- and early twentieth-century America.[9] Foreign immigration spurred nativist fears and politics, with immigrant identity often under attack. This is not unlike the divisive situation with regard to present-day immigrants and refugees.

With that in mind, perspectives from history, cultural studies, and linguistics inform this book. Though Germans settled across the state of Illinois, some areas, particularly those considered to be German heritage centers, garner more coverage than others. One example is southwest Illinois (i.e., St. Clair County and surrounding region), which comprised the earliest and one of the largest German migration clusters in Illinois. The same goes for situations and people, with the political refugees of the 1830s and 1848 era—owing to their education, leadership, and achievement—dominating the narrative on more than one occasion. To a large extent, these choices of focus reflect limitations of space and, in select cases, limited source material rather than relative importance, though we did attempt to cover those that would attract widespread levels of interest.

For convenience, this book is organized in such a way that chapters are stand-alone and topical. Yet, if read sequentially, they create a fluid narrative of German life in Illinois. That is not to say that this book is exhaustive. How could it be, when a great many books and articles devote themselves to single episodes in history—for example, the role of German Americans in political affairs, particularly during the pre– and post–Civil War years, or the effects of World War I on German American cultural life? What this book *does* do is present readily accessible information on a set of issues, pared down to the following: Chapter 2 describes the leading reasons on both sides of the Atlantic that motivated Germans to head en masse to Illinois, a migration flow that surged in the mid- and late nineteenth century and resulted in distinct settlement patterns across the state. Chapter 3 details the reliably unpleasant, if not hazardous, journey to Illinois. Here we have first-person descriptions that reveal to us the experiences and impressions of transatlantic life. Chapters 4, 5, and 6 collectively address how German settlers adjusted to, yet also profoundly transformed, nineteenth-century Illinois. The first generation to arrive set up farms in rural areas, profiting from the cheap land prices and fertile soil, while those who came later and in much larger numbers found opportunity in Illinois' emergent urban and industrial centers, the topic of chapter 4. The economic success and perceived fortitude of both groups made them worthy newcomers in the eyes of the host culture, but their imported language and customs set them apart and, as chapter 5 explains, made them the subject of nativist bigotry and politics. This chapter goes on to probe the role and perception of Germans in major events and conflicts, including Chicago's Lager Beer Riot, the American Civil War, and the American labor movement, which not only throws light on ideological and cultural differences between Germans and Anglo-Americans but between different groups of Germans and on the evolution and formation of Illinois more broadly. To be sure, Germans took pride in their cultural heritage and ethnic identity, with chapter 6 tracing important institutions and organizations of the era that fostered German language and culture. Chapter 7 centers on the first decades of the twentieth century when American perceptions of Germany hit an all-time low. In this chapter, the focus is World War I, which is covered alongside integration and "Americanization" efforts. Bringing us full circle, the final chapter, chapter 8, describes traces of German culture found in the Illinois landscape today. We also treat the complex and ever-evolving meaning of German American identity.

Firsthand accounts, including excerpts from newspapers and letters, are peppered throughout, whereas events and personal narratives of special interest tend to be presented as side stories at the end of chapters. And if any major topics in this book spark particular interest, the select annotated bibliography provides notes on major source material. We draw inspiration from these immigrants and their stories, marveling at their bravery, complexity, and accomplishments. If nothing else, this information is relevant not only for the people of Illinois but for all Americans. "The German ingredient flavors the whole American pie," as Frederick Luebke, a prominent German American historian, voices it.[10] Before we can really dive in though, it is worth acknowledging some basic issues and ways to think about ethnicity and scholarship on immigration.

What constitutes "German" ethnicity is not wholly intuitive. Germany did not exist as a nation until 1871, after a great many migrants had arrived in the United States. This meant that while language was a unifying factor, many German-speaking immigrants identified themselves as coming from specific duchies, principalities, regions, or states, such as Bavaria or Baden, as often documented in census data recording place of birth. The next three figures (1.2, 1.3, and 1.4) should provide a general idea. The first highlights one St. Clair County resident as documented in the 1870 census, while the second shows the member states of the

Page No. 184 } ☞ Inquiries numbered 7, 16, and 17 are not to be asked in respect to infants. Inquiries numbered 11, 12, 15, 16, 17, 19, and 20 are to be answered (if at all) merely by an affirmative mark, as /.

SCHEDULE 1.—Inhabitants in Belleville, in the County of St. Clair, State of Illinois, enumerated by me on the 25 day of July, 1870.

Post Office: Belleville Charles Duering, *Ass't Marshal.*

	Dwelling-houses, numbered in the order of visitation.	Families, numbered in the order of visitation.	The name of every person whose place of abode on the first day of June, 1870, was in this family.	Description: Age at last birth-day. If under 1 year, give months in fractions, thus, 3/12.	Description: Sex.—Males (M.), Females (F.)	Description: Color.—White (W.), Black (B.), Mulatto (M.), Chinese (C.), Indian (I.)	Profession, Occupation, or Trade of each person, male or female.	Value of Real Estate Owned: Value of Real Estate.	Value of Real Estate Owned: Value of Personal Estate.	Place of Birth, naming State or Territory of U. S.; or the Country, if of foreign birth.	Parentage: Father of foreign birth.	Parentage: Mother of foreign birth.	If born within the year, state month (Jan., Feb., &c.)	If married within the year, state month (Jan., Feb., &c.)	Attended school within the year.	Education: Cannot read.	Education: Cannot write.	Whether deaf and dumb, blind, insane, or idiotic.	Constitutional Relations: Male Citizens of U. S. of 21 years of age and upwards.	Constitutional Relations: Male Citizens of U. S. of 21 years of age and upwards, whose right to vote is denied or abridged on other grounds than rebellion or other crimes.
	1	2	3	4	5	6	7	8	9	10	11	12	13	14	15	16	17	18	19	20
1	1131	1341	Baetz, Michael	49	M	W	Laborer	400		Bavaria	/	/							/	
2			" Franziska	45	F	W	Keeping hous			"	/	/								
3			" Joseph	13	M	W	at home			"	/	/			/					
4	1132	1342	Vost, Adam	45	M	W	Blacksmith	4500	1000	Baden	/	/							/	

Fig. 1.2. Portion of an 1870 census page for Belleville showing Michael, Franziska, and Joseph Baetz from Bavaria. Their neighbor was from Baden. Data from the 1870 U.S. census, "Population Schedules," NARA microfilm publication M593 (Washington, DC: National Archives and Records Administration, n.d.), 442B. Accessed May 30, 2014, from www.ancestry.com.

German Confederation, a loose federation of some thirty German states (as compared to some 360 before the rise of Napoleon) as formed in 1815, which replaced the earlier Holy Roman Empire. Nearly fifty years later, in 1871, political unification was realized as displayed in the third figure.

As the maps illustrate, geopolitical boundaries can shift over the course of history. Much of what belonged to Germany in the 1800s, for example, is now part of present-day Poland, Hungary, Czech Republic, and Russia. Germany's cultural and political center of gravity, as Sinnhuber puts it, was oriented eastward, meaning that numerous Russians, Poles, Hungarians, and folks of other national origins emigrated from German-speaking settlements scattered across Central and Eastern Europe in the nineteenth century.[11] Indeed, German eastward expansion left in its wake many distinct German-language communities, traditionally called "speech islands" (from German *Sprachinseln*). In the historical records, references to immigrants of "German" extraction are often indicative of these German-speaking minorities.

Also significant are the immigrants who came to the United States from countries like Austria and Switzerland, each having a German-speaking majority. Enumerators, or census takers, tended to group them together under the category of "German." Though we tend to think of these countries individually, it's important to remember the historical setting at the time. It was not until 1871 that Austria was ousted from unified "lesser Germany,"

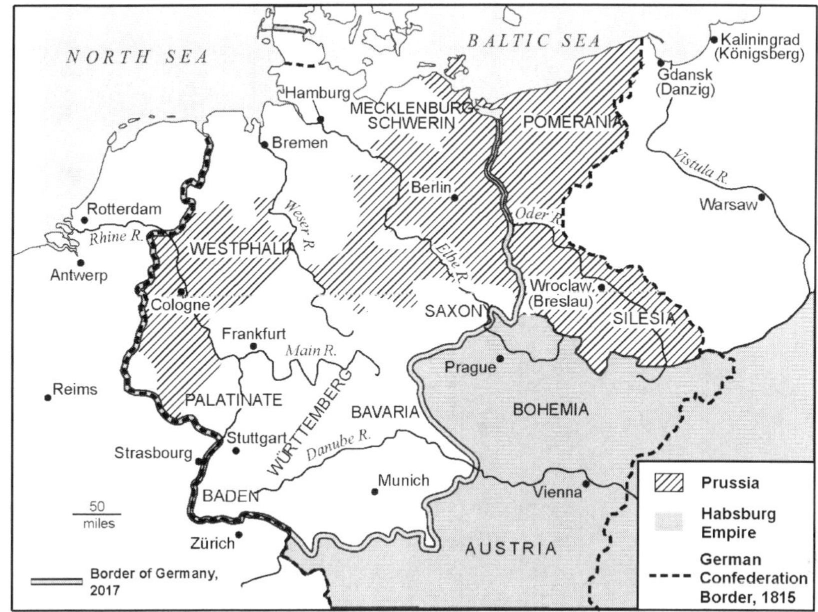

Fig. 1.3. German Confederation, 1815. Adapted from map 6 in Mary Fulbrook's *A Concise History of Germany*, 2nd ed. (Cambridge: Cambridge University Press, 2004), 102.t

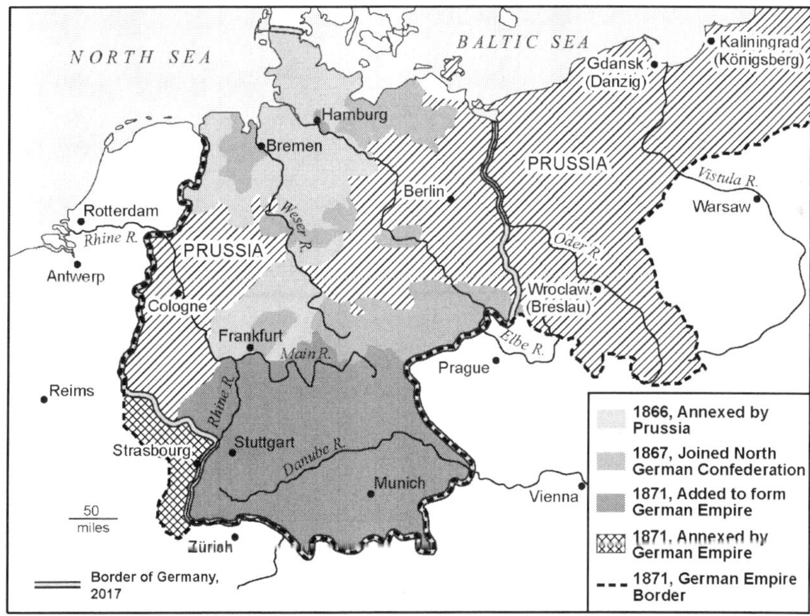

Fig. 1.4. Political unification of Germany, 1866–71. Adapted from "Creation of the German Empire (1866–1871)," originally published by Oxford University Press and available online at German History in Documents and Images, http://ghdi.ghi-dc.org/map.cfm?map_id=2195.

which was under Prussian rule. Even in the years thereafter, Austrians often considered themselves German, at least up until the end of World War II, decades after mass migration to the United States had ended.

Lastly, we should add that German Jewish immigration coincided with (and contributed to) the much larger German immigration patterns of the middle decades of the nineteenth century. While comparatively much smaller in number, German Jews came from the same regions and classes as other German-speaking immigrants of this period and, barring some exceptions, had similar motives for leaving. Their strong association with German culture and civilization, which was overall held in esteem, aided in their acceptance and success in America.[12] In short, our observations in the course of subsequent discussions only highlight German Jews—who made up a very slim 1 to 1.5 percent of Germany's population at the time—in instances where their experiences sharply contrasted from the broader experience of non-Jewish German immigrants and the streams in which they participated.[13]

For ease of reading this book, we refer to German speakers as German and coming from Germany, regardless of historical complexity or geographical fluidity. Linguistic similarity does not mean, however, that all German immigrants and their descendants were alike. To the contrary, they were quite heterogeneous; that is, they hailed from diverse regions of Germany (and beyond), entered the United States at different points in history, spoke varieties of German (in the form of dialects) not always mutually intelligible with Standard German, and had differing religious affiliations, professions, and political beliefs, among much else. In comparison to other ethnic groups—like the Poles, Irish, or Italians—there was considerable internal diversity among Germans.

Moving on to German immigration and immigration patterns more generally, much of what we know is anchored in U.S. census records, which provide a surprisingly detailed snapshot of life at the time. Apart from place of birth, historians can uncover a number of details about any individual, depending on census decade, such as place of residence, personal description (e.g., sex, age, race, etc.), occupation, literacy, native language, year of immigration (in 1900, 1910), and so on. While generally quite comparable, specific queries change from one census year to the next as demographics shift, with usually more targeted questions in the later census schedules as compared to the earlier ones (with the first census facilitated in 1790). These records are readily accessible to the general public as digitized images, with genealogists often making use of them to trace family history. Ancestry.com, for example, taps into the largest online collection of (worldwide) genealogical and historical data, such as census, birth, marriage, and death records, just to name a few.

As a representative example of the detail provided, look back at figure 1.2. From this image, we know the following about Michael Baetz in 1870: Born in Bavaria, he lived in a three-person household in Belleville, Illinois. He was a white, forty-nine-year-old naturalized U.S. citizen married to Franziska, a woman four years his junior. They were literate, with him working as a laborer while she stayed at home and kept house. His thirteen-year-old son, Joseph, attended school. Michael's parents were both born abroad, presumably in Bavaria, as were his wife's.

Based on Michael's birthplace, linguists also can deduce that he spoke *Bairisch*, a variety of High German, at home. Typically, most Germans' native tongues were actually related West Germanic languages, meaning that the immigrants were bilingual in their native languages as well as some form of Standard German as used in institutional settings. Even today, you'll find that if a speaker from southern Germany eavesdrops on a conversation folks from northern Germany are having, it's likely they won't fully grasp the exchange due to dialectal differences.

Having this kind of information on a single resident or residents within a household is useful on a much broader scale, too. It grants insight into the community at large, including how it may have shaped—or been shaped by—migration patterns. If we find, for example, that the majority of residents living in one community came from the same region of Germany, we can surmise that the community was the result of "chain migration." This is when relatives and friends followed in the footsteps of their loved ones, forming tight-knit communities in their newly adopted homeland, with many families likely being related. This shadowing, which we discuss in chapter 2, was often the direct result of immigrant letters, which tended to give favorable accounts of life in America. And if we consider the pockets of Lutherans and Catholics, it becomes clear that religious societies stimulated colonization efforts to some degree as well.

Other valuable documents that inform contemporary scholarship on immigration include applications for emigration (filed by emigrants prior to leaving Germany), passenger lists (collected by shipping agents), church records, personal letters and diaries, organizational records, German-language newspapers, and county histories, to name a few. Of course, owing to human error or omission, such historical documents, including the census, are rarely flawless. That's true, too, for published histories of the German immigrant experience, with the earliest ones either authored by the immigrants themselves or by their direct descendants. First-hand accounts provide tremendous historical insight, but they also teeter on rose-colored, if not entirely filiopietistic, interpretations of the German element in and their contributions to American society. Other flattering narratives can be found in the decades

A Note about German Pronunciation

To make the German names and terms in this book more accessible, here are a few basics about German and its alphabet. Apart from having all the same vowels as English, German has three additional ones. They look nearly the same as the others except for one small distinguishing characteristic: they have two dots (e.g., *ä*, *ö*, and *ü*), called an *Umlaut* in German, but you may have heard them—at least in musical circles—referred to as "heavy metal umlauts" or "röck döts" (think Motörhead or Mötley Crüe). While a metal umlaut is used for decorative purposes, a German *Umlaut* changes the quality of the vowel sound, rounding it out. So, the last name of a prominent German immigrant discussed in this book, Gustav Körner, should be pronounced more like "Kerner," not "Korner." Many folks using the American keyboard layout, which excludes umlauted vowels, just insert an "e" after the vowel (i.e., Koerner).

Another matter worth clarifying as it relates to vowels is a couple of common combinations. Anytime you see the vowels "ei" together, pronounce the last letter only (think *Heinz* ketchup). The same holds true for the combination "ie" (think *diesel* fuel).

A final discussion point is consonants. As with vowels, German has the same ones English does, yet their pronunciation is not always the same. For example, the letter "v" in German is pronounced like "f" in English, whereas the letter "w" in German is pronounced as "v" in English. A classic case in point is the breaded and deep-fried veal (or sometimes pork) cutlet known as *Wiener Schnitzel*, a Viennese specialty. The first letter sounds like "v," not "w," when pronounced in true German fashion. And German has one additional consonant, the letter *ß*, which is the equivalent of "ss" (and sounds like "s"). Its German name is *Eszett* (meaning "sz") or *scharfes S* (meaning "sharp S"). In standard spelling today, it is used only after long vowels and vowel combinations, whereas a singular "s" is used after short vowels. American beer drinkers may encounter this if they drink *Weißbier* (wheat beer), a summertime favorite.

after World War II, when the urge to resuscitate the German American image was great.

Even scholarly articles sometimes conflict in their telling of the historical record. Natural biases and varying perspectives of individual historians aside, many past histories relied almost exclusively on the German-language press as a primary source. The press is indeed an excellent source of information, but some authors assumed that the prolific editorials found in German newspapers across the country reflected the opinions and experiences of the German population at large. They therefore extrapolated based on this, a common mistake that was also made by the American public at the time the editorials were written.[14] Scholars in more recent years have recognized the limited scope of the press in making sense of past events and perspectives, with newspapers of different political viewpoints—the labor press versus the mainstream press versus religious publications, for example—even found to mirror the perspectives of only a small elite. The inflated accounts of Germans' influence on the 1860 presidential election are just one example of this. Newspaper editorials tended to support Lincoln across the board, but an analysis of the actual voting record reveals a more complex story, one we delve into in chapter 4.

Still, taken together, these myriad sources allow historians to connect the dots, establishing a connection between the peaks and trickles of migration. Complementing each other in numerous ways, they provide statistical information *and* contextualize the immigrant experience, offering a multilayered look at the lives of the settlers themselves. All this is a very roundabout way of explaining how we arrived at the facts and figures we share in this book about German immigrants. Since we primarily drew information from secondary sources, the quantitative and qualitative data on this group had already been compiled and synthesized, allowing this book to focus on telling the story and on bringing the narrative to life by sharing photos and letters. So, in the chapters that follow, we offer a highly condensed version of what scholars have learned about the arrival, grit, and adaptability of German immigrants as well as the distinct ways in which they have impacted and been impacted by our landscape, literally and figuratively, in ways both readily apparent and less obvious.

2

NINETEENTH-CENTURY GERMAN IMMIGRATION AND SETTLEMENT

Leaving Germany: Push Factors

Throughout the 1800s, Germans emigrated for a variety of independent, yet related, reasons, including agricultural disasters, changing economic conditions, and political unrest, among much else. With one (think crop failures) triggering others (think famine, inflation, unemployment, etc.), no element of German society went untouched. But it was the most vulnerable who left the homeland, with the majority coming from the lower and lower-middle classes. As conditions for emigration ripened, the New World offered a fresh, welcoming start.[1]

While it wasn't until the early 1850s that transatlantic migration became a mass movement, Germans began emigrating in increasingly large numbers in the early decades of the nineteenth century. Revolution and war were fresh memories, and the 1815 reconfiguration of the German states into the German Confederation did little to promote political and social reform. Government rulers, fearing insurgency and the loss of aristocratic privilege, adopted a specific set of restrictions in 1819, known as the Carlsbad Decrees, to stymie liberal developments and nationalist movements. In addition, Jews suffered from discriminatory legislation and inequities in many member states.[2] The mood in Germany was one of weariness and discontent, and in the heavily populated region of the southwest, where home manufacturing and subsistence farming were ways of life, it was one of desperation. In the period from 1816 to 1817, Württemberg, the Palatinate, and Baden experienced severe famine and inflation. Those events, compounded by a rapidly rising population, a partible inheritance system, and the arrival of factory competition from England, stimulated emigration among peasants and cottage craftsmen from these and other nearby states along the

Rhine.[3] Entire families left, with an estimated twenty thousand individuals escaping to the United States.[4] Many had to labor for their tickets, agreeing to work as indentured servants or apprentices for those already living in America.

By the 1830s, when German immigration to the United States rose to new levels, economic depression and unemployment in Germany were widespread. Land policies and prices as well as overcrowding burdened small farmers, and craft occupations cratered in the cities and villages as home-based products and handiworks were usurped by factory-based industry and mass production.[5] The replacement of the handloom with the power loom, for example, resulted in declining standards among skilled artisans in hand production centers, such as Osnabrück, northern Westphalia, Saxony, and Silesia (now part of Poland). Arousing upset and concern as well were the restrictive marriage laws enforced by legislators in many German states like Bavaria, Baden, and Württemberg, among others. Meant to regulate population growth and poverty, the laws limited marriage only to those deemed financially qualified and morally fit to start a family, which stripped countless couples of their right to wed and have (legally) legitimate children.[6] The response among many struggling farmers and village artisans was to cash out and leave.[7] Emigration was heaviest in the southwest but was starting to spread northward and eastward as well. The removal of tolls, restrictions, and trade barriers on the Rhine, Main, and Neckar, as well as the introduction of river steamboats, during this decade made leaving easier and within reach for a wider range of people.[8] Many headed for the farmlands and small towns of America's developing Midwest, where perceived place images of agricultural opportunity and enterprise were pulling forces.

Other causes for emigration during this period were religiously and politically motivated. Angered by a Prussian mandate to unite the Lutheran and Reformed churches, a group called the Altlutheraner, or Old Lutherans, headed westward in the late 1830s in pursuit of religious freedom. By 1854, seven thousand are presumed to have emigrated.[9] In fact, the Missouri Synod is a direct descendent of this group. Around the same time, Catholics emigrated after the Prussian government, which was Protestant, took over the Rhineland. Many settled in northern Illinois, but Clinton County's Germantown holds the distinction of being the earliest German Catholic colony in Illinois.[10]

News of the successful revolution of 1830 in France inspired uprisings in Germany as elsewhere in Europe. The desire to bring an end to the status quo was strong, but it came short of its purpose. Failure and repression of the liberal reform movements, which included the Hambacher Fest of 1832 and the Frankfurter Wachensturm of 1833, resulted in stricter reinforcement of the Carlsbad Decrees, that is, limitations on speech, press, and universities as well as a group of intellectual exiles to the United States known collectively as the "Dreißiger" (Thirtiers). Illinois attracted many extraordinary personalities, not least Gustav Körner (see his side story at the end of this chapter), who settled in St. Clair County, joining a small community of farmers already established in the rural Shiloh Valley Township near Belleville.[11]

Illinois experienced its first significant population growth starting in the 1830s and 1840s, mirroring the first of three major waves of immigration to the United States from Germany (see figure 2.1). The first wave came largely from southwestern Germany as well as the German-speaking areas of the Austrian Empire and Switzerland between the years 1845 and 1860 (see figure 2.2).[12] The food shortages of the mid- to late 1840s (the "hungry forties"), which resulted from repeated crop failures (including flax, from which handwoven linen cloth is made) and the potato blight, made matters unbearable, compelling many laborers, professionals, and

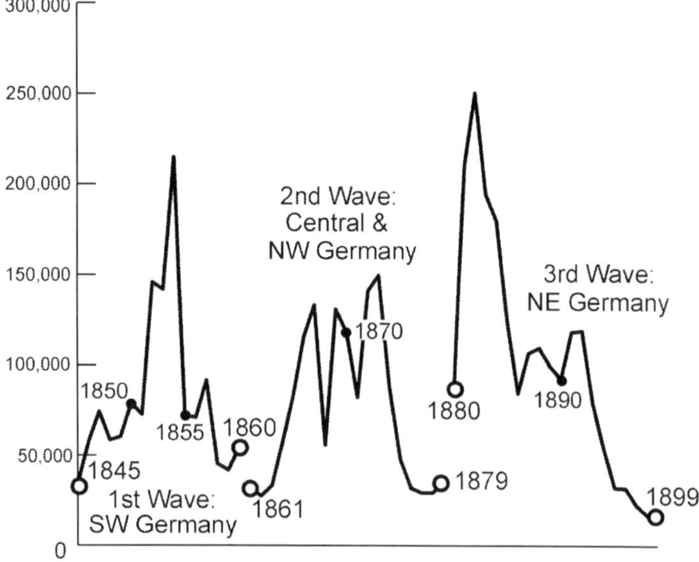

Fig. 2.1. German immigrants to the United States, 1845–99. Statistics from *International Migration and Naturalization, Series C 89–119*, "Immigrants, by Country: 1820 to 1970."

farmers to pursue a better life abroad. In select cases, those who were financially destitute were encouraged, if not forced, by government entities to emigrate from Germany in an effort to offset the quickly rising population.[13] Indeed, between 1815 and 1850, the population of the German states is estimated to have grown about 55 percent.[14] The country, rural areas in particular, was teeming with people in the mid-1800s, with Europe nearly having doubled its entire population within the span of a century. Fewer people meant fewer mouths to feed, and Germany certainly stood to benefit from emigration given its mounting population. In the case of German Jews, who were restricted from certain types of professions (or heavily regulated from advancement within them), the situation was particularly taxing.

Like the emigration of the 1830s, observers call this a movement of the lower-middle class, and as Mack Walker puts it, these were the self-sufficient folks who "had something to lose, and who were losing it, squeezed out by interacting social and economic forces."[15] Indeed, flight to America was spurred largely by economic matters, something Jacob Gross, an emigrant from the village of Kadelburg in southwestern Germany, freely indicates in his letter addressed to his brothers and sisters. In it, and as this excerpt will show, he describes his family's good fortune in

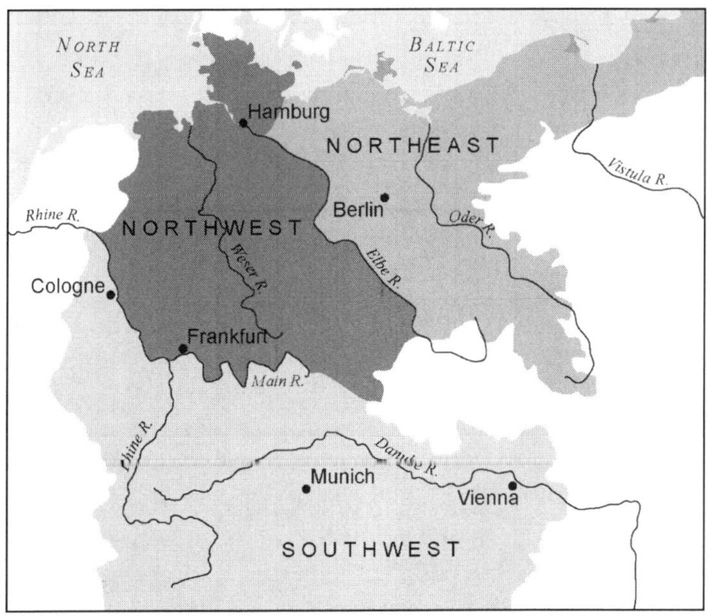

Fig. 2.2. Nineteenth-century sources of German emigration. Adapted from Thomas Purnell, Eric Raimy, and Joseph Salmons, *Wisconsin Talk* (© 2013 by the Board of Regents of the University of Wisconsin System) with permission of the University of Wisconsin Press.

Chicago, emphasizing improved financial conditions and overall economic worth. He wrote the following in 1856:

> Every beginning is hard. But we never have had to battle with Want and Hunger, and if the Good Lord lets us keep our health, we have good prospects. We now have 1 cow, 5 sheep, and 2 hogs. We feed the hogs with entrails and lungs from the slaughter house. When the snow is gone we let the cow and sheep run on the prairie—they come home again at night. Not once have we wished to be back; we are satisfied. But we do wish that all Kadelburgers had it as good as we. What we earn is ours. When we have paid $1.50, then our obligations are discharged. When we asked Marie whether she would like to go back home again, she answered: "No sir-ee—I have more meat than at home." She is very plump.[16]

Worsening agricultural and economic conditions do not account for the full scope of why Germans set sail for America though. Dissatisfaction among the European populace only continued and, in 1848, escalated to new heights. Throughout the year, Europe experienced several political and socioeconomic upheavals, beginning with the downfall of King Louis Philippe in France. By March, such news inspired revolutionary forces in Germany to try and effect change within their borders again, which included dueling powerhouses, Austria and Prussia, and a number of smaller, buffering states (refer back to figure 1.3 for a map of the German Confederation). Many saw what came to be referred to as the Revolution of 1848 as a step toward national unification (each state in the confederation was sovereign at the time), constitutional reform, and improved economic conditions, but there just wasn't enough widespread support for or coordination and consensus among liberals to overturn conservative regimes, who were reluctant to centralize powers and replace them with a democracy. While it was, in a sense, the revolution that *wasn't*, it did fuel modest development in Germany.[17]

However, those developments hardly appeased a group of educated liberals, radicals, and religious dissidents, known as the Achtundvierziger (Forty-Eighters), who made their way to America, seeking, in effect, political refuge.[18] Though they only comprised a small number of newcomers to the United States overall, they were dynamic. Generally pro-Union and antislavery, they wielded great influence on the social, cultural, and political life of Germans in the United States, topics to come in subsequent chapters. Prominent among the revolutionaries who settled in Illinois (Mascoutah Township) was Friedrich Hecker (see the side story on Friedrich Hecker at the end of chapter 5), a figure of considerable importance around the time of the American Civil War. The next large politically minded group of German immigrants did not come to the states until the Nazis came to power, close to a century later.

To provide some broad perspective on sheer numbers, nine hundred thousand Germans, primarily from the south and west, immigrated to the states by 1854.[19] That's an impressive number of men, women, and children, with many heading westward, settling in Ohio, Illinois, Michigan, and Wisconsin. The emigration trade was picking up steam, with German newspapers featuring emigration advertisements, railroads offering discounted fares, and communities establishing information guides, among much else.[20] The largest European emigrant sources at the time were the German states, Ireland, and England, with the Germans surpassing the Irish during this decade in America, generally, and in Illinois, specifically.[21]

The second great wave of over one million occurred between the years 1861 and 1879 (refer back to figure 2.1). Immigration to America dropped during the Civil War years but resumed thereafter, with 1866 marking the first year in many that the annual count of German newcomers surpassed one hundred thousand.[22] Though the idea of emigration was well-rooted throughout Germany by now, the majority of émigrés came from central and northwestern Germany (refer back to figure 2.2).[23] The grain-growing region of the north couldn't keep pace with the import of cheap, American wheat, which had weakened the market. Farmers left, as did urban craftsmen (e.g., bakers, carpenters, etc.) and industrial workers looking for a better standard of living in cities like Chicago where skilled workers were in demand. Beyond that, many fled to escape the wars of 1864, 1866, and 1870 for German unification, which for young men meant compulsory military service. Numbers, however, began to plummet in 1873 due to the financial crisis in America known as the Panic of 1873, which took a particularly heavy toll on Illinois.

The third and largest wave of German immigration to the United States broke in 1880, with the majority being displaced agrarian workers from the northeastern lands of Pomerania, Mecklenburg, and Prussia (refer back to figures 2.1 and 2.2). They were "workers rather than prospective farmers, and they were in pursuit of jobs, not land."[24] Also unlike their predecessors, they didn't emigrate as families.[25] Largely on their own, they gravitated toward urban locations like Chicago to take advantage of gains in industry, generally working low-wage jobs at mass-producing factories. With 250,630 newcomers setting foot on American soil, 1882 was a peak emigration year.[26] And yet, that trend reversed just one year later, with 1883 seeing a sharp and permanent decline in numbers. In fact, German emigration became almost negligible after 1884, with the annual movement never exceeding forty thousand, likely owing to Germany's economic resurgence.[27]

Of the three waves, this last group was the largest, poorest, and youngest. They were also much less critical of Germany as compared to earlier immigrants. After the Franco-Prussian War and with the formal unification of Germany in 1871, emigrants around this time and after began to see themselves as nationalistically German.[28] That wasn't necessarily the case before. Another distinguishing characteristic about this wave is that it concurred with a tide of new immigrants to America largely from southern and eastern Europe.

Coming to Illinois: Pull Factors

In the course of a century, more than five million Germans had abandoned Germany, with most of them settling in the United States.[29] But to say that Germans fled their homeland because of desperate conditions only tells half the story. Prospects in the United States seemed bright and, in Illinois, they were positively glowing. A state that scarcely counted two people per square mile between the years 1818 and 1833 became the third most populous state in the nation at 4.8 million in 1900. The state's foreign-born population was 20.1 percent of the total population, making Illinois one of the states having the largest percentage of foreign-born residents.[30]

This phenomenon occurred because developments happened that made immigration to Illinois not only feasible but highly desirable at the same time that many Germans were making plans to leave Germany. In terms of feasibility, improvements in transportation technology, such as inland waterways and railroads, reduced barriers to interior travel, making it logistically easier for Germans to get to Illinois. The 1825 completion of the Erie Canal, which provided access to Lake Erie from the Hudson River, created a speedier and more direct connection between the East Coast and Chicago. The coming of the railroads made the trip even faster and cheaper, and by the 1850s Germans—and others—were flowing into Illinois at a faster rate than ever before.

Considering what Illinois had to offer, the draw becomes obvious. To begin with, and though there were some resident slaveholders in its early years, Illinois was technically a free state.[31] As the United States inched its way toward civil war, Illinois' free-state status increasingly attracted German immigrants, most of whom were staunchly antislavery. Additionally, Illinois was one of several Midwestern states to offer a public education system, something valued by most Germans. In terms of legislation, the state was attractive to immigrants wishing to participate in America's political system. Compared to many other states, Illinois had very liberal suffrage laws.[32] For example, Illinois' first state constitution gave voting rights to any white man twenty-one years of age who had resided in the state for six months or more. In 1848, when the state's second constitution was ratified, the length of residency was extended to a minimum of one year.[33]

Grays vs. Greens

America offered Germans in the early to mid-nineteenth century something that German rulers did not, namely unlimited freedom of organization and association. Indeed, the existing order in post-Napoleonic Germany was politically oppressive. Popular desire for reform and change, particularly among students and the middle class, resulted in rampant censorship and prohibitive laws, such as the banning of public meetings, by the ruling monarchies and duchies who feared liberal and nationalistic inclinations among the populace. So, after the thwarted revolutionary uprisings in 1832 and 1848, a string of radicals, the Thirtiers and Forty-Eighters, made their way to America and, while small in number, shaped the public image of the German population in Illinois and else where where heavy numbers of Germans resided.

Notwithstanding their shared republican convictions and goals, there was friction between the newly arrived Forty-Eighters, referred to as "the Greens," and their predecessors, the Thirtiers, or "the Grays." The Greens considered the Grays to be complacent and lacking of political vision or assertiveness, not unlike how the younger cohort often views the older one.[1] The Grays, on the other hand, who had lived some years in the United States by this time and had a better grasp of American institutions, found the Greens to be overly vocal and self-righteous in terms of their left-leaning politics and "Utopian schemes, including the German state idea," which most Grays had long abandoned.[2] As recent arrivals, their ostentation and seemingly harsh critique of America struck many Grays as well as some native born Americans as unearned and off-putting. Where they found common ground and, in this way, reconciled, was on the abolition of slavery.[3]

Economic factors also played a large role in attracting Germans to Illinois. Illinois had relatively low taxes compared with those in the German states, and land was cheap and plentiful in the 1830s and 1840s, with word quickly spreading of the state's rich, loamy soil so loved by farmers. This countered the earlier yet short-lived belief that land without trees must have poor soil. Only after more migrants came to Illinois, fanning out into the northern prairies, did they discover some of the richest agricultural soil in the nation. With its soil of "exhaustless fertility," Illinois came to be marketed and known as the "Garden State of the West."[34]

The railroads had farmland that was available and ready to sell to newcomers. The Illinois Central Railroad in particular had been given a large land grant in 1851 from the federal government for the construction of its line from Chicago to Cairo—this was the first railroad land grant in America and resulted in large amounts of desirable land for sale at reasonable prices. At first, the company focused its sales on the English-speaking population, but in 1854, fearing a loss of business to neighboring Iowa, they began promoting settlement in Illinois to Germans both in the eastern United States and in Germany.[35] In addition to sending German-speaking agents to meet immigrants in New York and entice them to come to Illinois, they produced German-language pamphlets for distribution to Germans already living in Illinois, elsewhere in the United States, and in Germany. Advertisements ran in German-language newspapers both stateside and in Europe, and, at one point, the railroad commissioned *Reisen im Nordwesten der Vereinigten Staaten*, a six-hundred-page book describing conditions along the line throughout the Midwest.[36] Eventually, in 1862 the Illinois Central recruited German immigrant and Illinois lieutenant governor Francis Hoffmann as their German land agent, selling property exclusively to German immigrants.[37] As a result of these efforts, many German immigrants in the mid-nineteenth century purchased farmland from the Illinois Central; doubtless, the railroad company played a large role in the settlement of Germans in Illinois.[38]

In fact, the mid-nineteenth century saw a great deal of German-language literature published on the subject of the United States and the Midwest, the majority of it promotional in nature.[39] For example, if you needed to illustrate the idea of nineteenth-century America as a land of opportunity, you could hardly improve upon Gottfried Duden's *Report on a Journey to the Western States of North*

America. A lawyer and civil servant, Duden was born in Remscheid in the Ruhr Valley. He worked as a civil servant in the early 1820s, living through the tough economic and political environment in Germany at the time. Duden saw emigration as a possible solution to problems he believed were caused by overpopulation. After researching the scant literature that was available to him, Duden decided that the Mississippi Valley in the United States might be the best settlement location for emigrants. So, in 1824, he traveled to Missouri; impressed with what he found there, he purchased land for farming. Duden spent the next three years traveling in the region but farming very little (this was left to the hired help). Upon his return to Germany, he wrote about Missouri in glowing terms, describing its abundant wildlife, beautiful landscape, healthy climate, and fertile soil. He also described the robust economy and strong democracy of America.

The *Report* struck a chord with a population searching for a better life. Published in 1829, it became an international bestseller, reprinted once in Germany and twice in Switzerland.[40] The *Report* was, in fact, one of many German-language books, pamphlets, and periodicals sensationalizing immigration to the United States.[41] Between 1815 and 1858, over one hundred German-language travel books were published, the majority of which discussed the topic of moving to America, including where to go and what to bring. The periodicals *Allgemeine Auswanderungszeitung* and *Der Deutsche Auswanderer* both had a target audience of emigrants, and not all depictions of American life in these and other publications were rosy.[42] The role of women in the success of that move was considered integral, with one emigrant adviser offering up this insight:

QUALITIES

Which the emigrating woman must possess:
A strong resilient body
Robust health
A resilient soul
Strong nerves
A great lack of consideration for herself
Friendly obligingness to others.[43]

In sum, though many factors contributed to the surge in German immigration to Illinois in the 1830s, Duden's book—and others like it—no doubt had a substantial impact.

Newly resettled, German immigrants often gushed in their letters about how much better the economy was in their adopted home than back in Germany, which brings us to one of the most important pull factors yet: letters from family and friends. Without knowledge about conditions in the United States and in Illinois, especially, few immigrants would have ever made the journey at all. Letters home provided reliable and honest descriptions of conditions in the region. Indeed, the back-and-forth exchanges allowed for specific and detailed questions to be answered about a particular locale, informing would-be emigrants not only about whether conditions were right for settling in Illinois but also about what tools, skills, and supplies might be needed. Disabusing the recipient of false rumors about life in America, be they positive or negative, the correspondence provided instead a realistic sense of what life was like for an immigrant.[44] A case in point is a letter from Johann Bauer, in which he describes his life working and living on a farm in Princeton, Illinois, in 1855. It is addressed to his parents and siblings back in Baden.[45]

> [I]n my entire life I've never gone sledding so much as here. You have probably often thought how will Johann spend the winter; oh, I spent it much better than you could imagine. In Germany they still have the impression that there are no happy hours here, but this is mere foolishness. The people here know how to make life just as pleasant as in beautiful Germany . . .
>
> I am presently located in an area which 21 years ago was still fully in the hands of the Indians or savages. Only a few years ago you wouldn't have found a single farm here. Then, 4 or 5 years ago the land was put up for sale for 1 1/4 dollars per acre . . . and now it is no longer to be had for under 10 to 15 dollars . . . you can see from this that it takes quite a bit of money at the start here, because almost all of the uncultivated land is in the hands of speculators. . . . From the above description you can see how thriving the conditions here & that with a bit of hard work and stamina it is easier to get ahead than in Germany. I know people here who 4 or 5 years ago didn't even have 25 dollars to their name and now 2 to 3000 dollars. You mustn't think of America as a wilderness or nothing but shrubs & bushes & mountains. Sometimes you find areas 30 to 50 miles long & wide nothing but the most lovely fruitful hilly prairies or plains; with sufficient water but not always enough wood . . .

This letter gives a truthful account of the high price of land in the Princeton area (due to land speculators) but also paints an overall positive picture of life in Illinois. Such letters obviously continue to provide a wealth of information to historians and others interested in learning firsthand what life was like for German immigrants in the nineteenth century.

Published literature and advertisements—as well as letters home—didn't just boost the numbers of immigrants coming to Illinois, they also helped determine the growth and shape of Illinois' German immigrant communities. The following excerpt from *Immigrants in the Valley* reflects this trend:

> A missionary in Macoupin County, Illinois, reported that when he arrived in 1851 "there was but one German family within four miles of Brighton." But by 1854 "there are probably more than one hundred, and still they come," he wrote. "Each new family in turn brings a circle of relatives and acquaintances who settle around them, and these again, by their glowing description of the New World, attract others."[46]

The historical record supports this observation. Germans largely settled among and married within their own heritage group, with the following figures on marriages in Quincy paralleling those of larger samplings elsewhere in the Midwest:

> Over ninety-eight percent of the American marriages by women who came to Quincy from Münsterland were to men who were either born in Germany or were of German ancestry. Over three quarters of these marriages were to men who were born or whose ancestors were born in a Low-German speaking region of Germany. Nearly 60% of those above women married someone who was born in Münsterland or who had one or both parents born there. Only five of the 322 marriages of Münsterland women in Quincy were to non-Germans.[47]

Germans formed distinct settlement patterns (as shown in figure 2.3). In the early years of migration, the southwestern portion of Illinois, the American Bottom, was the quintessential settlement area, known for its fertile soil and proximity to St. Louis, a budding German American city and commercial center. This region also presented itself as a viable alternative to Missouri, a neighboring slave state. Ironically, while Duden specifically promoted settlement in Missouri and, in fact, had nothing favorable

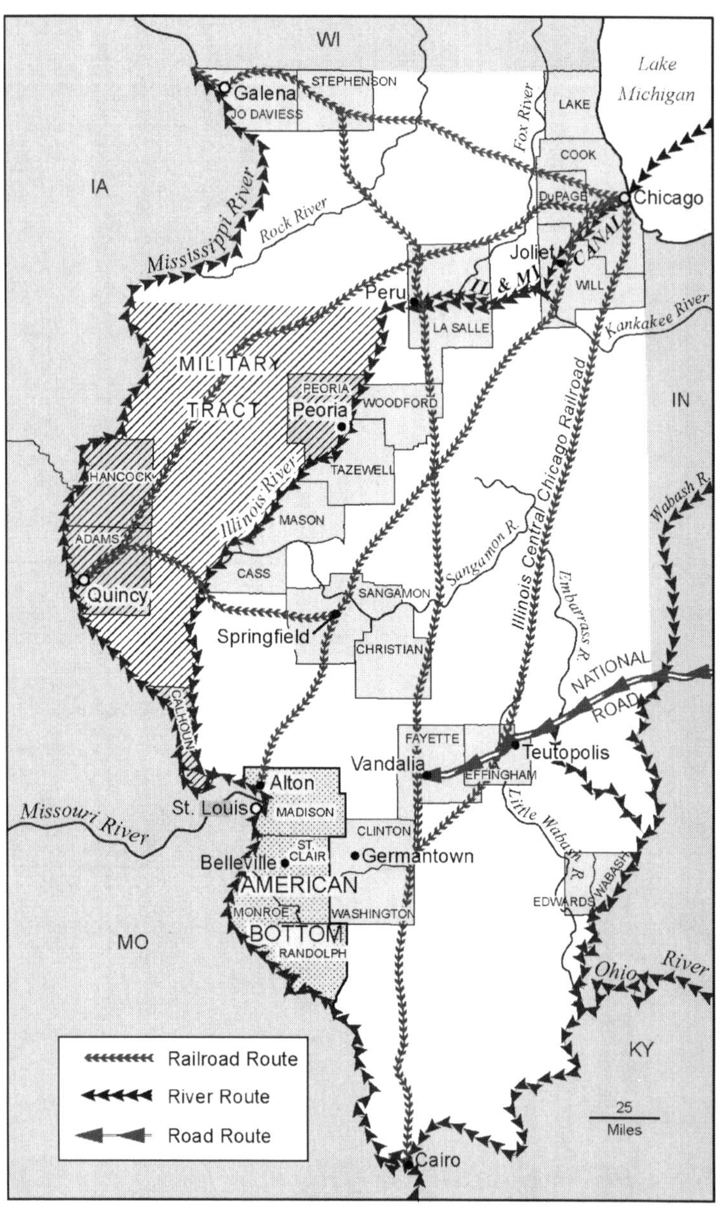

Fig. 2.3. Nineteenth-century migration routes and clusters within Illinois. Arrowheads represent migration routes to and diffusion within Illinois. Counties emphasized represent areas of considerable German concentration as discussed in Douglas K. Meyer, *Making the Heartland Quilt: A Geographical History of Settlement and Migration in Early Nineteenth-Century Illinois* (Carbondale: Southern Illinois University Press, 2000). Railroad locations based on an 1859 publication of the Illinois Central Railroad.

to say about the state of Illinois, his book inadvertently increased German migration to Illinois.

As is generally the pattern, the success of these early settlers along the Upper Mississippi brought about increased immigration to the state, amassing considerable German concentrations in the neighboring counties of Randolph, Madison, Monroe, and St. Clair, with St. Clair boasting the largest. Belleville, a town located in St. Clair County, makes for a great example of German saturation (though its first settlers, like those of this region, were Anglo-Americans). A glimpse at any nineteenth-century census record will show, as Mark Wyman reminds us, that whole neighborhoods reported Germany as their country of origin.[48] This general area, with Belleville at its center, was commonly referred to as a "Latin" settlement, denoting the classically educated Thirtiers and Forty-Eighters who lived and farmed there.[49]

Churches also played a central role in chain migration; for example, Robert Frizzell describes the Saint James Lutheran Church in Quincy. In the 1850s, the Reverend August Heinrich Schmieding answered letters from his community back in Westphalia regarding opportunities in Quincy. By the time he retired in 1873, over a quarter of his congregation consisted of immigrants from a single town in Westphalia, and 82 percent of the congregation was from within a thirty-mile radius.[50] Some groups of German Catholics were also known to move wholesale into Illinois communities, including St. Marie, Teutopolis, and Columbia.[51]

The fact is, churches provided the stimulus for many communities, with Protestant and Catholic churches alike sending missionaries to Illinois at a time when the state was still part of the American frontier because they feared that life in America would put German traditions and culture in jeopardy. As a result, Catholic and Protestant missionaries competed heavily with one another in Illinois in the 1830s and 1840s. Settlement patterns in the decades that followed largely reflect this effort; most German churches on the outskirts of Chicago, for instance, were Catholic because those living there had come from regions in Germany that were predominantly Catholic.[52] Catholic churches in particular worried that exposure to American Protestantism would weaken immigrants' beliefs.[53]

After the Revolution of 1848 in Germany, which happened to correspond with a progressively well-developed infrastructure for travel to and within Illinois, Germans pushed in great numbers further into the interior, settling in the towns of Quincy, Alton, Peoria, Springfield, Galena, Peru, and, of course, Chicago. Quincy in Adams County and Galena in Jo Daviess County served as government land offices for the "Military Tract," which refers to the land between the Mississippi and Illinois Rivers that the U.S. government gave to veterans of the War of 1812.[54] Most of the veterans had roots elsewhere and were uninterested in moving to the Military Tract, and therefore many sold their lots to land speculators, attracting Germans eager to homestead. In fact, Germans began to arrive in Quincy, later coined the "Gem City," as early as 1832. Its reputation as an agricultural and industrial hotspot drew a steady stream of newcomers up until the late 1880s.[55]

Settling in Chicago

The opening of the Illinois and Michigan Canal in 1848, which connected the Great Lakes to the Mississippi River, as well as the formation of a statewide railroad network contributed to Chicago's early growth, as did the usual Illinois boosters and real estate developers advertising land and attractive houses for purchase at affordable prices.[56] But Chicago's main draw was the availability of jobs. In the 1850s and 1860s, the growing city offered ample opportunity for skilled artisans and tradesmen fleeing German industrialization and the demise of the guild system to practice their crafts. Many would eventually work independently as their own bosses running small shops. For these individuals, Chicago was a place of promise.[57] And after the Chicago Fire of 1871, immigrants in the building trades found even more opportunity in the rebuilding of the city.[58]

The subsequent explosive industrial growth of Chicago, which created jobs in meatpacking plants, mills, and factories, coincided with the 1880s wave of working-class German immigrants who contributed to Chicago's rise as an industrial giant. For perspective's sake, consider these numbers: in 1845, there were about 1,000 Germans in Chicago; in 1850, 5,073; and in 1860, 22,230.[59] By 1890, 161,039 of Chicago's residents—that's roughly 15 percent—were German-born, and that percentage doubles when one includes second-generation German Americans.[60] That same year Illinois ranked as the country's third largest industrial state.[61] By 1900, Illinois was the third most populous state in the nation at forty-eight million.

Germans established themselves throughout Chicago and its suburbs over time, with some of the city's earliest residents being small numbers of German Jews, mostly from Bavaria, who arrived in the 1830s and 1840s.[62] The most significant area of settlement was the North Side, which included the area between Division and North, eventually expanding to Fullerton (for settlement patterns, see figure 4.3 in chapter 4). During the late 1800s this neighborhood continued to grow northward until eventually, by the twentieth century, the German community had mostly migrated north to the area between Fullerton and Devon. Other significant

Fig. 2.4. Advertisement for brick homes in Chicago, 1883. Courtesy Chicago History Museum; ICHi-06577.

neighborhoods settled in the 1880s include the Northwest Side (Ward 14), the West Side (Wards 6 and 7), and the South Side (Ward 5). Nearby towns with large German populations were Buffalo Grove, Elgin, Elmhurst, and Maywood.[63]

As we have seen, the westward current of German immigration to the Midwest, including its ebb and flow, reflects the social, political, and economic histories of both Germany and Illinois. Promising opportunity in a time of distress and discontent in the homeland, Illinois emerged as a top destination for Germans eager to start afresh and prosper. In the years to come, the state and its immigrants would shape each other in profound ways.

A German State in the Upper Mississippi Valley

The people writing promotional literature on emigration did much more than romanticize life in the American West: They campaigned for an organized group settlement of the area, particularly Missouri, for the express purpose of establishing permanent German communities where the language and culture could thrive unencumbered. In his *Report*, Duden speculated on the promise of a "rejuvenated Germania" by saying,

> If a small city were founded with the intention of serving the American Germans as a center of culture, one would soon see a rejuvenated Germania arise and the European Germans would then have a second country here, such as the British have. If only a live interest for such a project would develop in Germany! No plan of the present day can be more promising . . . than such a plan for the founding of a city as a center of German culture in western North America, and especially in the areas west of the Mississippi.[1]

Captivated by the idea, Friedrich Münch and Paul Follenius founded the Giessen Emigration Society and published the *Call*. In it, they outlined the society's plan for emigration as follows:

> It is our idea that the better part of the many Germans who have decided to emigrate should settle as a group, united as a whole in keeping with the purified and presently existing political form and received into the great federation of states, so that in this way the survival of German customs, language, etc., should be secured, so that a free and popular

form of life could be created. This is our idea, whose execution appears grandiose and desirable, appears to us to be possible and not too difficult.[2]

Capitalizing on the social ills and unrest in Germany, Münch and Follenius soon gained a following, with six hundred members, from varied backgrounds, selected to emigrate in 1834. Though the endeavor ultimately failed—or at least was considered to have—due to disease and other misfortunes along the way, it brought over Georg Bunsen, an individual who went on to make contributions in the realm of education in Illinois (see the sidebar on Georg Bunsen in chapter 6).

Across the Atlantic, and just a couple of years later in 1836, the German Settlement Society of Philadelphia was formed with much the same goal: to establish a settlement "farther west where German culture, German language, and German traditional values could be perpetuated."[3] What's especially striking in this particular case is that the society was founded in Pennsylvania, a state that had a solid German presence. Indeed, already by 1800, an estimated 150,000 Germans called Pennsylvania home. It might come as a surprise, then, that the founders of the society, recent immigrants from Germany and other German-speaking countries, deemed Philadelphia unsuitable. But, according to Schroeder,

the new immigrants had found the old stock settlers distressingly Americanized and became convinced that only by seeking a new and isolated location in the western United States could they safeguard German culture and create a more favorable environment for future generations while at the same time continuing to enjoy the rights and privileges of their new adopted country."[4]

So, to fulfill their utopian dream of a German state, they chose to settle in Hermann, Missouri, located in the Missouri River Valley. While it never became a "new Germany," it did become known as "Little Germany."

Gustav Körner

Gustav Körner was an exceptional figure in Illinois. Adamantly opposed to slavery, he chose to make Illinois, a free state, his adopted home after being forced to flee Germany in 1833 due to his

Fig. 2.5. Gustav Körner, 1836. Courtesy Northern Illinois University.

involvement in a failed coup to evoke revolution there.[1] Among a great deal else, he became the first German in Illinois to be elected to state office. His life story and achievements are remarkable, so much so that they merit distinct recognition.[2]

Born in 1809, Körner came of age in post-Napoleonic Europe. As a law student at Jena, and like many liberals, educated professionals, and intellectuals at the time, Körner rejected the repressive political conditions of a feudal, conservative hierarchy. He joined the *Burschenschaft*, a student organization at German universities that advocated for reform and national unification of Germany. Hopeful of change, he and his peers studied, among much else, English and American constitutional law. He continued his studies at Munich where he experienced his first encounters with authorities. Believed to be a threat to the state, he was jailed for four months, during which time he "learned more law . . . than I had in Jena for two years."[3]

Completing his studies at Heidelberg, where he was awarded a doctorate of law in 1832, he moved back to his hometown, Frankfurt, to practice law. It wasn't a particularly restful or peaceful time though; revolt was in the air. The revolutions in France, Belgium, Italy, Switzerland, Spain, Poland, and parts of Germany, although mostly short-lived and ineffective, hit home, especially with students and intellectuals who were eager for liberal reform. Calling on local chapters of the *Burschenschaft*, he and his peers, including Theodore Engelmann, planned a revolt (a one-day attack on military forces and government offices to gain control of the treasury) in Frankfurt, later known as the Frankfurter Wachensturm. Almost as quickly as the April 3, 1833, revolution began, it ended, with someone having informed the authorities of the offensive in advance. Wounded in battle, Körner had to leave Germany in order to avoid arrest.

With the help of his family, Körner, disguised as a woman (grudgingly, we might add), met up with Engelmann, dressed as a country gentleman. Together, they quickly fled Germany and made their way to the port city of Le Havre on France's western coast. With Engelmann's family, they set sail for America on May 1, 1833. At sea, Körner proposed to Sophie, Engelmann's sister. The group traveled west upon arriving in New York City, taking advantage of the east-west water route afforded by the Erie Canal.[4] Continuing their route to St. Louis on the Ohio River, Körner observed slavery firsthand, seeing slaves labor and toil along the banks of the river. Finding the institution hideous and vile, he knew he could never put down roots in a slave state like Missouri, as noted in his memoirs:

> At Louisville we put our feet for the first time on slave soil. What we heard here and what we saw, (for instance, negroes chained together hauling water from the river,) contributed to our detestation of the institution of slavery and confirmed our determination not to settle in Missouri.[5]

So, he and his fellow travelers settled in the free state of Illinois in 1833. Körner's experiences in Germany, political and educational, prepared him for leadership in his newly adopted home state.

His first order of business included passing the state bar exam in 1835 and then marrying Sophie a year later (with whom he had nine children). At the same time, he tried his hand at farming (though it was not his intention to farm for a living), working alongside the Engelmann family, and strived to improve his English. With political aspirations, Körner joined the Democratic Party, a party that was considered favorable toward immigrants and, thus, more liberal than the nativist-leaning Whig Party (which dissolved in the 1850s because of splintering views on the matter of slavery in the new territories). In 1837 he served as delegate to the Democratic State Convention, and a mere five years later, in 1842, he was elected to state legislature. On a roll, he was appointed to the Supreme Court in 1843. Ever active in politics, he was subsequently elected lieutenant governor in 1852.

His course as a Democratic superstar seemed set. Yet Körner, in staunch opposition to slavery, couldn't get behind 1854's Kansas-Nebraska Act, which enabled settlers—white males—to have the final say regarding slavery within each territory, thus annulling the Missouri Compromise of 1820. On the whole, Germans disapproved of slavery. In 1856, Körner broke from the Democrats and joined the new Republican Party, as did many other opponents to the act in Illinois. Quickly rising in the ranks, he served as president of the Illinois Republican State Convention in 1858, a position that was influential in locking the U.S. Senate nomination for Abraham Lincoln. Lincoln, in return, appointed Körner as minister to Spain in 1862, frequently soliciting his advice and assistance on attaining the German vote in Illinois during his presidential campaign. Throughout the Civil War, Körner offered his services in support of the Union cause. The relationship between Lincoln and Körner was one of mutual respect and admiration, with Körner being one of twelve Illinois pallbearers at Lincoln's burial in Springfield.

All the while, and set atop these achievements, Körner was an avid journalist and author, writing numerous articles in papers like the *Belleviller Zeitung* and St. Louis's *Anzeiger des Westens*, typically of a political persuasion, both in the states and abroad; books; and, in his final years, his two-volume memoirs. One of his earliest articles published in Germany, "Review of Duden's Report Concerning the Western States of North America," contradicted Duden's idealized view of life in America and, perhaps more importantly, criticized his promotion of Missouri as a promising state for Germans on account of slavery, thus advocating for Illinois in its stead. His books were, in a word, informative, offering a social history of events and people at the time. His book *Das deutsche Element in den Vereinigten Staaten von Nordamerika 1818–1848*, for example, provides an exhaustive and early account of Germans in the United States from the early to mid-1800s. Moreover, he wrote extensively on the life of Germans in Illinois, providing some of the earliest documentation we have on families and settlements there.

In the course of a long career (he died in 1896 at the age of eighty-seven), he served his country and the people in it, championing the causes of the underprivileged as a lawyer, politician, statesman, judge, and journalist. And those were merely his practical achievements. The voice he gave a growing immigrant population—and the clout his voice afforded them as Germans in the New World—was equally significant. The home he shared with his family is listed in the National Register of Historic Places in Belleville, Illinois.

3

THE JOURNEY TO ILLINOIS

Now that we have considered both the push and pull motives for migration, it might seem obvious that someone would decide to leave Germany in the nineteenth century. But leaving meant obtaining emigration consent from the authorities, abandoning loved ones and familiar places, enduring an arduous and often dangerous trip across the Atlantic, and having the wherewithal to forge a new life.[1] It also meant having enough money to make the journey in the first place. In spite of all adversity, many secured passage abroad, with the early 1850s seeing over half a million Germans cross the ocean.[2]

Bremen and Hamburg were the primary ports of departure, as were Le Havre (in France), Antwerp (in Belgium), and Rotterdam (in the Netherlands; refer back to figures 1.3 and 1.4 in chapter 1 to trace the rivers that provided a sea route for these emigrants).[3] Yet, a ticket bought only passage, not comfort, to the New World. It took sailing vessels, on average, a grueling six to seven weeks to make the crossing. Though steamships came into regular use in the 1850s, thus reducing the journey to half that time and, consequently, the hardships of the journey, they were high priced and not favored over sailing boats until years later.[4] It wasn't until 1869, for example, that "the mode of conveyance was 517 to 183 in favor of steamboats."[5]

Endeavoring to make a profit, companies and ticketing agents in the mid-nineteenth century overbooked their vessels, with many passengers lacking a bed to sleep in. Others were housed in the filthy cargo holds of the ship. All the more aggravating was the fact that the crew was not favorably disposed to passengers, often forcing them to help maintain the ship and do chores. Conditions were deplorable, with accounts reporting that there

Vor und während einer Seereise.

Sind Sie zum ersten Male zur See?	Is this the first time you are going to sea?	is this dhe förßt teim juhahr goh-ing tu ßih?
Ja wohl, ich bin noch nie zur See gewesen.	Yes, I was never at sea before.	jeß, ei was newwer ät ßih bifohr.
Fürchten Sie sich vor der Seekrankheit?	Are you afraid of sea-sickness?	ahr juh äfrehd ov ßih-ßikkneß?
Ich glaube, ich leide schon daran.	I think, I suffer from it already.	ei think, ei ßöffer from it ahlreddi.
Ich fühle mich sehr schwach und muß mich oft erbrechen.	I feel very weak and must vomit often.	ei fihl werri wihk änd mößt wommit oft'n.
Ich habe heftige Kopfschmerzen.	I have a severe headache.	ei häw ä ßiwihr heddehk.
Haben Sie Geduld, es wird bald vergehen.	Have patience, it will soon be over.	häw pehschens. it 'will ßuhn bih ohwer.
Es ist eine Folge der Seekrankheit, welche vom Schwanken des Schiffes herrührt.	It is in consequence of sea-sickness, caused by the rocking of the ship.	it is in konßekwenß ov ßih-ßikkneß, kahß'd bei dhe rokking ov dhe schip.

Fig. 3.1. "Before and during a Sea Voyage," a page from an immigrant guidebook to the English language. Afflictions of nausea and seasickness were emphasized, as was the pronunciation of English words by way of phonetic German on the right-hand side. From *Amerikanischer Dolmetscher, der unfehlbare Rathgeber für Einwanderer und Eingewanderte* (Philadelphia: Demokrat Publishing Company, circa 1880s–1890s), 120; courtesy Max Kade Institute for German-American Studies at the University of Wisconsin–Madison.

was often only one toilet per one hundred passengers on these ships. Mortality rates were high as crowded ships became breeding grounds for deadly diseases, such as cholera and dysentery. News of the dreadful conditions even reached Congress, who, in 1855, intervened, limiting the load to one passenger per two tons of vessel weight.[6]

The dietary conditions weren't much better. One immigrant ship from Hamburg, the *Howard*, arrived in New York in 1858 "with no drinking water left, a food shortage, and 37 dead from Cholera."[7] Indeed, within days of the journey, hunger and thirst plagued a great number of passengers who typically lived off of "heavily salted meat (often rotten and full of maggots), meal pudding, prunes, potatoes, and watery soups made from dried beans."[8] And safe drinking water was, at best, scarce and, at worst, nonexistent.

Despite these dreadful ordeals, scores of newcomers landed on American soil. Nothing better exemplifies the experience than letters from those who endured the voyage. In a letter to his parents on March 13, 1854, Carl Sieveking vividly recounts the horrors of his transatlantic trip:

> *[O]n the North Sea the passengers began complaining; on the first day we got nothing at all hot to eat, though it was very cold, on the 2nd and 3rd we got only a piece of meat, which we could hardly eat as we had no water for our thirst, on the 4th day we received our rations, but very little; . . . The first 14 days were O.K., it was still edible, but in the 3rd and 4th week it was so moldy that we could just get 1 lb. of good bread from a 8 lb. loaf, but we received nothing else to eat. If we went to the captain we were beaten, or were threatened with being clapped in irons. But nevertheless we were obliged to sing the praises of the man who helped us on board such a pirate ship . . . we had a barber on board, who was supposed to be our doctor on board; if we told the barber to help the sick, he said he could do nothing. . . . It was terrible for the sick people. Most died in the first 4 weeks, indeed most of them died of thirst. . . . Along on our ship 85 people died, if we had not received drinking water at all, then we would have all died. We also had trouble with vermin, you can hardly imagine the filth.*
>
> *Carl Sieveking, St. Louis*[9]

After weeks or even months at sea, the journey didn't end for Illinois-bound German immigrants. Their initial experience upon arrival was often one of chaos as they looked for lost bags, tried to find food and housing, searched for relatives, or just generally tried to get their bearings.[10] Many didn't even have a chance to explore their port of embarkation, heading directly to the trains and ships that took them West (see figures 3.2 and 3.3 for common routes immigrants took to reach Illinois).

There were four primary ports of entry for European immigrants in the nineteenth century: New Orleans, New York, Philadelphia, and Baltimore.[11] Before the explosion of railroads in the 1850s, most Germans traveled to the Midwest via rivers, canals, and lakes (though some did make the long journey overland on the National or Cumberland Road). Those bound for Illinois often landed in New Orleans, where they then could take a steamboat and travel up the Mississippi to St. Louis. An uneventful trip up the river, which was the distance of about twelve hundred miles, would take about a week. From there, many Germans settled in the counties directly across the river from St. Louis, as we have seen. Others traveled further north, arriving in Quincy or Galena, with Galena being a major steamboat hub. Germans landing in

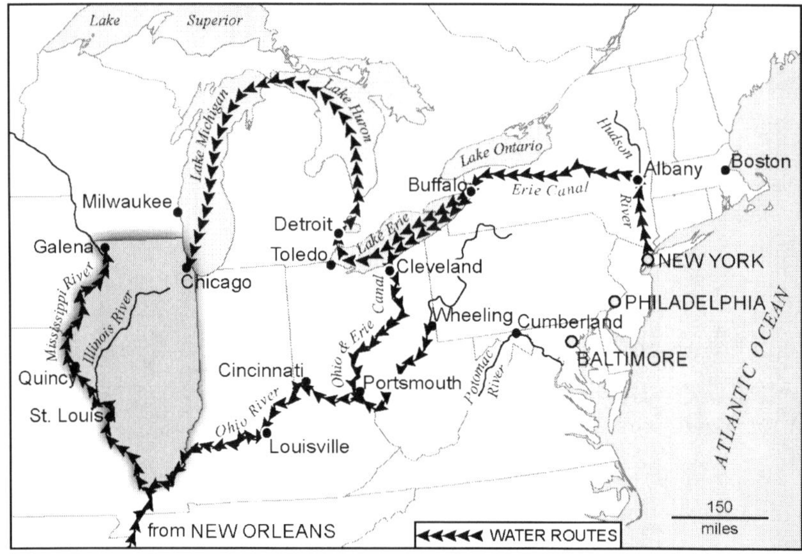

Fig. 3.2. Water migration routes to Illinois in the nineteenth century. Arrowheads represent flow of immigrants by water to Illinois. Arrivals to Baltimore, for example, also would have had to travel overland to reach Wheeling (see figure 3.3).

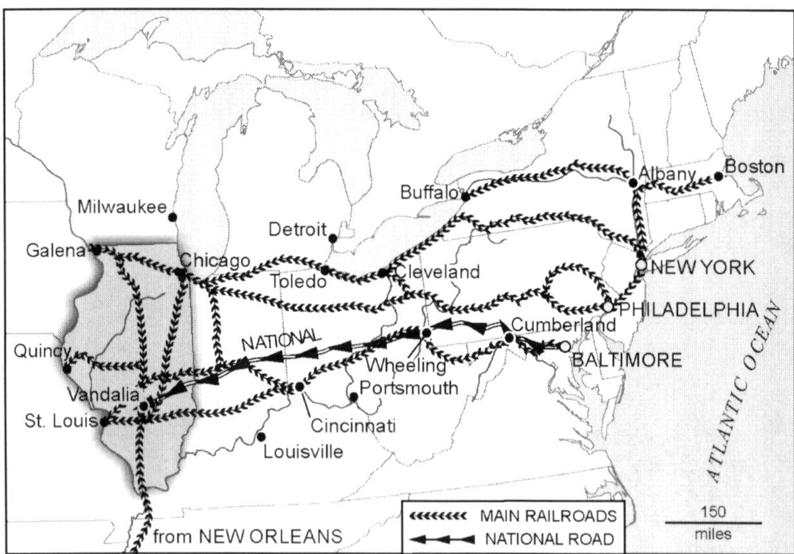

Fig. 3.3. Overland migration routes to Illinois in the nineteenth century. Arrowheads represent flow of immigrants overland to Illinois. Railroad locations are based on information available online at "Railroads and the Making of Modern America," a digital history project of the University of Nebraska–Lincoln, http://railroads.unl.edu.

Baltimore or Philadelphia, on the other hand, typically traveled overland to the Ohio River where they could then board a boat headed toward Illinois or other neighboring states. Arrivals to New York, which was the leading port of entry throughout the period of mass migration from Europe, made use of waterways as well, often traveling to Detroit via the Erie Canal.[12] They then journeyed by way of the Great Lakes to Chicago and its vicinity.[13] By 1841, improvements in steamship technology reduced travel time between Buffalo and Chicago to nine days.[14]

By the 1850s, rail travel offered an even faster option for traveling inland, cutting the journey from New York to Chicago to a mere thirty-six hours.[15] This decade saw railroad operation in Illinois go from 110 to 2,867 miles of track, with Illinois enjoying more railroad mileage than any other state except Ohio by 1860.[16] Around the time of the Civil War, New Orleans lost its status as a major entry port for European immigrants due to the Union's blockade as well as the staggering growth of rail networks along the eastern seaboard (though it did see a bump in traffic in line with the 1880s wave of southeastern European migrants).[17] Chicago, with its robust rail network, became the Midwest hub for railroad travel in 1860, taking in scores of immigrants from eastern seaports like New York. These new arrivals swarmed into well-known communities but also formed new ones in the interior and northern parts of the state (refer back to figure 2.3 for migration routes and clusters within Illinois).

Despite these improvements, immigrants still faced crowded conditions, abuse, and exploitation as they made their way by train to Illinois and arrived at their destination. From the moment they landed in America, German immigrants were vulnerable to an array of unprincipled individuals and businesses whose sole interest was in bilking new arrivals out of as much of their money as possible. To turn a profit, railroad workers on special immigrant trains en route to Chicago, for example, were paid by hotel and saloon owners to make unnecessary stops along the way. Price gouging, unfair money exchanges, and downright robbery were common.

In Chicago especially, boardinghouses and restaurants were in the practice of sending "runners," who were usually German themselves, to meet newly arrived immigrants at train stations and docks where they would hustle an immigrant over to the boardinghouse. There the immigrant would be quoted a reasonable price for room and board and enticed to stay for a few days; upon leaving, the charge would suddenly double or triple in amount.[18] Partly in response to this exploitation, the *Deutsche Gesellschaft von Chicago*, or German Aid Society was founded in 1854. Its aim was to help Germans assimilate and avoid being swindled.[19] Despite published warnings in the *Emigrant Guides*, immigrants were often exploited given their unfamiliarity with the language and customs. By offering free employment services, the German Aid Society did much to prevent a great many Germans from being conned by employment agents.

However taxing the journey was, it was understood as a means to an end. And the end was Illinois, a state that openly welcomed and acknowledged newcomers from the East Coast as well as from Europe, most especially Germany. As their mass migration spanned a half century, German immigrants brought with them a wide variety of perspectives and experiences, and they entered Illinois with diverse goals and at different stages of the state's development. These factors impacted where they settled, what they did, and how they fared. With that, let's see how their influence unfolds in the following chapters.

Cornelius Schubert: Diary of a Journey

Written from the viewpoint of a single, often ordinary individual and usually without any particular audience in mind, diaries can provide unique perspective into an event or time period. A peek into the diary of Cornelius Schubert as he made his way from Dessau, Germany, to Belleville, Illinois, shows us intimate examples of many experiences common to early immigrants. In 1834, when he was twenty years old, Schubert left Dessau, landed in Baltimore, and traveled to Belleville (overland via Wheeling and then, presumably, via the Ohio River to the St. Louis area), where he lived for several years until he married his wife, who was from Missouri. They lived in Atchison County, Missouri, for a number of years until they moved back to Belleville in 1859. An artistic family, they ran a photography and sign shop in Belleville and worked in local theater. Schubert died in 1876, leaving his wife and one surviving son. Here we present some excerpts from his 1834 diary.[1]

First, though, it's worth acknowledging a few particulars about his westward journey. For one thing, it began on Harriersand, an island in the Weser River between Bremen and Bremerhaven.

Because the ship Schubert was originally supposed to sail on, the *Everhart*, never arrived, he spent a good month waiting it out on this island—where meals and lodging were cheaper—before he was eventually assigned to the *Medora*. The shipping agent involved in the booking was of little use in helping him and his companions recoup the costs associated with their stay, proving to be, in Schubert's words, a "swindler and rogue," who in the end profited from their misfortune. So when the *Medora* finally did arrive, the reaction was one of joy and relief.

The *Medora* had three masts, one bowsprit, and 32 sails, and it measured 112 feet long, 26 feet wide, and 112 feet high, including the mast. The crew consisted of 20–25 men, including the captain, and there were 200 passengers on board. Among those passengers were many members of the famed Giessen Society, including cofounder Friedrich Münch (or "Pastor Münch," as Schubert called him), bound for Missouri (see chapter 2's side story, "A German State in the Upper Mississippi Valley").[2] Like most sailing vessels, it took the *Medora* about seven weeks to cross the Atlantic, and considering that Schubert shared a bed with three other people, there was imaginably little room for privacy, and, to be sure, no comfort. The trip itself was mostly without incident, but, as Schubert makes known, nothing about it was easy:

> *Monday, May 19th*
>
> *[T]here came a steamship from Bremen . . . brought us the joyful news that the ship* Medora *commanded by the American captain, Griffith, in which we were to sail, had arrived and would unload day and night so that by next Saturday we could move in. . . . Shouting of "lebe hock" many times and throwing hats high in the air we greeted the coming* Medora *. . .*
>
> *Thursday, May 29th*
>
> *Now at last the day arrived when we could leave this place of exile. I arose with the sun and took to the boats what I still had with me. . . . There she lay, the stately* Medora *which has to take us to the land of freedom and equality, our new Fatherland. Scarcely had we arrived on deck where everything was still in the greatest disorder . . .*
>
> *Saturday, May 31st*
>
> *With distribution of the eating and drinking the following method is used. Everyone gets his coffee, which is served at 7*

o'clock in his own cup. At 10 o'clock we receive whisky, but of which I do not partake as everyone must drink out of the same vessel. . . . Our dinner is brought in a little tub always enough for ten people, who have to divide that among themselves. The evening meal is just the same. The water is in a keg on deck, holds about five or six buckets of water, where everyone can drink as long as it lasts and it is replaced by a full one every morning. But to wash we have to get it up on board with a bucket.

Tuesday, June 3rd

Today Captain Griffith gave us some rules and Pastor Münch translated them into German. 1. No one could comb or wash on deck after 7 a.m. (children under one year excepted.) 2. No one could comb or wash in steerage at anytime (unless sick). 3. Soiled clothes shall be washed before breakfast on Tuesday. 4. Every morning before breakfast and after each meal the deck must be swept, To do this the passengers can portion it off into several sections. The dirt to be thrown overboard. 5. Smoking is forbidden in steerage. 6. Only by special permission of the Captain can light be had in steerage. 7. Must scrub and clean steerage twice each week (Wednesday and Saturday) 8. Without permission no one can descend to storage room. 9. Fresh water must not be used in washing in any manner. It is one of the most necessary things of the sea and one which can not be substituted. For that reason all passengers are requested to use as sparingly as possible. Namely, to use it only for cooking and drinking. If any wasting of it is noticed, smaller portions will be allowed. 10. If there should be any quarreling among passengers, the court of arbitration shall immediately settle it, as no violent altercations are permitted. 11. We expect that no passengers converse with the sailors, as that could keep them from fulfilling their duties. 12. If there are any complaints, they shall be laid before the Captain, who is ready at all times to hear and help. These rules were made to insure the wellbeing of the passengers, and the Captain trusts that the passengers will recognize the Captains good intentions to keep the rules listed above. Again it is recommended that the greatest cleanliness in all ways be practised [sic], for without which so large a company could not escape the worst diseases.

Wednesday, June 4th

[T]he boat was thrown around until many became seasick and soon I became quite dizzy, accompanied by a complete weakness. . . . There I lay scarcely conscious . . . forsaken by everything

that I hold dear. . . . I began to realize what I had left behind. Surrounded, not really by strangers, but by those who were not bound to me by ties of friendship. Only the uplifting thought of the freedom before me could cheer me somewhat.

Monday, June 9th

This morning we had a calm which lasted until about noon and we lay opposite a high limestone cliff. Afternoon we had a strong wind that took us close to land past the summer home of the King of England and we were so close that it was necessary to turn the ship sharply which was done at the sharp command of the Captain.

Tuesday June 24th

Today is St. John's day and under the 48°N B and DI from Greenwich our population was increased by the arrival of a little girl. . . . The father immediately named her Medora Johanna after the ship and for St. John's day. We are now about half way.

Thursday June 26th

Today our ship was in danger of sailing into another ship. There appeared, about three o'clock, a sail on the horizon at our left . . . Scarcely had we noticed this than it seemed to turn and come straight toward us. The Captain thinking they wanted to talk to us had one sail after the other reefed (shortened) in order to give it time to come near. It was so close that we could see the people on the ship and saw how they were busy with continual pumping. Where-at we concluded the ship was leaking and needed our help. At that moment the Captain thought that it would turn in order to come to our side but in spite of all shoutings it sailed right in front of us and only a few feet more and we would have sunk it to the bottom of the sea. Our Captain, greatly frightened, had our ship turned quickly so that it passed quite close along side. Furious, especially at the inactive gaping of the sailors on the other ship, our Captain scolded and swore at their negligence. Instead of apologizing they laughed and made the most devilish faces and one of them asked if we were going to America. On the ship was neither captain nor mate to be seen and only one sailor seemed to be on the ship. Our Captain had never found himself in such danger in his entire life and thought that the ship had wanted him to run into it so he would have to pay the damages. Toward evening the youngest child, not quite six months old, of Druggist Bruhl, died.

Sunday July 20th

At 11:30 the cry of "Land!, Land!" from the craw's nest awakened me out of my reveries and about 2 P.M. I had the pleasure of seeing land again, after six weeks of water. But how different it was from what I had imagined it would be! Not the bare cliffs of England, or the flat strips of Germany did I see here—no I saw a dark green expanse of rolling land covered with trees.

Monday July 21st

At 9 A.M. we had before us the wide expanse of Cape Harry and the wind was weak so we sailed into Chesapeake Bay about noon.

N.D.

As I have had no time to write for four weeks, I will now narrate further. . . . The first person who met us in the new world was a collector for a hospital for sick immigrants and each had to give him $1. 50. After this man left us the physician appeared . . . who examined the health condition of our people while enjoying several bottles of wine with our Captain. . . . Now my first need was to find a place to stay in company with Bunkwitz. We found a place in half an hour and agreed to pay $2.00 per person for a week. As the Captain did not want to unload the baggage until the next morning, we started to do it ourselves and brought the boxes, many weighing 600 pounds from the lower decks to the wharf where many men with two wheel wagons were waiting to take them one mile for half a dollar. The custom officials were on the wharf ready to examine them for 25cts. . . . After one week in Baltimore I, with two other families, hired a freight wagon which is built very light but durable and with six horses can take from 5000 to 6000 pounds. We loaded our baggage on-it and drove out of the city. Two women, one maid-servant and six children of which none has reached the age of seven years, climbed on the wagon and with much jolting passed through the uneven streets. We men walked in front, behind, and on both sides of the wagon in order to pick up such small articles as fell off. I carried a double-barreled shot gun, a couteau de chasse (hunting knife), and a game bag. . . . After we had been on this trip two weeks we arrived on the top of the last high hill from which we had a fine view of the Ohio Valley and soon drove into Wheeling.

1868 New York Immigration Commission Report on the *Leibnitz*

The following excerpt from the New York Immigration Commission's 1868 report of the sailing vessel, *Leibnitz*, is remarkably similar in description to the Sieveking letter. What makes this report especially powerful is that it not only substantiates the claim that many U.S. directives for provision allowances, such as water, were violated, it also bears direct testimony to the sufferings, including extortion, many America-bound (and in the case of this ship's passengers, Illinois- and Wisconsin-bound) German emigrants faced. In it, the spoiled provisions as well as the sullied, poorly ventilated quarters and the arresting death toll are, among much else, detailed.

> The *Leibnitz*, originally the *Van Couver*, is a large and fine vessel, built at Boston for the China trade, and formerly plying between that port and China. She was sold some years ago to the house of Robert M. Sloman, and has since sailed under her present name . . . she left Hamburg, Nov. 2, 1867, Capt. H. F. Bornhold, lay at Cuxhaven, on account of head-winds, until the 11th, whereupon she took the southern course to New York. She went by the way of Madeira, down to the Tropics, 20th degree, and arrived in the Lower Bay on Jan. 11, 1868, after a passage of 61 days, or rather 70 days—at least, as far as the passengers are concerned, who were confined to the densely crowded steerage for that length of time.
>
> The heat, for the period that they were in the lower latitudes, very often reached 24 degrees of Reaumur, or 94 degrees of Fahrenheit. Her passengers 544 in all—of whom 395 were adults, 103 children, and 46 infants—came principally from Mecklenburg, and proposed to settle as farmer and laborers in Illinois and Wisconsin; besides them, there were about 40 Prussians from Pomerania and Posen, and a few Saxons and Thuringians.
>
> It is not proven by any fact, that the cholera (as has been alleged) raged or had raged in or near their homes when or before they left them. This statement appears to have been made by or in behalf of those who have an interest in throwing the origin of the sickness on its poor victims. Of

these 544 German passengers, 105 died on the voyage, and three in port, making it a total of 108 deaths—leaving 436 surviving. The first death occurred on Nov. 25th. On some days, as for instance on Dec. 1, nine passengers died, and on Dec. 17, eight. The sickness did not abate until toward the end of December, and no new cases happened with the ship had again reached the northern latitudes; five children were born; during the voyage some families had died out entirely; of others, the fathers and mothers are gone; here, a husband had left a poor widow, with small children; and there, a husband had lost his wife. We spoke to some little boys and girls, who, when asked where were their parents, pointed to the ocean with sobs and tears, and cried, "*Down there!*"

Prior to our arrival on board, the ship had been cleansed and fumigated several times, but not sufficiently so to remove the dirt, which, in some places, covered the walls. Mr. Frederick Kassner, our able and experienced Boarding Officer, reports that he found the ship and the passengers in a most filthy condition, and that when boarding the *Leibnitz* he hardly discovered a clean spot on the ladder, or on the ropes, where he could put his hands and feet. He does not remember to have seen anything like it within the last five years. Captain True, who likewise boarded the ship immediately after her arrival, corroborates the statement of Mr. Kassner.

As to the interior of the vessel, the upper steerage is high and wide. All the spars, beams, and planks which were used for the construction of temporary berths had been removed. Except through two hatchways and two very small ventilators, it had no ventilation, and not a single window or bull's-eye was open during the voyage. In general, however, it was not worse than the average of the steerages of other emigrant ships; but the lower steerage, the so-called orlop-deck, is a perfect pesthole, calculated to kill the healthiest man. It had been made a temporary room for the voyage by laying a tier of planks over the lower beams of the vessel, and they were so little supported that they shook when walking on them. The little light this orlop-deck received came through one of the hatchways of the upper-deck. Although the latter was open when we were on board, and although the ship was lying in the open sea, free from all sides, it was impossible to see anything at a distance of two or three feet. On our enquiring how this hole had been lighted during the voyage, we were told that some lanterns had been up there, but that on account of the foulness of air, they could scarcely burn. . . . And in this place about 120 passengers were crowded for 70 days, and for a greater part of the voyage in a tropical heat, with scanty rations and a very inadequate supply of water, and worse than all, suffering from the miasma below, above, and beside them, which itself must create fever and pestilence.

The captain himself stated to us that the passengers refused to carry the excrements on deck, and that "the urine and ordure of the upper-steerage flowed down to the lower." As that main-deck was very difficult to access from the orlop-deck, the inmates of the latter often failed to go on deck even to attend to the calls of nature. There were only six water-closets for the accommodation of all the passengers. They have been cleansed, of course; but the smell that emanated from them was still very intense, and corroborates the statement of the above-named officers—that they must have been in an extraordinary frightful condition . . .

There was not a single emigrant who did not complain of the captain, as well as of the short allowance of provisions and water on board. As we know, from a long experience, that the passengers of emigrant ships, with a very few exceptions, are in the habit of claiming more than they are entitled to, we are far from putting implicit faith in all their statements. There is as much falsehood and exaggeration among this class of people as among any other body of uneducated men. We have, therefore, taken their complaints with due allowance, and report only so much thereof as we believe to be well founded.

All the passengers concur in the complaint that their provisions were short, partly rotten, and that, especially, the supply of water was insufficient, until they were approaching port. We examined the provisions on board, and found that the water was clean and pure. If the whole supply during the voyage was such as the samples handed to use, there was no reason for complaint as to the quality. But, in quantity, the complaints of the passengers are too well founded; for they unanimously state, and are not effectually contradicted by the captain, that they never received more than half a pint of drinkable water per day, while by the laws of the United States they were entitled to receive three quarts. Some of the biscuit handed to us was rotten and old, and hardly eatable; other pieces were better. We ordered the steward to open a cask of cornbeef, and found it of ordinary good quality; the butter, however, was rancid. Once a week herrings were cooked instead of meat. The beans and sauerkraut were often badly cooked, and, in spite of hunger, thrown overboard.

The treatment of passengers was heartless in the extreme. The sick passengers received the same food with the healthy, and high prices were exacted for all extras and comforts. A regular traffic in wine, beer, and liquors was carried on between the passengers on the one side and the steward and crew on the other. A man by the name of Frederick Hildebrand, from Wirsitz, in Posen, who lost two children, paid 35 Prussian thalers extra for beer and wine to sustain himself and his sick wife. A bottle of rum cost him one dollar; a bottle of bad wine even more. "This extortion, at such a time, cannot be too strongly condemned," says Captain True, in his report, which confirms the information received by us from the passengers.

When the first deaths occurred, the corpses were often suffered to remain in the steerage for full twenty-four hours. In some cases the bodies were covered with vermin before they were removed.

There was no physician on board. Although we found a large medicine-chest, it was not large enough for the many cases of sickness, and was, in fact, emptied after the first two weeks of the voyage.

The captain seems to have been sadly deficient in energy and authority in matters of moment, while he punished severely small offences; as, for instance, he handcuffed a passenger for the use of insulting words; but he did not enforce the plainest rules for the health and welfare of his passengers. Instead of compelling them, from the first, to come on deck and remove the dirt, he allowed them to remain below, and to perish among their own excrements. Of the whole crew, the cook alone fell sick and died, as he slept in the steerage. Three passenger girls who were employed in the kitchen, and lived on deck, enjoyed excellent health, during the whole voyage.

The physicians above mentioned, to whose report we refer for particulars, most positively declare that it was not Asiatic cholera, but intestinal and stomach catarrh (catarrh ventriculi et intestinorum), more or less severe, and contagious typhus, which killed the passengers. From what we saw and learned from the passengers, we likewise arrive at the conclusion that the shocking mortality on board the *Leibnitz* arose from want of good ventilation, cleanliness, suitable medical care, sufficient water, and whole-some food.

The present case is another instance of mortality on board the Hamburg sailing-vessels, and increases their bad reputation. Of 917 passengers on board of two ships of the Sloman line, not less than 183 died within one month! . . .[1]

4

RURAL AND URBAN LIVING

Settling Illinois at a time when land was cheap and abundant, early arrivals to the fertile Mississippi Valley, or "American Bottom," unsurprisingly set out to work the land, or at least have a go at it. Those with means tended to purchase already established farms in rural areas or towns rather than start their own. An observation in the *History of St. Clair County* reads,

> The German . . . is not exactly a pioneer or frontiersman. He prefers to make his home in districts where the American pioneer has performed the arduous task of opening the wilderness to cultivation. The plow is the German's "forte" not the axe nor the rifle.[1]

Though in a few years' time immigrants could acquire land at almost no cost by way of the Homestead Act, the capital required to clear it and prepare the prairie soil was often prohibitive.[2] Indeed, less than one-fifth of the five hundred million acres distributed by the General Land Office between 1862 and 1904 went to farmers.[3] It was therefore more economical to purchase plots of land from the Illinois Central Railroad rather than acquire it "free and clear" by way of the Homestead Act.[4] And purchase they did; among newcomers to the state, Germans quickly became Illinois Central's top clients, with sales cresting in the late 1860s.[5] Establishing a farm along the planned railroad route from Chicago to Cairo also made good practical sense; farmers had the assurance of quick and easy access to markets by rail. They also had "the benefits of religious and intellectual culture" since churches had already been "planted" and schools "organized" along the route.[6]

The Illinois Central sold tracts of land starting at forty acres, with the per-acre purchase price ranging from six to twenty-five

Fig. 4.1. Drawing of a farm owned by Jacob Wagner, a prominent Adams County citizen and second-generation German American who came to Illinois from Pennsylvania. The residence is described as "a frame building, has two stories, good cellar, seven rooms. . . . The yard is shaded with fruit, evergreen, and other forest trees. The barn was built in 1867, and is well arranged. Among the prominent out-buildings are an ice house, smoke house, &c. The orchard is quite extensive, containing over six hundred fruit trees, of all varieties. . . . As to fence, there are three hundred and twenty rods of hedge, three miles of rail, and seventy rods of board. One hundred and eighty acres are under cultivation, and seventy are in grass and pasture. Mr. W. has nine horses, twelve cows, and twenty hogs. He also has seventy acres of timber in Section 33. The city of Quincy is six miles distant. It is only one mile to a good public school. The soil is well drained, fertile, and of a dry nature. Large crops have been raised. The farm is valued at eighty dollars per acre. The neighborhood is well settled, and the society will compare, for intelligence and morality, with any in the state." Image and description found in A. T. Andreas, W. P. Campbell, D. W. Ensign, and N. Friend, *Atlas Map of Adams County, Illinois: Compiled, Drawn, and Published from Personal Examinations and Surveys* (Davenport, IA: Andreas, Lyter & Co., 1872), image on p. 76, caption on p. 94. Courtesy of Quincy Public Library.

dollars according to an 1859 guide put out by the railroad office.[7] Starting a family farm meant more than procuring land, however. It also required buying lumber and other materials to build a homestead, fencing, and other accommodations. Then, of course, there was also the matter of purchasing seed, cattle, and field tools, placing the average total cost of a forty-acre farm at midcentury just above $1,000. That was a pittance compared to prices in Germany, which resulted in Germans purchasing much larger landholdings than they would have back home. Descriptions of farms or farm life found in primary source material, such as pamphlets put out by the Illinois Central Railroad, point to most farms measuring at around 160 acres. An 1889 description of a farm in St. Clair County reads,

> A farm of 140 acres, three miles southwest of Georgetown in Prairie du Long, 100 acres in cultivation, 20 acres pasture, a pretty creek runs through it, with sufficient and healthy water for the animals, also growing on the same is the prettiest young wood for miles in the whole area, the other 20 acres are regular heavy woodland, also there is a spacious house on the same, with 4 rooms, garret, cellar and porch, barn 20x20, fruit house 16x18, surrounded with fence, also smoke house, chicken house, oven, cisterns, and a well . . . young orchard with the latest types of fruit, apples, peaches, plums, blackberries, strawberries, 100 fruiting grapevines of various types, all the best, a number of ornamental and shade trees, etc.[8]

Farm Life

Germans readily adapted to life on the American farm, which often included gardens and orchards, though it has been described in the literature as seemingly "lonely" and "isolated" by comparison.[9] To be sure, American farmsteads were much larger and more remote than those in Germany, which also made reliance on farming machinery both necessary and common in grain-growing regions like the Midwest.[10] Typical crops included corn, wheat, oats, and hay. Corn, often referred to as "Turkish wheat" in immigrant letters, was a new, swiftly embraced grain crop for Germans. By contrast, staples from the homeland, such as rye, potatoes, and barley, were in less demand here than in Germany.

Labor was shared among family members. As they had in Germany, wives and children often took on heavy duties, reportedly more so than their American counterparts whom many Germans viewed as entitled by comparison. Letters from the immigrants themselves declare as much as the following excerpt from *Contented among Strangers* affirms:[11]

> A common opinion among German-speaking immigrants was that women had many rights in America, perhaps even more than was good for them. One recently arrived immigrant from Illinois wrote, "America is the best land for women. It is not the custom for them to work and they have many rights here. Therefore all the German women like it here. My wife thinks

> a lot about home, but she is quite healthy, for she weighs one hundred and eighty pounds." The sequence of his ideas may indicate that he feared America was spoiling his wife, causing her to become fat and lazy.[12]

Perhaps a more fundamental conclusion that we may draw from the foregoing excerpt is that the family and social structure among Germans was markedly male-dominated. So, while German women were essential to the smooth running of the household and farmstead, for which they enjoyed some level of autonomy and respect, their efforts did not result in full marriage equality.[13] That disparity wasn't particularly bothersome to German women in rural America though; if anything, it "suited the work patterns and long-term family goals of the subsistence frontier farmer."[14] Cultivating a family farm that provided for subsequent generations was the foremost goal, with production support (in the form of manual labor), subordination to husbands, fiscal prudence, and producing (and rearing) successors counting among the strategies wives took in enabling that continuity.[15]

That Germans were viewed as capable, if not exceptional, farmers is likely the result of two independent yet related phenomena. First, based on raw numbers alone, the Germans outnumbered all other immigrant groups in agriculture.[16] While there's no evidence to suggest that their farming practices or yields outshone those of their Anglo-American neighbors, the fact that they were the largest foreign-language group working the land certainly made a lasting impression, as did the visible productivity of women and children on those farms.[17] Second, Germans tended to hold onto their land when others lost theirs. Indeed, coming from an overpopulated country with little room for socioeconomic mobility, they placed a great deal of value on landownership and stewardship. Sons were raised to be farmers and clustered their farms around those of their fathers. That practice provided security and a bedrock for future generations.[18] They were thus less susceptible to the feverish speculation that consumed so many settlers as described here by a German farmer in Missouri:

> There are people here who are always moving around. They buy themselves a piece of land, live and work like animals and when they don't get rich in a few years, then they curse about the area, sell everything for a trifle, go somewhere else and do even worse, and sometimes come back again and would often

> be happy just to have their land back again; they often move 5 to 6 times like this before they come to their senses and learn that riches don't fall into everyone's laps.[19]

The family patterns and land practices that distinguished German from Yankee farmers can be ascribed to their cultural relationship to the land.[20] Germans saw land as a family possession, one that united generations, and farming was a means by which parents could help establish their children.[21] The Yankees, by contrast, were entrepreneurs who saw land as a commodity and farming as a business. Sons were not expected to farm and follow in the footsteps of their fathers; rather, they were encouraged to pursue their own ambitions.

These cultural differences resulted in each group having misconceptions about the actions of their neighbors. The eagerness at which Yankees bought and sold land or borrowed on credit for short-term returns, as mentioned above, seemed irresponsible and foolhardy in the eyes of Germans. Anglo-Americans were equally bewildered if not sincerely disturbed to see anyone other than men or hired help labor in the fields. But German farm families viewed the roles and efforts of women and children as central to the welfare and future of the family enterprise, so they willingly joined in the workforce, with some children having to cut their education short in order to do so. Illuminating is the following excerpt from a short story written in 1893. In it, the author describes the daughter of German immigrants in comparison to Yankee and Norwegian girls:

> She had a little schooling . . . but her life had been one of hard work and mighty little play. Her parents . . . could speak English only very brokenly. . . . Her life was lonely and hard. . . . She knew that the Yankee girls did not work in the fields—even the Norwegian girls seldom did so now, they worked in town—but she had been brought up to hoe and pull weeds from her childhood, and her father and mother considered it good for her.[22]

That English was spoken "only very brokenly" points to the ethnic homogeneity of most early settlements.[23] Because there wasn't any compelling reason to learn English in isolated areas or communities heavily settled by Germans, many didn't. To be sure, quantitative and qualitative sources alike reveal that

German was the primary language in numerous communities in the Midwest for decades after mass migration from Germany had ceased. And for some second- and third-generation descendants of immigrants, it was the only language. This led to a situation in which German language and culture flourished, a matter we take up more fully in chapters 6 and 7.

Farming wasn't the only draw or endeavor in which Germans distinguished themselves. In the mid-nineteenth century, there was a widespread and testified demand for craftsmen as villages, towns, and cities emerged and grew in response to westward expansion and immigration. Unlike other newcomer groups like the Irish, Italians, and Poles, the Germans, by and large, had marketable (and transportable) skills that increased their prospects in the growing American workforce.[24] For traditional artisans, who had faced stiff competition for business back in Germany, pursuing their trade in American towns and cities provided a situation that allowed them to make money and build a reputation for themselves. Germans dominated as shoemakers, tailors, cabinetmakers, carpenters, coopers, blacksmiths, wagonmakers, butchers, bakers, and brewers, to give a few examples.[25] Even today, a good beer is frequently credited to German influence. To be sure, they were conspicuous in a variety of other, classically trained professions, too, but, in terms of numbers they were not nearly as representative.

In the case of women, particularly wives and older daughters, work almost always meant managing the household, and when it came to domestic affairs, German women had a reputation for cleanliness, efficiency, and reliability.[26] Most were listed in the census records as having "none" or "keeping house" under employment. A rather standard and commonplace arrangement in the nineteenth and early twentieth centuries, they raised the children and tended to the house, garden, and any livestock. Women in rural environments tackled arduous farm duties as well, and some even ran cottage industries out of their homes to turn a profit, selling commodities like butter, eggs, and produce.[27] Those women who did seek employment outside the home often did so in urban areas. Census records at midcentury show single women working as domestic servants, laundresses, and seamstresses. It wasn't uncommon for teenagers and adult children to contribute to their family's household, with young unmarried women usually earning supplemental income by working as seamstresses or in retail.[28]

Industrialization and Urbanization

While most early German immigrants to Illinois found ample reason to settle in rural areas or small communities, the second half of the nineteenth century saw increasing settlement in urban centers as America's cities experienced unprecedented growth (for the 1870 distribution of German immigrants in Illinois by county, expressed in percentages, see figure 4.2). Jacob Gross, in a different excerpt from the same letter presented in chapter 2, provides an eyewitness account of Chicago's emergent industries and burgeoning German American institutions in 1856:

> Chicago is the largest trading city in the world. There is such life and urge that one's life is in danger when one crosses the street! Besides eight railroads, there are 37 branch roads in the town, where daily over 200 trains go back and forth. Also, the biggest fruit and lumber trade in the world. . . . More than 300 ships wintered in the harbor. The city is growing rapidly that an average of 3,000 houses are built yearly. Also, last summer a German Hall was built (on shares) which is four stories high and is to be used for a theater, singing and reading clubs, and school purposes.[29]

This description offers a perfect illustration of Chicago as it stood on the brink of explosive industrial growth and profound social transformation. Indeed, between 1830 and 1890—in just sixty years—Chicago grew from a tiny settlement to America's second-largest city.[30] By the 1850s, when the above excerpt was written, Chicago was already a growing region of transportation, commerce, and trade. Not yet a manufacturing center, the city was a place where commodities—often agricultural goods produced elsewhere in the state—were exchanged and transported, due to its proximity to the Illinois and Michigan Canal and the growing railway system.[31]

Beginning in the 1860s, the city rapidly transformed into an industrial powerhouse. The Civil War provided economic stimulus and opportunity to Chicago and to Illinois as a whole. The military's demand for uniforms, food, and other supplies boosted the state's agricultural economy as well as Chicago's iron, steel, and garment industries. Many of Chicago's urban rivals, such as St. Louis and Cincinnati, were unable to transport goods due to proximity to the front lines or river trade blockades, so wheat

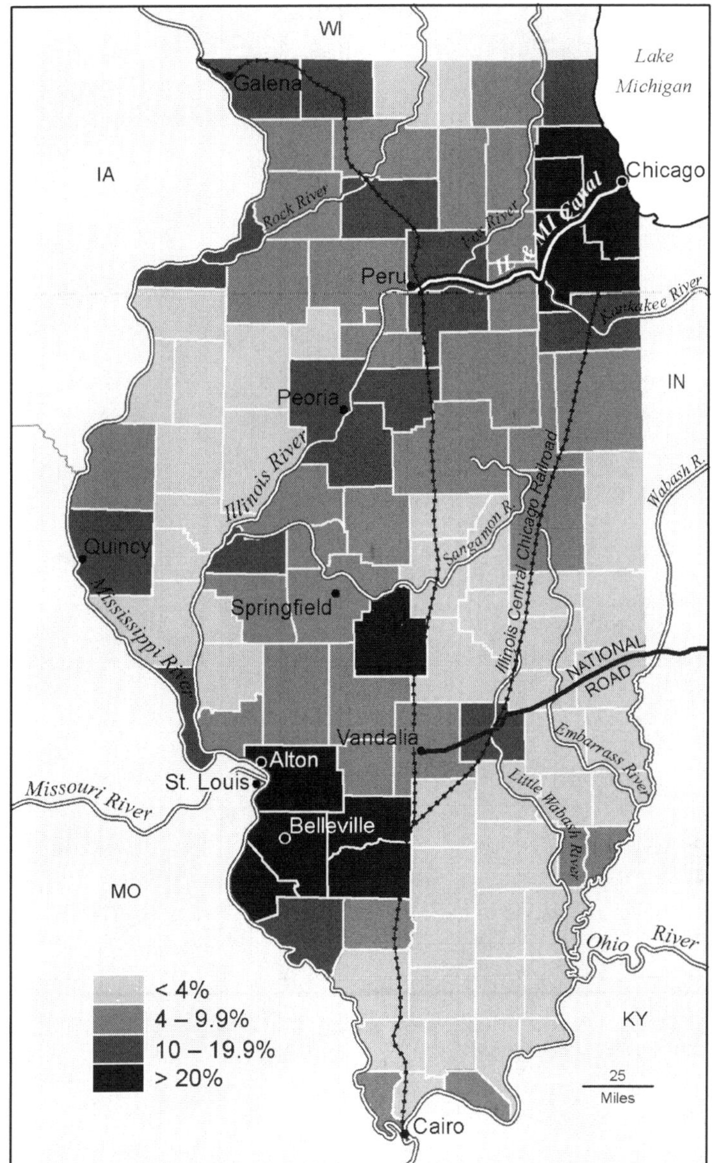

Fig. 4.2. Percentage born in Germany living in Illinois, by county, 1870. Population data from the 1870 U.S. census, "Selected Nativities by Counties," table VII.

export and meatpacking were diverted to Chicago. This came at a moment when industrial technology and expanded access to capital allowed new industrialists like Cyrus McCormick and George Pullman to invest in large-scale manufacturing endeavors.[32] The 1871 Chicago Fire, though devastating, provided even more opportunities for expansion and growth as the city rebuilt.

By 1880 Chicago was the fourth-largest city in the United States, continuing to dominate the meatpacking, wheat export, agricultural equipment, iron and steel, and lumber industries.[33]

Other Illinois cities were profoundly affected by industrialization as well. Those in northeastern Illinois, such as Joliet, Chicago Heights, and Waukegan, boasted strong iron and steel industries, as did the region across the Mississippi from St. Louis—including the German stronghold of Belleville. Peoria dominated the liquor market, and Moline was second only to Chicago in the agricultural equipment industry. Other major industrial cities included Rockford, Springfield, and Freeport.[34]

As urban industry grew, much of the population shifted from farm to city at the same time that German immigration was at its peak. By 1870 over one-fourth of Illinois' German immigrants lived in Chicago, and by 1890 nearly one half of the state's German immigrants lived there.[35] This figure doesn't even include other significant urban centers in Illinois, such as Rockford, Moline, and the areas surrounding Chicago proper. For comparison, in 1890, 28.7 percent of Illinois' total population lived in Chicago, still a significant increase from 11.6 percent in 1870, but not nearly as high as the percentage of Illinois' Germans and other immigrants living in Chicago at this time.[36] By some estimates, first- and second-generation Germans made up nearly 30 percent of Chicago's population between 1860 and 1900. An estimate of this scale points toward the profound impact Germans had on Chicago as a developing industrial metropolis.[37]

The influences at work in the urbanization of Illinois were many. First, land in desirable locations had become increasingly expensive and scarce from midcentury onward. As Chicago evolved into a major transportation hub, many immigrants who were originally passing through ended up staying, taking whatever employment they could find.[38] And as the Industrial Revolution transformed mid-America, rural areas were affected in ways that were not always advantageous to its farmers, ultimately causing rural labor outflows. Urban industrialization and rural commercialization grew in tandem. Factories in cities produced the agricultural equipment that made farming more productive than ever before. The expansion of the railroads made it affordable and efficient to ship farm products elsewhere. Meatpacking plants like the Union Stock Yards expanded to process meat products prior to shipping. During the Civil War, this increase in agricultural productivity was a boon to small and large farmers alike, as the state of Illinois purchased all the crops they could produce. Many farmers even mortgaged their land to expand production during this period.[39]

The times were good but short-lived. After the war, farmers' continued high yields resulted in a glut in the market, which steeply lowered prices for their products. As agricultural methods became more efficient, fewer farmhands were needed to work the fields, and the railroads that had been key in developing Illinois' agricultural economy now used their power to overcharge small farmers for shipping their products. On top of all this, and finally, the end of the war coincided with reduced demand for imported American produce in Europe, so Illinois farmers experienced an agricultural depression. These factors, combined with the Panic of 1873 and the ensuing nationwide depression of the 1870s, created an environment in which small farmers found themselves unable to compete with large industrial farms. Many were forced off their land and either relocated to urban areas, moved westward, or became tenant farmers.[40]

City Life

Obviously, life for Germans in Chicago and other cities in the second half of the nineteenth century was distinctly different from that of those in rural areas and small towns. The class, religious, regional, linguistic, and generational differences between Chicago's German immigrants made for a multiplicity of experiences within the city as well. Immigrants of the 1850s were often artisans and skilled workers from Bavaria and Württemberg, for example, while those immigrating in the 1880s tended to be poor laborers coming from the west, north, and northeast. Of the unskilled laborers who immigrated to Chicago, some were industrial workers who brought a culture of labor activism with them from Germany, whereas others were farmers experiencing a city for the first time.[41]

For those immigrating to Chicago from rural Germany, the initial shock of Chicago's urban industrial environment must have been especially overwhelming. Adjusting to urban living as well as to the economic structure of emerging industrial capitalism, and all in a new country, these immigrants experienced profound cultural and economic change. It is no wonder that these and other German immigrants sought the familiarity of family and friends who had arrived before them, quickly organizing themselves around class, religion, and region of origin and into the ethnic neighborhoods and communities that became the mainstay of German American life in Chicago.[42]

Indeed, as Keil and Jentz point out, "neighborhood defined the world of everyday life" for most of Chicago's Germans in the second half of the nineteenth century.[43] By the 1870s, German neighborhoods supplied nearly everything residents needed, as workers usually lived in close proximity to their places of employment, and neighborhood shops and services provided for household and family needs. Cultural events often took place inside the structure of neighborhood life as well. In this way, family life, social life, and work were integrated into the fabric of daily life within a geographically limited area.[44]

This was especially true in the North Side neighborhood, which supported German-run hospitals, schools, churches, clubs, orphanages, and lodges.[45] Settled in the 1840s (see figure 4.3), it was the oldest and largest German neighborhood in Chicago, and it accommodated middle- and upper-class Germans as well as working-class Germans. As you might imagine, the middle and upper classes lived closer to Lake Michigan, with skilled workers and artisans living in the central part of the neighborhood and unskilled laborers living in the industrial area along the Chicago River. The central part of the neighborhood was characterized by small independent shops and individuals working from home. Many if not most German houses had small businesses on the bottom floor, providing the neighborhood with bakeries, groceries, hardware or shoe stores, saloons, or barber shops. Many of these businesses advertised in German only. As was the case on German farms, these small businesses were predominately family operated, with wives and children assuming significant responsibilities in running the shops.[46] Residents of the North Side also worked locally in the building trades, machine shops, textiles, cigar making, furniture making, and printing. These trades were representative of many midcentury artisan immigrants from Germany and continued to be highly represented in that neighborhood into the latter part of the century.[47] In the 1860s and 1870s, breweries and distilleries as well as brickyards and tanneries cropped up in this area as well.[48]

During the final wave of German mass immigration, which began in the late 1870s and continued until the 1890s, working-class

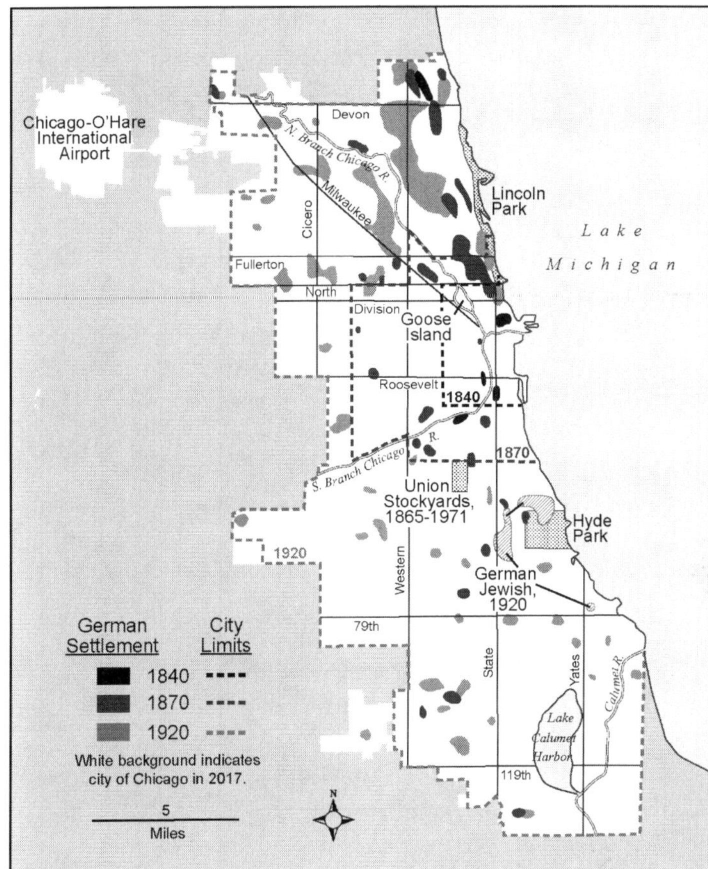

Fig. 4.3. German distribution and settlement in Chicago, 1840–1920. Data from *Historic City: The Settlement of Chicago* (comp. and pub. by the Department of Development and Planning, 1976).

German neighborhoods emerged on the West, Northwest, and Southwest Sides; reflecting the immigrants of this era, these later neighborhoods had a higher proportion of unskilled workers and fewer home-based industries than the North Side. Conditions in the crowded Northwest neighborhood, which contained two-story wooden apartment buildings built in close proximity, rapidly deteriorated. Those Germans with the means moved to houses on the edge of the city.[49] In the late nineteenth century, workers in the Northwest neighborhood were often employed locally in leather and tanning, iron and steel, and large-scale furniture and machine factories. By 1900, as workers moved farther out on the Northwest Side, industries like brewing, baking, clothing, building, and tobacco became more heavily represented.[50] German workers on the West Side tended to work in lumber and furniture, and on the South Side, where the Union Stock Yards were located, most toiled in meatpacking plants and slaughterhouses.[51]

The heavy influx of immigrants in the 1880s corresponded with a particularly difficult and intense moment in Chicago's industrialization process. Different trades were affected differently, but it was during this time that many skilled workers found their positions eliminated and replaced with low-paying unskilled jobs. This happened at workplaces like slaughterhouses and meatpacking plants, where division of labor, rather than mechanization, was causing the devaluation of skills. Other skilled trades were in transition. For example, furniture making—though fairly mechanized and concentrated in large plants by the 1880s—still commanded a large number of skilled and semiskilled workers who earned decent wages. Still others, such as bakers in small shops, didn't experience a dramatic change in their working conditions, but they did increasingly struggle to compete with larger bakeries.[52]

By 1900, most of the above occupations had become industrialized. Furniture makers experienced division of labor and devaluation of their skills, while metalworkers were required to learn new skills for operating complex machinery.[53] That said, many Germans by then were no longer concentrated in these trades, as second- and third- generation Germans often gravitated toward professional work. By now, many more German women were also working outside the home. Still often employed in the clothing industry, many also worked in retail and clerical settings.[54] In addition, women in the apparel industry increasingly worked at machines in large factories rather than at home.[55]

These changes in occupation, as well as changes in the city itself, resulted in a reconfiguration of German neighborhood life. By 1900, more than half of first- and second-generation Germans were concentrated in newer neighborhoods on the outer edges of the city. While the neighborhoods in the North and Northwest Sides were losing Germans, those in the South and West were gaining them. German Jews had largely vacated the downtown area by 1920, and, as figure 4.3 shows, settled quite a ways south, in the Hyde Park and South Shore areas.[56] Advances in transportation added to this dispersal, with the development of streetcars and elevated railway lines allowing workers to live further from their jobs, as did the inflow of southern and eastern European immigrants who crowded into the formerly established German communities. Census records indicate that younger families were moving out into the suburbs and that the older North Side neighborhoods had an aging population. Suburbs certainly created a more distinct separation between work life, family life, and social life and weakened the traditional community ties that had characterized German neighborhoods in the middle decades of the nineteenth century.[57]

While the vast majority of Germans in nineteenth-century Chicago were working class, some German-owned businesses became quite successful. Chicago, particularly between 1871 (when the city began to rebuild from the fire) and World War I, gave rise to a number of German entrepreneurs in a variety of industries. Germans, of course, dominated the brewing industry (see that side story at the end of this chapter). William Haas and Konrad Sulzer founded the first brewery in 1836. Eventually, almost all German breweries either closed or were swallowed up by larger corporations; but for a time, the small brewer in Chicago prospered.[58] Chicago's thriving meatpacking industry also included successful German Jewish immigrants in its ranks, such as Nelson Morris, who emigrated from Germany in 1852.[59] He started a meatpacking business that eventually supplied the entire U.S. Army with beef during the Civil War, which made him a small fortune.[60] Another German immigrant who got his start in meat-making and selling was Oscar F. Meyer. In 1883 he and his brother opened a meat market in Chicago and sold old-world sausages; they quickly built a successful brand, originally trademarked Edelweiss (alluding to the well-known flower found in the Alps). The company's products, which have expanded to include other meat products like bacon, are wildly popular even today.

Notable men aside, the more common examples of business success among Germans were the smaller German-run shops and manufacturing endeavors that employed just a handful of people. It wasn't unusual for these businesses, often run by established Germans who had immigrated in the 1850s, to employ more recent, third-wave German immigrants. During the labor strife of the late 1800s, then, working-class Germans could find themselves in direct opposition to the German capitalist class, a topic explored in more depth in the next chapter.

All in all, the vast majority of German immigrants in Illinois did really well for themselves, whether they lived in rural or urban communities. They not only got by, but they prospered. Many realized their dreams of landownership, and those living in cities had more professional opportunities than the other leading immigrant group at the time, the Irish, who were poor and unskilled by comparison. German immigrants were slow to adopt English but didn't suffer any economic loss because of it. While industrial advances later forced many craftsmen into low-wage positions in factories, their downward mobility was not unlike that of anyone else, foreign or native born. Economically, they performed on par with or, by some accounts, even better than their American counterparts. That's true even for the working-class immigrants of the 1880s who tended to have less capital to invest. In Chicago, many second-generation Germans, for example, entered middle-class occupations; that success takes a particular poignancy in consideration of the fact that the large majority of first-generation immigrants were working class.[61] Admired for their "industriousness, thrift, and honesty," Germans were desirable Europeans believed to fit "easily and well" into American society during a period of rapid growth and change.[62]

Fig. 4.4. Tonk Manufacturing Company workers, 1893. The German-owned company became the largest piano stool manufacturer in the United States. Courtesy Chicago History Museum; ICHi-034809.

Observations of Industrial Working Conditions

The following translated excerpts from Alfred Kolb's book *Als Arbeiter in Amerika* are an eyewitness account of working-class life in industrial Chicago nearing the turn of the twentieth century.[1] Though Kolb himself later returned to Germany, only having worked in the city for a few months, his descriptions illuminate the homogenizing effects of mechanization on the lives of German workers.

Work in a Bicycle Factory (Western Wheel Works)

That morning it was like a railway station there [in the German Society]. The door was barely ever still. People of every age and appearance pushed their way in and asked about work. As everyone else had received a negative answer, I took out my letter of recommendation without much hope. But it worked . . .

The assembly room was a huge hall twenty-seven windows long, its entire length traversed by wide work benches full of vises, tools, and miscellaneous equipment. The finished bicycle parts were carried here in a continuous stream on a rattling conveyer belt and then fitted together to make whole bicycles. The principle of the division of labor was thereby applied extensively, and the human hand was replaced by a machine wherever possible. Even the turning of screws was done mechanically by devices similar to that thin, whirring tube whose painful acquaintance we make when a tooth is filled.

The foreman led me to one of the long benches and instructed me in the work. It required neither skill nor much exertion, consisting of a few constantly repeated hand movements on the front wheels of the bicycles. The man to my left prepared the axles. I stuck them through the hub, and after I had checked the ball bearings, pulled a greased felt washer over it. The neighbor to my right put on nuts. The next ground down the ends of the spokes, slipped the rubber tires over, inflated them until they were firm, and so forth, until the wheel, all ready to go, arrived at the end of the table, where it was then inserted into the front fork of the frame.

I do not want to dwell here any longer on the details of our work. Suffice it to say that at the time it bored me beyond all measure. Through it, I gained an appreciation for certain accusations against the modern division of labor. Such division is of course indispensable. Today's entire technology would be unthinkable without it. But that is all the more reason why we may not close our eyes to the joyless, eternal monotony of an occupation which parches the senses and mind, which requires a few uniform muscular movements and so little thought that—to a certain degree—the process takes place beneath the threshold of consciousness. It would be difficult in such work to still find that measure of moral dignity that no occupation can forgo without, in the long run, ethically endangering those who practice it. Such work takes into consideration neither the individuality nor the talent of the person, but reduces him to a part of a machine, "a mere stopgap necessitated by human ingenuity." For me a further reason to hope for the curtailment of exactly this kind of industrial work.

The workday in the bicycle factories lasted the ten hours typical of the city; in the beginning there were also two to three hours overtime in the evening, but they were short-lived. The entire operation of the plants was cut up into seasonal work. At the beginning of winter, one worked day and night; that had already stopped when I began there. As summer approached, more than three-quarters of all the workers were gradually let go or else stayed away of their own accord because they found a more appealing job somewhere else. And those of us who remained still only got five days a week until finally that stopped, too, and the business shut down for weeks on end. But as far as I know, the daily wages were not reduced.

I repeatedly heard it expressed, and mainly from the mouths of newly arrived immigrants, that work was not so strenuous back home in Germany as here in America. There may be some truth to that; in American, in any case, one never stops hearing the warning, "Get going! Hurry up!" But no rules without exceptions. At first I had worked with all my might so as not to fall behind my comrades. Until one of them asked scornfully, "Hey, are you crazy? Working just like you're on piecework? Don't be a fool!" And when I answered that I didn't want to promote my dismissal, he laughed at me. "That's no reason to run yourself into the ground, greenhorn [Grünhorn]. Look at me: am I knocking myself out? The main thing is to get in good with the foreman. His father runs a saloon. Whoever goes there and spends a bit doesn't have to worry about being thrown out."

This last tip was not completely unfounded. Despite the unrelenting pressure, there were several loafers among us who dawdled away the time without being punished for it, trusting in such behind the scene influences. The worst of the lot was a Bavarian, a true genius at doing nothing, and who on top of it all worked himself into a rage over the heavy labor. He worked near me, and I can still see him today, short and fat, alternately taking snuff and grumbling: "Holy Jesus, what a treadmill. Don't it never end? Holy Mother of Altötting!"[2]

The work began at seven in the morning and lasted until 5:30 in the evening. The half-hour lunch break was at noon. Sitting on the work benches, the married workers then ate the snack they had brought from home. We single workers hurried to the nearby cheap kitchens or saloons. At noon, as well as during overtime at night, we were allowed to get beer, for which most kept special tin containers. A half liter cost five cents. It was fetched by the errand boys working in the hall, who on payday got a few extra cents for it. Aside from these times, the consumption of alcohol was not permitted, and the rule was strictly observed. Whoever got thirsty during work drank from the bad tap water . . .

Among my new fellow workers, I also made the acquaintance of a few teetotalers. None of them spoke German. That may have been purely coincidental, but the fact is that the great majority of our fellow countrymen over there want to hear nothing of temperance. That is perhaps the only question about which they agree, and nothing was more loathsome to them about McKinley's colonial policies than the tax on spirits. It is further true that comparatively more alcohol is drunk in Germany than in the United States. . . . Yet for all that, it seems to me as though I saw more real drunks over there; more people who go the limit, and who, once they have started, don't stop drinking until they are under the table. . . .

When I began there, the bicycle factory employed about 2,500 workers, lots of them German. The number of trained machinists was remarkably small; after all, everything was done by machine. Among the masses of unskilled were people of the most varied backgrounds who, whether permanently or merely temporarily, had fallen into the midsts of the industrial proletariat. In motley rows stood merchant and farmhand, teacher and craftsman, musician and who knows what else, all together at the vise. We had educated people in the assembly hall, too. A theologian, a philologist, and three lawyers: all Germans. As I found out later, the fallen schoolteacher indulged in Socratic love, which was doubtless also the reason for his having had to leave his homeland. The theologian had found the beer in Erlangen too good to resist until finally his money ran out, and instead of stepping up to the pulpit, he stepped onto an immigrant ship. That was probably twenty years ago—one long chain of disappointment, recklessness and misery. As a factory worker he merely scraped through the winter, while in the summer he ran around soliciting advertisements during the day, and at night, for free beer, sat at the ticket window of a honky-tonk. . . .

Standing before me, the man betrayed no sign, either inwardly or outwardly, of better days. It was apparent that he had long since buried whatever hope and courage may once have swelled in his breast. His theology had been extinguished along with his religious conviction in order to make room for that superficial materialism which hypnotizes the masses of the German-American proletariat. Idealism and spiritualism cast aside, all intellectual content in life evaporates, leaving but hopeless resignation: eat, drink, and be merry, dear soul, for tomorrow you'll be dead.

Work in a Brewery

Although Chicago is an industrial city with some 200,000 workers, it does not have industrial districts in the true sense of the term. Its innumerable shops are spread throughout its various quarters; tall smoking chimneys can even be found in the inner city. The T. brewery is located on the South Side, a German mile from the city center . . .

Right next to the entrance gate in a low wing was the bottling department. Such an operation is not quite so simple as one might think. The beer is pushed out of the vats by compressed air into the filling machines which do the bottling by themselves. Filled in this manner and thereupon corked, the bottles are sterilized in a steam bath, and the better brands are then decorated with labels, wires, and tinfoil caps. The washing, brushing, rinsing, bottling, corking, wiring, and labeling was done by machines which were operated by young or female workers.

Besides this, there were many considerably more strenuous tasks which were done by men. A greenhorn, I found them doubly difficult. Even today I remember with misgiving handling wet barrels and heavy beer cases. Among these cases were many old ones studded with glass splinters, splints, and nails. Within eight days my hands were covered with bloody cuts and cracks. My back had become stiff, my gait and carriage clumsy and heavy. I like to think that as a rule I'm not unusually awkward; at least not to such a degree as one might be tempted to take for granted of a bureaucrat. Once, however, shortly before quitting time, a heavy case of empty bottles which I was to bring into the basement slipped out of my tired arms. Of course, the foreman really told me off, and a small office penpusher with a four-inch stand-up collar who happened to be passing by turned up his nose and said: "That guy's probably soused!"

Now and then, when there wasn't anything to be toted, the men were temporarily put to easier work too—nailing cases, stacking bottles, washing the floor, cleaning up, etc. We took weekly turns at other such chores—for example, cleaning the toilets. These were water closets with enamel bowls and lifting seats, neat and clean—and by the way characteristic of the standard of living. When I did the cleaning, they were even outstandingly clean.

My fellow workers, some seventy in number, were without exception unskilled, younger people, mainly of German origin. And German was also the language spoken among us. We addressed each other—even the foreman—by first names.[3] An occasional "you silly ass!" was taken as inoffensively as it was meant. In the beginning I sometimes had difficulty suppressing a smile when some fresh youngster shouted at me: "Alfred, come here and pick up the case!" But not for long; hard work makes one dull. And our work was certainly hard and heavy enough. This I can state from experience, because later on I had a much easier time elsewhere. Probably a calmer pace prevailed at other times in the brewery. But just at that time—so the rumor went—there was a huge order in from Havana, and therefore whatever strength and energy we had was squeezed out of us. Small wonder that we were completely winded. If for once someone actually paused to catch his breath, the foreman appeared immediately to drive him on. I noticed a look of dull sullenness stamped on the men's faces about the roots of the nose and the corners of the mouth. My own face probably didn't look any different.

It need hardly be mentioned that under such conditions any exchange of ideas during work was out of the question. During the one-hour lunch break, too, everybody silently squatted or lay in some corner. At best, something like a conversation started after quitting time, when we had a drink together before going home. But nothing much came of it. Most pressed for home, and a recurring saying was: "Glad the grind is over for today!" . . .

To protect our clothes during work we used an outfit made of strong blue linen which, as the name *overall* indicates, is worn like a cover over the clothes. Since my return home I have looked around for such overalls in German factories. Of course they are also known here, but not nearly so commonly used. This may also be a reason why the workers in the streets of Chicago appeared to be cleaner than in Germany. With exceptions, naturally. My comrades in the brewery, particularly, were usually unclean and in rags. . . .

The regular workday in the brewery lasted from 6 to 12 and from 1 to 5, i.e., ten hours. There was no coffee or late afternoon break. But beer was handed out at 9 and at 3 o'clock. Admittedly, everyone drank at other times also, whenever we got thirsty. As long as you didn't lay your hands on stout or other good brands, the foreman looked in the other direction. By the way, this license was not at all abused. It is true that cheese was preferred at breakfast, "because it makes you so pleasantly thirsty." But I hardly ever saw anyone tipsy; except maybe during overtime, when the men restored their vanishing strength with alcohol. Overtime night work was almost routine; usually until 9, sometimes 10 in the evening. In that case a half-hour break was taken at 6 o'clock, which would have been very nice if the lunch break had not been shortened accordingly. Thus the total length of work was from 14 to 15 hours. In addition, we worked on Sunday mornings from 6 to 12 o'clock.

Most of the workers usually hurried home for lunch. Those who lived farther away brought along a cold snack or ate in a saloon. The snack consisted of bread, eggs, ham, sausage, and roast. Tartar with the long mild American onions seemed very popular. There was always meat, and always plenty of it. Also, I never saw the bread, fine wheat bread, without butter or jam. Along with the others who lived there, I ate at my landlord's. I must concede that his old battle-ax of a wife was a very good cook. Each of the three daily meals cost 15 cents, but was much better than in the 15-cent restaurants [Fünfzehncentsrestaurants] of the inner city. There was no menu from which to select; you just helped yourself to everything—and as much of it as you wished—that was put on the table. Even the empty meat dishes were promptly refilled. In the morning at 5:30 we received coffee, bread and butter, cheese, fried eggs, fried potatoes, and a warm meat dish, usually pork ribs. For lunch—soup, vegetables, potatoes, and always three different meat dishes; not infrequently goose giblets and delicious hasenpfeffer. In the evening at 6 o'clock the same was offered as lunchtime. Though the place was a saloon, we almost always had coffee with our meals. Only the boarders had breakfast there. But at noon and in the evening numerous diners showed up—maltsters, brewers, blacksmiths, fireman, beer draymen. There was such a great rush that people ate in shifts. While some were eating, others were impatiently waiting behind their chairs.

Thus there was little time for talk. Also, most men were too dull and rough for any half-reasonable conversation. Only crude teasing and coarse answers came of it, and one evening these even came to blows. Two deserters were involved—onetime corporals from the province of Baden—two incredibly rude customers. One, suspecting me a former comrade, once asked me why I had "cut out." Addressing people with "you scoundrel," "you heel," emphasized by dirty adjectives, was nothing unusual. Equally common were expressions like dumb Swabian, blind Hessian, horned bull of Baden, Bavarian swine, Prussian beggar—a microcosmic reproduction of the regional antagonisms which the German doesn't give up even on the other side of the ocean. . . .

If incidents at work were mentioned—at best only every now and then—they were skimmed over rather than discussed. . . . In such confined circles conversation crept along, at lunch and at night in the boardinghouses, not even faintly touched by matters of political, religious, or social interest—with ever-dwindling exceptions. One day the machine attendant was caught by the driving belt of the big steam engine and torn to pieces—no wonder, by the way, given the lack of any safety equipment. Returning on the night of the funeral, his acquaintances talked about the deceased. "Too bad for him," someone said, "he was a good guy! Now he's had it!" Whereupon someone else said: "Eat and drink, guys; because soon we'll all have had it, and that's that." The others were silent; they seemed to agree. . . .

If I mention the idle chatter I had to listen to in the boardinghouse where a few older people who spent [spenden] a good share of their weekly wages at the bar bored us with sanctimonious talk about an impending hunger riot . . . then I believe that I have pretty well recounted the social and political subjects which came up. But I believe it would be a mistake to infer quietism and contentment from the lack of more general topics for conversation going beyond daily events. These people were simply too dumb and worn out; they also had too little sense of community and solidarity to explain to themselves and others the vague sentiments that brooded in them. There was some indication—more felt than observed—that beneath the layer of dull apathy there glowed and smoldered the spark of gnawing, though yet confused, discontent. . . .

We received the standard wages for Chicago's unskilled manual labor—for boys 50 cents, for women 75, for young men 1 dollar, for adults 1¼ dollars per day. Overtime was paid separately, but not higher. A carpenter, my landlord received 60 dollars a month. Brewers and maltsters earned 17 dollars a week and up. After a failed walkout, their *union* and the brewery administration agreed upon this sum as the minimum wage; non-union members may not be hired.

The most I earned in a week was 10 dollars. Forty-two Marks, a tidy little sum. But bitterly earned with 20 hours overtime. Only those who have been through it themselves can understand what so much overtime at hard labor means. The question as to long hours and their consequences has been discussed countless times. I had read and heard enough about it. But I didn't think seriously about it until I felt these consequences in my own body. He who feels no weight has a light load.

Day after day, ten long hours of standing, toting, bending, lifting—it's no trifle. To say nothing of fourteen and fifteen hours. Evenings at 9 or 10, when I dragged back to my room which I'd left that morning at 5:30, ready to collapse from fatigue, I had only one wish: to fall into bed. And yet still, at the beginning, the thought of lying down as filthy as I was was so offensive that I preferred to sacrifice a portion of my meager time in bed and—it was the middle of winter with freezing temperatures down to minus 20 degrees R.[4]—first lit the oven to warm water. But these heroics didn't last long. When we began to have to work even on Sundays and weren't let off till it was impossible to bathe anyway, the need for cleanliness also began to gradually and gently fade away. It was like getting used to staying at a series of bivouacs during a rainy maneuver. First you think you'll suffocate in the filth and begin to disgust yourself, and then finally—inevitably—you notice with amazement how little soap a person needs to get by.

Of course I don't mean to imply that each and every one of my fellow workers didn't wash. . . .

Even when I just started working at the brewery, I thought I perceived that the people—especially the single workers—were much more poorly clothed that the workers I'd seen at the boardinghouse and on the streets.

The friendly young man who saw to it that I didn't oversleep on the first morning wore a suit which obviously hadn't been cleaned for a long time. Only the worst holes had been mended. Beneath it a brown woolen shirt as well as undergarments and stockings just like it. Like almost everyone there, he kept his underthings on at night so that he simply had to slip into his boots and clothes in the morning and then he was all ready. As long as I knew him I don't believe he once changed his undergarments. Otherwise an honest soul, though life had treated him hard. His father died on him when he was still young; his mother had remarried, and when he was 15, his stepfather showed him the door.

This I learned later. On that first morning, sitting across from him under the light at the breakfast table, I was secretly shocked by so much dirt and disorderliness. But wrongly so. It didn't take long before I was on my way to resembling him. Working with cases as we did, it was impossible to avoid getting holes and rips. If I returned home from work on into the evening it was too late to run off to a tailor. I had to turn to the needle myself; and what my exhausted hand was able to patch together looked just as disorderly as what which had originally so offended me on that poor devil. It was also too late to take my dirty things out to be washed; too late to buy anything. I couldn't even ask my landlord and his wife. They were already in bed by the time I got home. But leave was most difficult to obtain. If one also considers the incredible fatigue—and that general indifference toward everything awaiting one in the next hour which comes from it—one can perhaps imagine the way I looked. At the beginning I felt this life to be absolutely unbearable. Ultimately I did as my comrades: I took things as they came.

I had to force myself to take notes. I hardly wrote any letters. I looked at newspapers just as infrequently as others. I had no desire to seek out the reading rooms in the magnificent Public Library. I was most content to sit around home and smoke in dull apathy. At best, certain spontaneous desires would flare up and I'd recall that statistical problem which a Frenchman had so drastically formulated with the phrase: *Les enfants poussent dans la misère comme les champignons sur le fumier.*[5]

It needn't be pointed out that the unaccustomed work weighed three times as heavily upon me, the greenhorn. I'm aware of that myself. But this I know just as well: my comrades suffered too. Yes, in a certain sense even more. The knowledge that I merely had to go to a hotel and change my clothes to change the person, that at any time I could remove myself from all the misery—this knowledge lent me a spark of resiliency which the pressing weight of the situation had long since extinguished in these poor creatures. And if, at close quarters, they represented that which they appeared to, then the reason for it could also be traced to this situation.

Chicago's Brewing Industry

Germans dominated the brewing industry in Chicago, with the first brewery believed to have been founded in 1836 by William Haas and Konrad Sulzer. In its first year of operation, The Haas & Sulzer Brewery produced about six hundred barrels, no small feat considering the toil and primitive nature of early brewing (and the fact that Chicago counted a mere two hundred or so residents at the time).[1]

Its early success attracted the attention of William Ogden, Chicago's first mayor, who bought out Sulzer to join Haas as the new co-owner. To meet the increased demand for their ale, Ogden and Haas founded a larger brewery on Chicago Avenue at Pine Street (now north Michigan Avenue). Within a few years, William Lill, an English immigrant, and Michael Diversey, an immigrant from Alsace-Lorraine (now part of modern-day France), bought the brewery. Quickly known as The Lill & Diversey Brewery (also the Chicago Brewery / Lill's Chicago Brewery / Lill's Cream Ale Brewery), it employed anywhere from fifty to seventy-five men, comprised two city blocks, and was "considered the largest brewery west of the Atlantic Seaboard."[2] Indeed, by 1860, its annual sales had neared forty-five thousand barrels.[3]

Given the city's budding population, the demand for beer was growing, and in 1847 John Huck and John Schneider, two Germans, established John A. Huck Brewing, introducing lager beer to the Chicago brewing scene. Differing from ales (such as porters and stouts), which was the more familiar variety of beer at the time in the United States, lagers (named after the German word *lagern*, meaning "to store") used a different type of yeast and required cooler temperatures during fermentation. Having a taste reminiscent of the homeland, lager beer was heartily welcomed by Chicago's Germans, with Huck founding the city's first beer garden, an outdoor, picnic-like area—typically adjacent to the brewery—for enjoying beer.

By 1860, the city had exceeded one hundred thousand residents. In response, further breweries emerged, most notably Seipp & Lehman; Downer, Bemis & Company; Jacob Rehm & Company; Sand's Ale Brewing Company; and Busch & Brand. And in 1869 Chicago produced an astonishing 246,212 barrels, a conservative estimate considering that yields from other, smaller breweries often went unrecorded.[4] Chicago, with its insatiable thirst for beer and its geographic positioning, came to be viewed as a key market for the lager trade, with Milwaukee brewers such as Phil Best & Company (later Pabst), the Val Blatz Brewing Company, and Joseph Schlitz Brewing opening branches in the city. By this time, German lager had come into mainstream favor. It was readily understood among the populace as both affordable and socially responsible—that is, it was "the drink of moderation" (compared to higher-priced, distilled libations like whiskey).

Yet, Chicago's prospering beer industry took a turn in October 1871 when the Great Chicago Fire swept through the city, destroying many breweries in its path. For example, Lill & Diversey and John A. Huck Brewing, two leading breweries at the time, never recovered, which opened up the market share to other, surviving breweries (though Seipp & Lehman, later Conrad Seipp Brewing Co., maintained its status as the most productive brewery in Chicago). Schlitz may not have gained the stronghold on the city that it did then either. Finding the silver lining in the historical tragedy, enterprising Joseph Schlitz, a native of Mainz, Germany, increased export of his Milwaukee product. He not only quenched the thirst of many Chicagoans; he also made use of the city's railway infrastructure to market Schlitz nationwide. So, while Schlitz has come to be known as "The Beer That Made Milwaukee Famous," it was Chicago that rendered it so, as Bob Skilnik, the author of *Beer: A History of Brewing in Chicago*, reminds us.[5]

Beer was big business in Chicago throughout the late nineteenth century despite intermittent prohibition and temperance movements. In 1879 the city ranked sixth in U.S. beer production, having brewed approximately 340,000 barrels.[6] The Industrial Revolution, with its inventions and advances in manufacturing, had transformed the brewing industry, and Chicago was at the heart of many of these improvements.

One significant advancement in the realm of beer testing and analysis was made possible by Dr. John E. Siebel, a German immigrant from Düsseldorf, who founded the Siebel Institute of Technology (or Zymotechnic Institute) in 1872. A chemist, Siebel viewed brewing as a science, requiring close attention to process, detail, and sanitation. Publishing scientific research on subjects like malting and mechanical refrigeration, he altered the perception and practice of brewing. Offering a wide range of courses, the institute enjoys success even today, staying true to its primary goal, which, according to Siebel as quoted in an 1892 ad in the *Western Brewer*, a popular brewery trade publication printed in both German and English until 1892, is "to promote the progress of the industries based on fermentation, which is done by instruction, investigation, analysis and otherwise."[7]

Though Chicago breweries founded by Germans have either closed or have been absorbed into larger corporations by now, their owners influenced not only the prosperity of the people and city—through gainful employment and internal revenue—but also the city's development and character through charity and politics. Michael Diversey, for instance, had a hand in founding a German school on Chicago's North Side; the Catholic churches St. Joseph (1846), St. Peter (1846), and St. Michael (1852); and *Der Nationaldemokrat*, a German daily newspaper.[8] He also served as alderman in 1844 in the largely German Ward Six. In fact, many of Chicago's German brewers held public office, especially that of city treasurer.[9] Another example is that of Conrad Seipp, founder of Conrad Seipp Brewing Co. He and his wife donated generously to causes and projects, such as the German Hospital (later Grant Hospital) and the Art Institute. What's especially noteworthy about the Seipp family is their interest in documenting the influence of Germans (including those with German lineage) in the United States. As such, they funded Albert Faust's 1909 monograph *The German Element in the United States*, which gave both a chronological history of Germans in the states and an account of their specific contributions.

In terms of beer, they certainly made their mark, particularly by having introduced Americans to a new style of beer, lagers. In fact, a good number of what we consider today to be old-time Chicago brews, such as Atlas Prager, Fox Deluxe, Edelweiss, Nectar, Tavern Pale, Topaz, Monarch, and Sieben's Real Lager, were lager beers.

5

NATIVISM, POLITICS, AND THE CIVIL WAR

Nativism

Not everyone rolled out the welcome mat for Germans. The nativists took a dim, even hostile, view of the rising tide of European immigrants. Nativism refers to anti-immigrant sentiment, with nativists fearing the impact newcomers would have on their Protestant Anglo-American customs and values. This was especially true for cities like Chicago where large numbers of immigrants resided. By 1870 over half of Chicago's residents, for example, were foreign born, and by 1890 more than three-quarters of its residents were first- and second-generation immigrants.[1]

Nativism, as an ideology, existed well before the 1850s, but it was the sudden influx of immigrants, together with the Reform movement in Protestant churches in America, that spawned a political movement, the Know Nothings, in 1854. The majority of the criticism—and fear—was directed at Catholics, which targeted some Germans and practically all of the Irish.[2] Catholicism, with its papal teachings, was regarded as diametrically opposed to democratic ideals.

The premise of the party, officially known as the American Party, was to curb immigration and restrict the political power of immigrants. Its membership grew out of secret societies, such as the Order of the Star-Spangled Banner, which vehemently opposed immigration. It got its nickname, Know Nothing, from the fact that members would reply, "I know nothing," when asked about party affairs.

The party's platform assailed immigrants in three major ways. It moved to institute a twenty-one-year residency period for U.S. citizenship (which included voting rights), limit public office to native-born citizens, and restrict the sale of alcohol. The Germans, with their foreign ways and love for beer, became easy targets for discrimination, particularly since Anglo-Americans at the time had not yet developed a palpable thirst for beer (especially lager beer), drinking whisky instead. The consumption of beer, then, was seen as symbolically German. What struck nativists as even more alien, if not irreverent, was that its consumption was allowed daily, even on the Sabbath. For many Germans, this was not out of step with their religious cultural practices. Sunday was a day of activity; festivals and parades were often held in conjunction with Sunday church, and Sundays were considered a day for business transactions, trips to the beer garden, and other outings, not a day for quiet contemplation and rest.[3]

With the Know Nothings gaining power and anti-immigrant and anti-Catholic sentiment on the rise, conflicts between Yankees and immigrants "produced some of the most potent political issues of the late nineteenth century."[4] One of those, the Chicago Beer Riot (also known as the Lager Beer War), occurred over temperance and prohibition. In 1855, Chicago mayor (and great-nephew of Daniel Boone) Levi Boone invoked an antiquated ordinance and mandated that taverns close on Sunday, thus prohibiting the sale of alcohol on the Sabbath. A Baptist and temperance advocate, he also upped the cost of a liquor license from fifty to three hundred dollars while limiting its terms to three months.[5] To mitigate resistance, Boone, among other things, overhauled the city's police, appointing only native-born Americans to the force.

These actions were troubling to Germans who, like most workers, labored at their jobs six days a week. Sunday was often the only day in which families could socially gather in German taverns, scattered along Chicago's North Side.[6] The exorbitant increase in the fees for a liquor license was also offensive, especially since they seemingly were enforced only for beer, not whisky, since the taverns located on the South Side, where the "natives" lived, incurred little to no intrusion. Additionally, 625 of the city's saloons were immigrant owned compared to only 50 that were "native" owned.

In response to the growing number of German and Irish tavern owners being interned for selling alcohol on Sunday, the Germans staged a protest at the courthouse on April 21, 1855. As tension escalated, the protest turned into a riot, resulting in gunfire, many arrests, and one death. Shortly thereafter, the campaign against foreigners eased up, and the Know-Nothing Party, which had elected Boone to office, began to dissipate. For the 1856 election, Chicago's immigrant voters united and mobilized. With greater turnout, especially from the Germans and Irish, the nativists were defeated, and many of Boone's prohibitionist reforms were overturned.

Germans and the Election of Lincoln

Nativist leanings in U.S. political discourse hardly subsided with the disbanding of the Know Nothings. Economic concerns and the perceived political power of the Germans, a consequence of their growing numbers, continued to fuel prejudices and anxieties.[7] When it came to politics, however, the Germans were for the most part only ever unified against movements that disparaged their language and cultural life, such as temperance and prohibition.[8] The voting behavior of Germans in the United States as a whole—owing to their differences in provincial origin, religion, and class, just to name a few—was otherwise complex and variable, rarely determining the outcome of an election. That's true even for the presidential election of 1860, where solidarity among the Germans for the Republican candidate, Abraham Lincoln, was once considered by historians to be strong and significant. To be sure, antebellum politics had brought many established German leaders, who supported free-soil principles of opportunity, and their followers into the Republican camp.[9] And while a number of high-profile Thirtiers and Forty-Eighters did, in fact, stump for Lincoln and the Republican cause, their views did not mirror those of all Germans, such that Lincoln received less than half of the German vote nationwide.[10] The nativist attitudes and anti-Catholic rhetoric associated with the party (to the documented dismay of Lincoln) continued to alienate many German (and other immigrant) voters, particularly those affiliated with the Catholic Church.[11]

That said, Illinois was one exception to this rule. Along with Missouri and Minnesota, Illinois was one of the only states where Germans largely supported Lincoln's election. This was even true for some Catholics, who usually voted Democratic.[12] Prominent supporters of Lincoln and his party included Friedrich Hecker and Gustav Körner as well as Francis A. Hoffmann and George Schneider. Hoffmann, who immigrated in 1840 to Dunkley's Grove, had a wide and varied career as minister, newspaperman, banker, politician, farmer, and more. A passionate abolitionist and friend of Abraham Lincoln, he served as an alderman in Chicago in the 1850s and went on to become lieutenant governor of Illinois during the Civil War.[13] Schneider was editor of the *Illinois Staats-Zeitung* and used his position to condemn the Kansas-Nebraska Act and eventually exhort Germans to support the Republican Party. Additionally, he was heavily involved in the early formation of the Illinois Republican Party, introducing a resolution that promoted religious and intellectual tolerance and blatantly contradicted the platform of the Know-Nothing Party.[14] The lessening of nativist tendencies in the Illinois Republican Party could indeed have influenced Illinois Germans to vote Republican instead of Democrat, more so than in states where the Republican platform still smacked of nativist leanings. That Lincoln even secretly financed a German newspaper, the Springfield-based *Illinois Staats-Anzeiger*, which gave him extraordinary access to prominent, influential German revolutionaries, couldn't have hurt matters either.[15]

The Civil War

Lincoln won the election of 1860 and, with it, inherited a fractured union. Shots fired at Fort Sumter on April 12, 1861, commenced the American Civil War, and the Germans, like their Anglo-American and immigrant (i.e., Irish) counterparts, enlisted in droves, with the vast majority supporting the North.[16] That they "all fought like brothers, shoulder to shoulder, for one holy purpose—the preservation of the Union—and, with it, for the salvation of the last great bastion of freedom and for all the suppressed and the underprivileged of all nations" is, however, doubtful.[17] Surviving documents from this period, including letters from the soldiers themselves, overwhelmingly reveal a situation in which Germans kept to themselves, often fighting in German regiments or companies. Additionally, their reasons for fighting in the war were neither strictly political nor self-sacrificing.

Germans made up the largest foreign-born population in the Union (the Irish came in second), totaling 10 percent of all Union troops.[18] They were often older and, coming from a European context, had more military experience and training than their American counterparts. German soldiers in the Union numbered 176,817, and Illinois supplied 18,140 of them.[19] Segregation by ethnicity was common and practical; in short, it removed the language barrier. It also provided a sense of community and belonging among the foreign born, as one soldier was sure to point out to prospective recruits in an open letter to the *Illinois Staats-Zeitung* on August 12, 1862:

"Men will find many cheerfulness, joviality, song, and good comradeship with us, and all that makes the soldier's life comfortable."[20]

There were just over thirty German regiments during the course of the war, and three came out of Illinois: the Twenty-Fourth Illinois Volunteers (or Hecker Rifles Regiment), the Forty-Third Illinois Volunteers (or the Körner Regiment), and the Eighty-Second Illinois Volunteers (or Second Hecker Regiment). The Eighty-Second was unique in that it was one of only two regiments in thc Union that included a company of Jews.[21] Most Germans, however, fought in mixed regiments (i.e., regiments composed mainly of Anglo-Americans), though these regiments often included distinct German companies. German was the primary language of communication in these regiments and companies, which allowed those who didn't speak any English to enlist and carry out military orders. Those orders frequently came from Forty-Eighters who served as colonels and even generals in the Union.[22]

Fig. 5.1. Officers of the Eighty-Second Illinois in Atlanta, October 1864. Courtesy Chicago History Museum; ICHi-008203.

Firsthand accounts of service in Hecker's Eighty-Second, including camp life and conditions as well as battles, can be found in *Yankee Dutchmen under Fire: Civil War Letters from the 82nd Illinois Infantry*. Because Germans in this and other units were among their own, they practiced traditional German customs and activities.[23] They ate sauerkraut and sausages with beer, and in the first months of war, troops in German regiments even wore uniforms that resembled German military uniforms. They also felt a special sense of ethnic and regimental pride, sometimes to the harsh critique of their American counterparts, as the following letter excerpts show:

> According to what we have heard, our enthusiastic company made a thoroughly favorable impression in Springfield because post commander Fonda called us the best of the troops in camp here. Such a statement on the part of an American toward an exclusively German company certainly is saying something. Each individual is proud of this company and also to belong to this regiment. The spirit is excellent and the camaraderie could not be better. I do not need to explain further that it is a pleasure to serve under such circumstances. The members of our company are thoroughly strong young men, full of courage and lust for life—solely German. We are not exaggerating when we state that it excited us when we saw the joy of our countrymen and the admiration of the Americans in Springfield who enthusiastically observed us. Yesterday, the handsome uniforms and the military deportment of the men pleased everyone.[24]

> It is really a joy to see our regiment march, which was born only 2 months ago, in comparison to the dawdling one-year-old American regiments.[25]

> I do not want to conceal that we appear to be a thorn in the eyes of the American regiments here. It seems almost as if they could not endure the strapping appearance and the cheerful nature of the "Dutchmen." However, we will show them our superiority. We do not want to know anything about the boring and stupid chit-chat in their daily meetings and the chaplains from other regiments, who meanwhile creep through our camp, make sour faces, and see that their invitation to

> the meeting sits poorly with us; mawkishness and meetings are inadmissible commodities with us.—Therefore we drink our lager on Sundays, of course, when we can obtain it, even if there is some difficulty connected with it; otherwise, thank goodness, we have not yet experienced any deficiency of this noble substance although the Springfield beer cannot measure up entirely to the product from Chicago.[26]

Beer was a favorite topic in many of the letters, with one nineteen-year-old soldier pleading for "Best, Busch, and Brand, and all other manufacturers of the exalted liquid" to "have pity on 800 drooling throats." He beseeched them to "send beer in special trains, much beer," and for that their "name shall be emblazoned in golden letters in the memories of our soldiers."[27] Interestingly, beer was banned in camp for non-German soldiers, which created some degree of animosity as the third excerpt above indicates.[28]

Showcasing ethnic pride and solidarity as well as military triumphs made German support and bloodshed for the Union visible. That visibility, however, also raised their profile in a less desirable way: it marked them as different from (or unassimilated to) mainstream American society, which made Germans a convenient target for criticism, ongoing nativism, and, as one scholar frames it, "scapegoating."[29]

The defeat of the Eleventh Corps, referred to as the "German Corps" (even though it was only about half German), in the Chancellorsville campaign makes for a good example of scapegoating. Under Major General Joseph Hooker's command, the Eleventh, which included Hecker's Eighty-Second Illinois, was unfavorably positioned some distance away from the rest of the army. Exposed and unprotected, they were attacked and sorely defeated by rebel troops. This victory for the Confederacy has historically been considered one of General Robert E. Lee's greatest. The Eighty-Second was reported to have held strong despite an utterly disadvantaged position, but blame for the loss at Chancellorsville landed squarely on the Eleventh.[30] Seemingly at once, German soldiers were accused of cowardice, among other things, in many major and nativist outlets, which soured the reputation and self-esteem of all German Americans, not just those who had served in combat.[31]

Prejudice continued to fester in the postwar years, exacerbated by the events at Chancellorsville. This came as a slap in the face to Germans, who felt that they had fought bravely and sacrificed dearly. They reacted in the exact way one might imagine when persecuted and ridiculed; they turned to their community for support and acceptance. There was a sharp increase in activities and societies that served as cultural and linguistic bastions, and Germany's unification in 1871 only intensified their ethnic zeal and celebration.

Few Germans experienced the Civil War as an opportunity for integration. Motivations for fighting were varied, with many paralleling those of Anglo-Americans. Some saw it as an expression of American loyalty and sacrifice, with the hoped-for side effect of curtailed nativism. More recent immigrants, however, tended to enlist for economic reasons, simply seeking food, shelter, and a steady income. For many, it was necessitated by a desire to end slavery, not because of a moral opposition per se but rather out of a concern over job competition.[32] It was the ideology of free labor as opposed to slave labor that made slavery offensive to many and, ultimately, gave abolition in this country its momentum.

After the War: The Gilded Age

The Confederacy surrendered on June 2, 1865, and the Civil War finally came to an end. In subsequent years, those in the Forty-Eighter generation provided much of the passion behind the Liberal Republican movement (which abhorred the Grant administration), but the increasing identification of the Republican Party more broadly with temperance and English-only legislation as well as industrial capitalism in urban areas resulted in new political alignments and leaders within the German community. Many turned toward the Democrats, while others, particularly working-class arrivals of the 1880s, moved in the direction of left-wing radicalism (at least in urban environments).[33]

As discussed in chapter 4, the decades after the war, known as the Gilded Age, brought about rapid industrialization, urbanization, and economic growth in Illinois. This economic boom did not benefit everyone, however, and while many working-class immigrants were able to achieve some level of financial success—allowing their children to enter the white-collar world, for example—many found themselves working in exploitative conditions, laboring twelve to fourteen hours a day, six or seven days a week.

The Panic of 1873 and the five-and-a-half-year depression that followed resulted in economic and social upheaval throughout the United States and Europe, but especially in Illinois. Employers cut wages and laid off workers; in some cases, workers experienced nearly a 50 percent reduction in wages, and at its peak, unemployment in Chicago reached 40 percent.[34] In this environment, workers became increasingly radicalized, and in the last decades of the nineteenth century, Chicago in particular saw membership in socialist and anarchist organizations soaring as the city became a center of union activity. Two German-led political parties were even active for a short time.[35]

In 1877 railroad workers throughout Illinois united with workers elsewhere in the country in a strike protesting wage cuts. This strike turned into a call for a general strike, and many Chicago workers joined in. As the strikes turned violent, the governor called in the National Guard. These events inflamed class conflict and strengthened the power of unions.[36] By the 1880s, several national labor unions had formed in America, and the eight-hour-workday movement was gaining momentum, with Chicago leading the way.[37]

Fig. 5.2. Police confronting rioters at Turner Hall in July 1877 in the midst of the national Railroad Strike. From *Harper's Weekly*, vol. 21, August 18, 1877. Courtesy Chicago History Museum, ICHi-14018.

Germans often took the lead in this organizing activity. From a historical perspective, their familiarity with the functions of craft and trade guilds back in Germany, which were the forerunners of trade unions, provided a seedbed for concepts transferable to the political organization of the labor movement. In addition, the Forty-Eighters had brought their extensive experience with political organizing to early craft unions as well as to the antislavery movement. As a result, several German workers' organizations quickly took shape, such as the Chicago Arbeiterverein. Organized in the 1850s, it boasted a library, offered night school courses, arranged for lectures, and financially supported families of veterans killed in the Civil War.[38]

The role of Chicago's German workers in the labor movement cannot be overstated; they accounted for over 40 percent of Chicago trade union membership and 31 percent of organized labor overall in 1886. These figures take on a particular poignancy considering that Germans accounted for only 23 percent of the laboring workforce.[39] It was their response to industrial capitalism, however, that made Germans' actions in labor notable and politically significant.

The concerns of Germans extended well beyond mainstream labor movements; they were prominent in the movement for the eight-hour workday and in radical circles as well. Germans filled the ranks of Chicago's Socialist Party in the late nineteenth century. Worker-controlled, German-language newspapers, such as the *Chicagoer Arbeiter-Zeitung* (Workers' Newspaper), *Der Vorbote* (The Harbinger), and *Die Fackel* (The Torch), abounded, some going so far as to advocate for a workers' revolution.[40] By 1900, one-fifth of working-class Germans in Chicago were purchasing socialist newspapers, with the overall readership surely being much greater.[41] Germans were also prominent in Chicago's very active and sometimes violent anarchist movement, which called for overthrow of the capitalist system. Compared with the anarchist and leftist movements as a whole, the "bomb-throwing" anarchists were few in number, but they struck fear into the hearts of officials.[42]

The large participation of Germans in radical political movements had consequences for the community. Their strong visibility in organizing efforts resulted in unprovoked attacks on German workers by the authorities as well as an increase in anti-immigrant attitudes among the general populace.[43] Harassment of German radicals reached its peak with Chicago's Haymarket Affair (see the side story at the end of this chapter), but anti-radical and anti-immigrant sentiment continued to be intertwined through the early twentieth century (see chapter 7's side story on the hanging of Robert Prager for an example).

German support for leftist movements was, of course, far from unanimous. Many middle- and upper-class Germans, along with the mainstream German-language press, were just as anti-labor and anti-radical as others of their class.[44] And church-centered German communities, both rural and urban, often tended toward conservatism or were simply apolitical. Viewing it as corrupt and sinful—and as an Americanizing force—the Missouri Lutheran Synod discouraged involvement in American politics, and the Mennonites outright rejected it.[45] That is to say, German Americans' political leanings were as diverse as their backgrounds, religious beliefs, and cultural practices.

Needless to say, nineteenth-century attitudes and actions in Illinois as well as elsewhere were heavily influenced by German immigrants. They brought with them their own customs, languages, and religions, and their insistence on continuing these practices was viewed by some Yankees as a rejection of American culture and identity. But for Germans, the reality was more nuanced than that; preserving their imported culture and language was not, to their mind, incompatible with identifying as American. They saw themselves as dutiful, loyal citizens irrespective of their *Deutschtum* or religious affiliation. In this respect, Rabbi Bernhard Felsenthal of Chicago likely described many of his contemporaries when he said, "Racially I am Jew, for I have been born among the Jewish nation. Politically I am an American as patriotic, as enthusiastic as devoted an American citizen as it is possible to be. But spiritually I am a German, for my inner life has been profoundly influenced by Schiller, Goethe, Kant and other intellectual giants of Germany."[46]

In the 1887 meeting of the German American Catholics (*Amerikanisch-deutsche Katholiken Versammlung*) in Chicago, this perception is also clearly evident. In that meeting, amid talk of the prevailing anti-German sentiment of the times, attendees emphatically described themselves as "echt deutsch und echt katholisch zugleich . . . und obendrein hierzulande auch gute Amerikaner," that is, "genuinely German and at the same time genuinely Catholic . . . and on top of that good Americans here in this country."[47] Identity was for them as it was (and is) for all immigrants and their descendants in diasporic settings: multilayered and socially complex.

Friedrich Hecker

Friedrich Hecker is one of the best-known Forty-Eighters, or political exiles, to take up residence in Illinois. With military experience, an earned doctorate in law, and—according to many sources—a fiery personality, he became a forceful current in U.S. political affairs. He helped found the Republican Party, fought in the Civil War, and advocated on behalf of German Americans and their interests with faithfulness and rigor.[1]

Born in 1811 in Eichtersheim, Baden, Hecker grew up comfortably and with a civic sense of duty as the son of a royal Bavarian court councilor. He began practicing law in Mannheim in 1838, but it was his election to the lower (or second) chamber of the Baden State Assembly in 1842 that jumpstarted his political career. Revolutionary in his outlook, he was a catalyst for political and social reform, criticizing the established order of princely governments. He promoted liberal concepts, such as freedom of speech and assembly and freedom of conscience and teaching. His talents as a lawyer coupled with his energy and uninhibited rhetoric gained him support and popularity, and he quickly became a frontrunner of the assembly's liberal wing.

Fig. 5.3. Carte-de-visite of Friedrich Hecker, circa 1875. Courtesy the State Historical Society of Missouri Research Center–St. Louis, folder 60, Friedrich Hecker (1811–81) Papers, 1825–1987 (S0451).

The toppling of France's Louis Philippe spurred revolution against the governments of the German Confederation. In 1848, and in cooperation with socialist-leaning Gustav Struve, Hecker essentially sought to undo the aristocracy, demanding the formation of a federal constitution and the dissolution of a hereditary monarchy. Unable to gain parliamentary support at Frankfurt, he orchestrated an armed uprising on April 12 in support of a German Republic. The force, marching from Constance through the Black Forest, didn't accumulate in number as expected and was defeated on the Scheidegg at Kandern (also known as the Battle of Kandern) on April 20. Hecker quickly fled to Muttenz, Switzerland, where he made arrangements to depart for America.

A figure synonymous with the German liberal and socialist movements, Hecker arrived in the United States on October 5, 1848, to much fanfare. As he traveled the country, scores of German Americans rallied around him and held receptions in his honor. He gave a number of talks and in them stressed his intent to return to Germany and see the rebellion through. Despite some early sputtering, a second uprising never came. It was at this point that Hecker determined that the United States would be his family's new homeland.

This decision was deliberate and well-rooted in a desire for life in a democracy. America was, in his view, a country whose historical narrative most closely patterned his own ideals and political leanings. He believed in civil and personal liberties and marveled at a constitutional form of government. America achieved what Germany could not, and for this, he both revered and critiqued his newly adopted country.

He began his tenure in Illinois as a farmer. In 1849 he bought a farm just three miles southeast of Lebanon, joining the ranks of earlier political refugees in the Belleville vicinity, including Gustav Körner (who also happened to be Hecker's dueling opponent when he was a student in Heidelberg). They largely shared in his republican beliefs, but his intensity was bristling to some, particularly the Thirtiers, or "the Grays," who had lived in the states for twenty-odd years (see the sidebar on Grays vs. Greens in chapter 2).

Hecker's early years were spent growing his farm and avoiding political office. In letters, he wrote about being ill, weary, and discontent. He wasn't particularly well-suited to farm life, despite the success and high repute he held as a farmer. Hecker had more to offer, and the passing of the Kansas-Nebraska Act of 1854, an indirect endorsement of slavery, brought him full force into U.S. politics. The formation of the Republican Party was underway, dissolving the Whigs and splitting the Democrats.

Hecker promoted the new Republican Party, including its 1861 presidential hopeful, Abraham Lincoln, and countered temperance and nativist movements that were anti-foreign. He opposed the institution of slavery, but his position—like that of many at the time—was grounded more in the expansion of the white middle class than on the emancipation of slaves. The American Civil War broke out almost immediately after Lincoln took office, and as Sabine Freitag explains, for many Thirtiers and Forty-Eighters, opposition to the South was akin to opposition to European aristocracy.[2] So, in keeping with his values, Hecker traveled to Missouri with his oldest son, Arthur, to enlist as a private in the Third Missouri Volunteer Regiment of Colonel Franz Sigel. He was fifty years old.

Owing to his military exploits during the uprisings in Germany, particularly his leadership role in the revolt in Baden (also known as Hecker's Uprising), he was a hero in the eyes of most German Americans. As such, and unbeknownst to him, a volunteer infantry regiment quickly formed in his name, Hecker Rifles Regiment (or Twenty-Fourth Illinois). He served as the mostly German regiment's colonel from July 8, 1861, to December 23, 1861. While he provided able leadership, the Twenty-Fourth Illinois, an independent regiment, was never properly supplied or outfitted. That, together with some administrative complications, led to Hecker's resignation. Back home on his farm, he found it hard to ignore crucial developments in the war. The Emancipation Proclamation, a landmark bill that paved the way toward ending slavery, put Hecker back in the saddle, this time leading a new regiment: the Eighty-Second Illinois Volunteers (or Second Hecker Regiment). Known for keeping his camp "neat as a pin," Hecker displayed discipline, fairness, and exacting standards, for which his troops admired him greatly.[3]

The Eighty-Second, together with other German regiments, was assigned to the Third Division of the Eleventh Corps, the smallest corps in the Army of the Potomac. Hecker was badly wounded in the Battle of Chancellorsville in 1863, a defeat that historians now agree was unjustly assigned to the Eleventh. This came as a slap in the face to Hecker, who felt that his men had fought bravely and sacrificed dearly.

After the Civil War, Hecker involved himself in American politics. Reconstruction under the Grant administration had splintered Republicans, and Hecker strongly identified with the liberal reform movement in that party. For his part, he took special interest in civil service reform, which would not only curb corruption but also open up access to public office for Germans. Hecker was extremely popular, and his reputation provided him prominent newspaper coverage in which he railed against temperance legislation and its nativist overtones. Throughout the 1870s, he gave talks on a range of hot-button issues around the country (and in

Germany in 1873), such as the separation of church and state and women's rights. He was anti-clergy and anti-suffrage, the latter of which he ultimately rationalized on the grounds that political equality would wreck the family and state (i.e., demoralize women). Most Germans, including women and liberals, did not support emancipation for women.

Hecker passed away on March 24, 1881, at the age of sixty-nine from a lung infection. The very embodiment of a political citizen, he was at the heart of many dramatic and sweeping events in U.S. history. He even lived to see Germany unified in 1871. Hecker is buried in Summerfield, Illinois. A tall obelisk monument commemorating him can be found in Benton Park in St. Louis as well as in Washington Park in Cincinnati, Ohio.

Lincoln, Liberty, and the Know Nothings

Lincoln despised the Know Nothings, called *die Feinde der Ausländer* (the enemies of foreigners) by Germans.[1] To his mind, the Declaration of Independence protected the liberty of all, including "negroes, and foreigners, and Catholics," not just Anglo-Americans. In an 1855 letter to friend and native Kentuckian Joshua F. Speed, his exact words were,

> I am not a Know-Nothing. That is certain. How could I be? How can any one who abhors the oppression of negroes, be in favor of degrading classes of white people? Our progress in degeneracy appears to me to be pretty rapid. As a nation, we began by declaring that "all men are created equal." We now practically read it "all men are created equal, except negroes." When the Know-Nothings get control, it will read "all men are created equal, except negroes, and foreigners, and Catholics." When it comes to this I should prefer emigrating to some country where they make no pretence [*sic*] of loving liberty—to Russia, for instance, where despotism can be taken pure, and without the base alloy of hypocracy [*sic*].[2]

This letter was written after the Kansas-Nebraska Act was approved in Congress, an act that dissolved the Missouri Compromise of 1820 and, accordingly, endorsed slavery in the new territories. It was also an act that gave way to the new Republican Party and brought Lincoln national distinction as he sought to overturn it.[3]

Lincoln's disgust for slavery and nativism made its way into public discourse and debate, too, and he wasn't afraid to challenge his listeners:

> I should like to know, if taking this old Declaration of Independence, which declares that all men are equal upon principle, and making exceptions to it, where will it stop? If one man says it does not mean a negro, why not another say it does not mean some other man? If that Declaration is not the truth, let us get the statute book, in which we find it, and tear it out![4]

And then in 1859, at the urging of German Americans in Illinois, he condemned a newly passed Massachusetts state amendment (the Massachusetts Two Years' Amendment) that required a two-year waiting period before naturalized citizens could vote. To that, he said,

> I am against its adoption in Illinois, or in any other place, where I have a right to oppose it. Understanding the spirit of our institutions to aim at the elevation of men, I am opposed to whatever tends to degrade them. I have some little notoriety for commiserating the oppressed condition of the negroe; and I should be strangely inconsistent if I could favor any project for curtailing the existing rights of white men, even though born in different lands, and speaking different languages from myself.[5]

Similar inclusive language about immigrants found its way into the Republican national platform on which he ran and won the presidency in 1860.[6]

Lincoln was a documented friend and ally to many outstanding individuals in the German immigrant community, and he did not believe that state and federal activities had to take place exclusively in English. His actions throughout his presidential bid, during which his campaign materials were also published in German, and through the Civil War, during which he appointed German officers to command German regiments, certainly suggest as much. Those moves not only elevated the national status and perception of Germans as a group; it also gave rise to foreign-born political leaders in the decades that followed.

The Haymarket Affair

The movement for the eight-hour workday was officially launched by the American Federation of Labor on May 1, 1886, when tens of thousands of workers—in Illinois and elsewhere—walked off the job as part of a general strike. In Chicago, as many as eighty thousand workers marched up Michigan Avenue that day. The strike continued through May 4, as tens of thousands more workers joined in the protests. Though most of the protests were peaceful, the mainstream press vilified the radicals and labor leaders at the forefront of the strikes. Many—possibly a majority—of the radicals were German.

One such radical, August Spies, together with several other Germans and a few Americans, became the focal point for this backlash in what became known as the Haymarket Affair. Spies had immigrated in 1873, and by the 1880s he identified as an anarchist and edited the socialist newspaper, the *Chicagoer Arbeiter-Zeitung* (Workers' Newspaper). Unlike some more militant anarchists, Spies did not explicitly advocate violence.

On May 3, 1886, Spies spoke at a rally near the McCormick Reaper Works. There he witnessed an incident in which police fired into a crowd of protesters, killing two workers. Infuriated, he immediately rushed back to the newspaper and created a flyer titled "Workingmen to Arms!" According to Spies, unbeknownst to him, the typesetter then added the word, "REVENGE" (see figure 5.4). The next day, Spies met with several militant anarchists, including the Germans George Engel and Adolph Fischer, to plan a protest rally at Haymarket Square. Posters advertising the rally were printed with the line, "Workingmen Arm Yourselves and Appear in Full Force!" Spies refused to speak at the protest until the offending line was removed from the poster (see figure 5.5). While most of the broadsides that were distributed did not include that line, a few made their way into circulation.

The May 4 rally was utterly uneventful until the bomb went off. The speeches were no more inflammatory than usual, and the crowd was peaceful. Around 10:30 P.M., inspector John Bonfield, known for his hostility toward the labor movement, marched his force of about 175 men up to what remained of the crowd—only a few hundred people at this point—and ordered them to disburse immediately. Samuel Fielden, who was finishing up his speech, complied and got down from the wagon on which he was speaking.

Suddenly, a bomb flew just above the heads of the crowd and into the police ranks, killing at least one officer and injuring dozens more. Bullets flew and injured sixty police officers and dozens of civilians. Most evidence suggests that the majority of these came from the panicked and confused police themselves. At the end of it all, seven police officers and at least four workers were dead. To this day, no one knows who threw the bomb.

This event had the double effect of turning the general public against the radicals and inflaming prejudice against the "foreign anarchists." Police eventually charged eight prominent radical leaders with murder; six of them were German immigrants, including August Spies, George Engel, and Adolph Fischer. Lacking any

REVENGE!

Workingmen, to Arms!!!

Your masters sent out their bloodhounds — the police —; they killed six of your brothers at McCormicks this afternoon. They killed the poor wretches, because they, like you, had the courage to disobey the supreme will of your bosses. They killed them, because they dared ask for the shortenin of the hours of toil. They killed them to show you, "Free American Citizens", that you must be satisfied and contended with whatever your bosses condescend to allow you, or you will get killed!

You have for years endured the most abject humiliations; you have for years suffered unmeasurable iniquities; you have worked yourself to death; you have endured the pangs of want and hunger; your Children you have sacrificed to the factory-lords — in short: You have been miserable and obedient slave all these years: Why? To satisfy the insatiable greed, to fill the coffers of your lazy thieving master? When you ask them now to lessen your burden, he sends his bloodhounds out to shoot you, kill you!

If you are men, if you are the sons of your grand sires, who have shed their blood to free you, then you will rise in your might, Hercules, and destroy the hideous monster that seeks to destroy you. To arms we call you, to arms!

Your Brothers.

Rache! Rache!

Arbeiter, zu den Waffen!

Arbeitendes Volk, heute Nachmittag mordeten die Bluthunde Eurer Ausbeuter 6 Eurer Brüder draußen bei McCormick's. Warum mordeten sie dieselben? Weil sie den Muth hatten, mit dem Loos unzufrieden zu sein, welches Eure Ausbeuter ihnen beschieden haben. Sie forderten Brod, man antwortete ihnen mit Blei, eingedenk der Thatsache, daß man damit das Volk am wirksamsten zum Schweigen bringen kann! Viele, viele Jahre habt Ihr alle Demüthigungen ohne Widerspruch ertragen, habt Euch vom frühen Morgen bis zum späten Abend geschunden, habt Entbehrungen jeder Art ertragen, habt Eure Kinder selbst geopfert — Alles, um die Schatzkammern Euer Herren zu füllen, Alles für sie! Und jetzt, wo Ihr vor sie hintretet, und sie ersucht, Eure Bürde etwas zu erleichtern, da hetzen sie zum Dank für Eure Opfer ihre Bluthunde, die Polizei, auf Euch, um Euch mit Bleikugeln von der Unzufriedenheit zu kuriren. Sklaven, wir fragen und beschwören Euch bei Allem, was Euch heilig und werth ist, rächt diesen scheußlichen Mord, den man heute an Euren Brüdern beging, und vielleicht morgen schon an Euch begehen wird. Arbeitendes Volk, Herkules, Du bist am Scheideweg angelangt. Wofür entscheidest Du Dich? Für Sklaverei und Hunger, oder für Freiheit und Brod? Entscheidest Du Dich für das Letztere, dann säume keinen Augenblick; dann, Volk, zu den Waffen! Vernichtung den menschlichen Bestien, die sich Deine Herrscher nennen! Rücksichtslose Vernichtung ihnen — das muß Deine Losung sein! Denk' der Helden, deren Blut den Weg zum Fortschritt, zur Freiheit und zur Menschlichkeit gedüngt — und strebe, ihre würdig zu werden!

Eure Brüder.

Fig. 5.4. "Revenge" flyer, May 3, 1886. Courtesy Chicago History Museum; ICHi-019659.

evidence as to who actually threw the bomb, and despite the fact that most of the men were not at the rally at the time of the incident, the jury nonetheless found the charged guilty of incitement. Seven of the men were sentenced to death, and the eighth was given a fifteen-year sentence. Governor Richard Oglesby commuted the sentence of two of the men to life in prison, and another committed suicide before the remaining four men—Spies, Fischer, Engel, and the American, Albert Parsons—were executed by hanging on November 11, 1887.

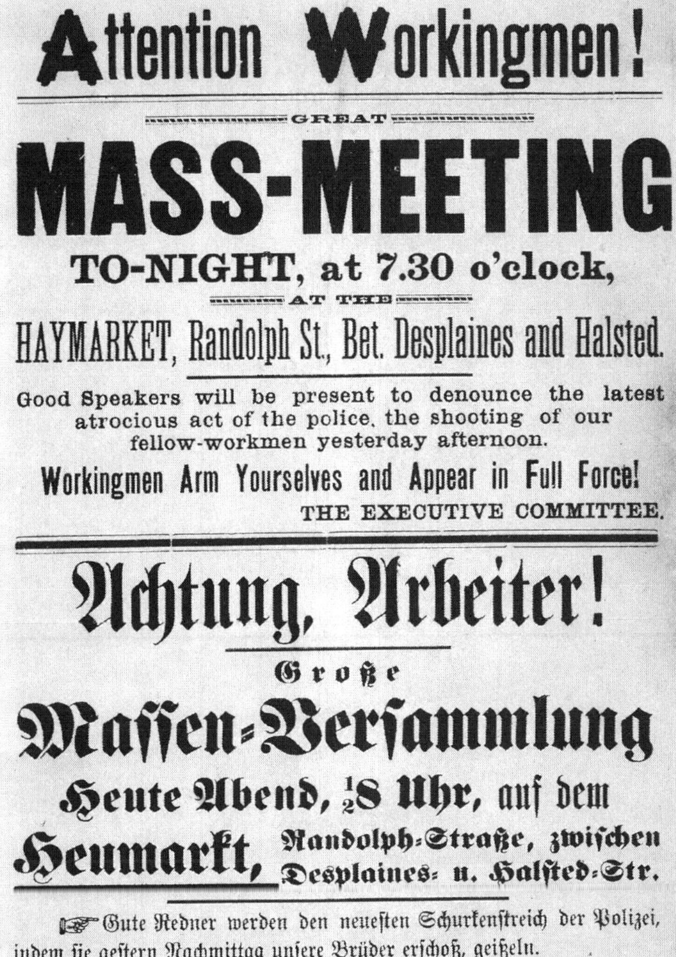

Fig. 5.5. "Attention Workingmen" circular, advertising the Haymarket protest, May 4, 1886. This is the version with the controversial line. Courtesy Chicago History Museum; ICHi-034602.

The German American community was deeply divided over the issue on class lines; while the *Chicagoer Arbeiter-Zeitung* called for the release of the prisoners, the more conservative, middle-class *Illinois Staats-Zeitung* called for their execution. John Peter Altgeld, a German-born immigrant who was elected to the governorship in 1893, examined the trial transcripts and found evidence of bias; he pardoned the three remaining prisoners in June 1893. It was due to this controversial move that Illinois' first and only German-born governor was not elected to a second term.

The executed men became instant martyrs to their cause. Their funeral processions drew enormous crowds—the *Chicagoer Arbeiter-Zeitung* described the November 13 funeral procession: "Wherever the procession went, people bared their heads. Not a word was spoken, but the only feelings, clearly recognizable, were those of resentful grief, bitter anguish, and a fury. . . ."[1] By 1893, a monument had been completed in their memory. Chicago police erected their own monument as well, funded by Chicago business owners. The anniversaries of the bombing and of the executions have since become focal points for rallies on both sides of the issue, with events surrounding the Haymarket Affair continuing to ignite public interest. International Workers' Day is celebrated on May 1 around the world to commemorate the Haymarket Affair and the struggle for the eight-hour workday.[2]

6

CULTURAL AND INSTITUTIONAL LIFE

Cultural and institutional life developed early and ran deep, as institutions that reinforced German identity and social customs were fashioned at lightning speed. Among the earliest and most important were churches and schools, which provided the bedrock of many communities. And those communities were teeming with activity that helped shape public life and discourse as well as the cultural landscape we know today.

Religion

German immigrants came from a variety of religious backgrounds, with the majority identifying as some form of Lutheran. Catholics, however, made up the largest cohesive religious group, accounting for approximately 35 percent of German immigrants in the United States. In Illinois in 1860, approximately 23 percent of the population was Catholic, and in Chicago around 33 percent of Germans identified as Catholic by 1890.[1] The remaining Christian immigrants were of various Protestant denominations, most notably Evangelical, Methodist, as well as some Baptist.[2] Jews were a small minority as were Free Thinkers, who rejected institutional religion altogether.[3] Despite their small numbers, Jews and Free Thinkers included among their membership a large share of the community's progressives, intellectuals, and local leaders.[4]

While individual congregations and denominations served as a unifying force for immigrants in particular areas, the absence of a common religion (along with the fact that Germany was not a unified country before 1871) often contributed to a lack of cohesiveness in the German immigrant community as a whole.[5] Back in Germany, the population had always been deeply divided over the issue of religion, with communities—and even historical political boundaries—forming based on religious affiliation. German immigrants imported these divisions to America, and many formed their community identity around their church first and their country of origin second.[6]

Some German Catholics and Lutherans, as well as Mennonite groups, tended to be insular and resistant to assimilation. Churches formed their own schools, hospitals, orphanages, newspapers, and fraternal organizations.[7] The Lutheran Missouri Synod, in particular, formed in Chicago in 1845 as an American organization intent on remaining separate from other denominations and from American culture.[8] This sect provided a safe haven for many newcomers, offering familiar language and customs, but many other German Protestant immigrants rejected its inflexibility.[9] These religious communities stressed German culture and language as a means of reinforcing religious identity and maintaining group cohesiveness.[10]

Other Protestant denominations were less isolationist. During the nineteenth century, some German Lutherans began to merge with the Reformed Church in Germany and elsewhere. This was especially true in Prussia and Westphalia, key locations from which many Germans had immigrated to the states. The isolation of frontier living provided further incentive for Protestant groups to band together, and this merger led to the formation of the Evangelical Synod of North America, which eventually became part of the United Church of Christ.[11] Evangelicals, though also supporting their own schools and other institutions, were less insular than the Catholics and the Missouri Synod Lutherans.[12] This was also the case for German Methodists and several other groups like Reform Jews. They were more likely to integrate into American culture or to participate in nonreligious German cultural organizations, as their cultural identity wasn't tied to their religious beliefs.[13]

Regardless of faith, for most German Americans, in Illinois as well as elsewhere, religious institutions were central to immigrant communities. They served not only as a meeting place but also as a means of keeping the German language and culture alive in an environment that sometimes seemed to threaten their traditional way of life. In this capacity, congregations also served as a social outlet, organizing clubs and societies for newcomers, as well as parochial German-language schools, which were considered central to maintaining and passing on cultural traditions.[14]

Education

Some of the first schools in Illinois were church affiliated, as a free public school system was not approved by state legislation until 1855. Even then many Germans preferred that their children receive a parochial education, as public institutions "were often anti-Catholic or at least had strongly Anglo-Protestant overtones."[15] Johann Bauer, whose letter excerpts can be found in previous chapters, even questioned the quality of an American education, writing in 1868 to family and friends in Germany to say, "I don't like the American school system, by the way. The Americans think there's nothing in the world better than the schools here, which is a great self-deception. There are even many people who cannot read a word, and when they have to write their names they make a + . . ."[16] Though this letter was written after Bauer had relocated from Illinois to Missouri, the perception that American schools were inferior to German ones was widespread. The fact is, educational standards in nineteenth-century Germany were exceptional by comparison, with school attendance compulsory since the eighteenth century. In Illinois, it wasn't until 1883 that similar legislation was enacted. Accordingly, the literacy rate among Germans was high, with those settling in Chicago estimated at 95 percent.[17] Besides that, Germans were ahead of the curve pedagogically, developing and practicing new methods in early childhood education and teacher training. Many of these theories and practices, like preschool, kindergarten, and teacher education, were imported by the educated refugees of the 1830s and 1848 era, finding their way into the present structure of the U.S. educational system.[18]

It should come as little surprise, then, that German parents placed great importance on the quality of their children's education in Illinois.[19] And that quality included the retention of native language skills.[20] German was, after all, the language of literary giants like Goethe and Schiller. It also dominated as the language of scientific communication.[21] The German language thus embodied a culture that, to their mind, was second to none other. Its perpetuation linked German American schoolchildren to their cultural heritage, including the achievements of their people.[22]

The insistence on German instruction wasn't exclusive to church schools or rural settings. In 1849 Germans in Chicago called for a school "in which both the German and English languages and the elements of the most needful sciences shall be taught."[23] After 1860 the number of German schools in Chicago exploded.[24]

Attending schools where lessons were taught in German was fairly common in areas of heavy German settlement, since schools were run locally for most of the nineteenth century, but controversy over the language's instructional use nevertheless began early. It wasn't that English-only instruction was thought to be more effective; rather, it was that its enforcement was seen as central to becoming American. A shining example of this comes from a minority statement filed in response to the St. Louis Board of Education's support of German instruction in public schools in 1860. In it, Dr. Pope, a reputed "gentleman and scholar," claimed,

> The constitution and laws of our country are in English, and the language of our public schools should entirely conform to that of the land.
>
> The sooner the German and all other naturalized citizens learn and adopt our vernacular tongue, the better, it is believed, for all concerned.[25]

With able representation on local school boards, however, German instruction in public schools was strongly supported and defended, so it persisted well into the early twentieth century. School records and teaching materials certainly attest to German's robustness in the public and private sectors. In some cases, English was even avoided as a school subject altogether because teachers lacked in their English proficiency. This has been the subject of overt comment, as demonstrated in the following example from Naperville: "For a while English was not taught at all in the Catholic school; the School Commissioner reported that the schoolmaster there, '. . . understands English very imperfectly, and therefore does not attempt to teach it.'"[26]

Children learning to read, write, and speak Standard German didn't have it easy though; it was akin to "learning a foreign language" because many of them spoke dialects at home (e.g., Low German) that were quite unlike the standard variety taught in schools.[27] For those who attended bilingual schools (or split their schooling between English- and German-language schools), the challenge was even greater. When reading, they had to contend with two different typefaces as German texts were published in Gothic type (known as *Fraktur*) whereas American ones were

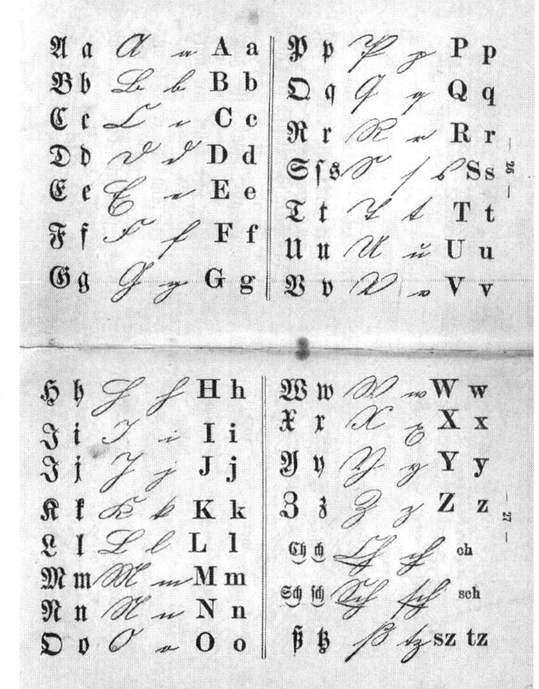

Fig. 6.1. Page from a first-grade reader used in German American schools showing *Fraktur* (printed Gothic type), *Kurrent* (cursive counterpart to *Fraktur*), and roman type. From Witter's *Deutsch-Englische Schreib- und Lese-Fibel* (1904); courtesy Max Kade Institute for German-American Studies at the University of Wisconsin–Madison.

printed in roman type. And when it came to writing, they had to master the old German script (known as *Kurrent*) for compositions in German and modern cursive for compositions in English.[28] Textbooks and other curricular materials were prepared specifically with these needs in mind for German American schoolchildren.[29]

Germans were interested in other aspects of public education as well. They advanced and contested the inclusion of academic subjects and found some success in doing so. The Turner society (defined later in this chapter) in particular was an organ of reform and change in public education. Its members, for example, most famously promoted German (as an academic subject, not just an instructional language), physical education, and music but adamantly opposed the teaching of religion in public schools, favoring instead the separation of church and state and the purging of tax exemptions granted to churches. Through their influence, Chicago became the first American city to add physical education to the formal education curriculum.[30]

The Press

Public expression of German cultural and ethnic identity can also be observed in print media. Already by 1848, German Americans in Illinois had launched several German newspapers, including *Der Freiheitsbote für Illinois* (1840), *Belleviller Beobachter* (1844), *Adler des Westens* (1844), *Stern des Westens* (1845), *Chicago Volksfreund* (1845), and *Illinois Staats-Zeitung* (1848), all products of that founding generation of Thirtiers and Forty-Eighters, many of whom worked as journalists and newspaper editors. By 1890, when the number of German papers published in Illinois reached its peak, there were approximately eighty.[31] The *Illinois Staats-Zeitung* of Chicago was by far the most influential foreign (not just German) newspaper, enjoying broad readership not only in Illinois but throughout the Midwest and beyond until its demise in 1922.

In *The German-Language Press in America*, Carl Wittke summarizes the function of the immigrant press as one "to initiate the immigrant into his new environment and to interpret for him, in words which he can understand, the political, economic, and social pattern of America."[32] In Illinois, a representative example is Gustav Körner's "Auszug aus den Gesetzen des Staats Illinois," an exposition published in 1838 to inform newly arrived immigrants of the laws and edicts of the state. German papers and periodicals not only helped assimilate newcomers to the state, they also maintained the language, carried news from the homeland, and upheld cultural ties and institutions. Chicago, Belleville, Quincy, Peoria, Springfield, and Bloomington emerged as the leading German press centers, but any town with a heavy concentration of Germans had at least one newspaper in the mother tongue.[33] Hermann Raster, chief editor of the Chicago-based *Illinois Staats-Zeitung* from 1867 to 1891, connected "the newspaper with the church and school as the 'backbone' of German culture in the United States, and stressed in particular the role of the press in creating 'German-American life' and culture in the United States, thus giving the German immigrant a feeling of pride in the cultural achievements of his people."[34]

Journalism was also a means to engage in local, state, and national affairs. German papers reported political news and activities with great enthusiasm, with newspapermen speaking out on a number of public issues. On the whole, they supported progressive views, such as public education reform, the abolition of slavery, and improved working conditions; they were vehemently opposed to any legislation in favor of prohibition and women's suffrage.[35] Along with their patriarchal ideals was their understanding of women's suffrage as tied to prohibition. Because women were key players in the fight for temperance in the late nineteenth century, prohibition laws were more likely to pass, they contended, if women could vote.[36]

The magnitude of the German press in America is remarkable. It easily outnumbered all other foreign-language papers, accounting for 79 percent of the immigrant press in 1885.[37] Though numbers declined in the decades that followed, German papers and periodicals still accounted for nearly half (46 percent) of all immigrant publications in 1914.[38] War-related strife, of course, took its toll, and by 1919 only twenty-six dailies remained, and most of those folded by the time of the Great Depression (for more on the broader societal forces driving the decline of the German press, see the side story on the shift from German to English at the end of this chapter).

Clubs, Festivals, and the Arts

Churches, schools, and the immigrant press weren't the only community structures that touched the lives of settlers and their descendants. Clubs and societies (or *Vereine*) that celebrated German language and customs were a large part of German American culture. The *Vereine* had roots back in Germany, where they had developed in the late eighteenth century and gained momentum throughout the nineteenth amid the social changes of early industrialization. These organizations, separate from government or industry, proved essential to the development of labor unions and political parties in Germany, particularly in the years immediately following the 1848 revolution. In the United States, even as *Vereine* arose with the intent to advance a collective German identity and ethnic consciousness, their true function was often to provide space for heterogeneous groups of Germans to organize themselves separately from each other. Thus, numerous *Vereine* of all types emerged, often organized by generation, region of origin, religion, political affiliation, cultural interest, or class.[39]

By 1910, Germans had the largest share of clubs of any ethnic group in Chicago.[40] Founded in 1865 as a singing club, the Germania Club ranks historically as perhaps one of the city's most important and long lasting. Its members, which included a long list of distinguished citizens, spearheaded many activities and pursuits of interest and benefit to the city's German community. Its lasting achievements include collecting literary works by German American authors, which resulted in a published survey in 1893, and founding the German American Historical Society in 1900.[41] It also welcomed and hosted a great number of prominent visitors from Germany, including Albert Einstein in 1921.[42] The club remained active until 1986.

Of the many organizations and activities of the nineteenth century, some of the liveliest and most pervasive were those that preserved a bit of the Fatherland. *Sängerbunde*, or singer societies, for example, attracted many members as they championed German music, culture, and, ultimately, fellowship, as multiple clubs often came together to organize large singing festivals.[43] Songs and poems reflect nationalistic leanings; that is, they speak to a "German" identity, as shown in the following poem written by Fritz Goldbeck:

Fort mit dem trügerischen Schein,
Ein Deutscher bin ich, will es sein!
Ob ich auch englisch reden kann,
Bin ich darum kein and'rer Mann.

Away with the deceiving appearances:
I am and want to be a German. Even though
I can speak English, I'm not
someone else because of that.[44]

These societies, which cropped up across Illinois as soon as Germans settled, are active even today, raising awareness of German customs and traditions. Another type of transplanted organization that was popular in the latter half of the nineteenth century was that of the *Schützenvereine*, or rifle shooting societies. With origins as civilian guards, these organizations had their own shooting ranges and sometimes hosted other forms of entertainment as well. Established by Germans to promote recreation and healthy competition in their adopted homeland, the sport, given its style of shooting and competition, also propagated Old World traditions.

One of the oldest and most influential of clubs to migrate to Illinois (and elsewhere) from Germany was the *Turnverein*, or Turner society. Turner (from German *turnen*; "to practice gymnastics") clubs, were at the center of Germany's nationalist and revolutionary movements of the early to mid-nineteenth century. They emphasized athleticism and its connection to liberal activism.[45] Society founder Friedrich L. Jahn (1778–1852) believed that "Germany's morale, which had received a staggering blow under Napoleon's yoke, could be restored by building up physical and moral powers through the practice of gymnastics."[46]

The Forty-Eighters, who had fled Germany as a result of their heavy involvement in the failed Revolution of 1848, founded the first Turner clubs in the states. The first American Turner society was established in Cincinnati in 1848, and its description of purpose reads as follows: "Cultivation of rational training, both intellectual and physical, in order that the members may become energetic, patriotic citizens of the Republic, who could and would represent and protect common human liberty by word and deed."[47] A mere three years later, in 1851, Illinois established its own Turner societies in Peoria and Chicago.[48] By 1860 there were 157 Turner societies in the United States with an estimated 10,000 members, most of whom were working or middle class.

Fig. 6.2. German *Turnverein* class, mid-1880s. Courtesy Chicago Historical Society, ICHi-14858.

Their membership grew steadily in the postwar years when German immigration to this country climbed and a wide array of women's clubs were created. In 1894 it reached its peak at 317 clubs with around 40,000 members.[49]

American Turners kept the physical culture of sport and exercise while also fostering a German cultural lifestyle, with their *Turnhalle*, or gymnasiums (large halls, really), serving as popular venues for social gatherings and recreation as well as political discourse. But it was their devotion to social change and equality—in no small part due to the intellectual contributions and political goals of their founders—that made them memorable in this country.[50] They opposed nativism, slavery, temperance legislation, and religious instruction, and when the Civil War erupted, Turners were among the very first to volunteer and fight for the Union. Though the umbrella organization changed its name from *Socialistischer Turnerbund von Nordamerika* (Socialist Gymnastic Union of North America) to the *Nordamerikansicher Turnerbund* (North American Gymnastic Union) after the war ended, individual clubs and societies continued to mobilize leftist, if not wholly radical, political agendas.[51] That was especially true in Chicago where Turner clubs were centers for working-class and anarchist movements.

Patriotic in spirit and democratic at the core, the Turners were a political force to be reckoned with, at least up until the World War I era. While club membership numbers remained the same until the war's end, the attitudes and goals of its members did not. It wasn't just that the socially progressive, anticlerical Forty-Eighters—the founding generation of Turners—were by now deceased but that the successive generations had become increasingly more assimilated into mainstream American society. The anti-German crusade synonymous with the war also worked to transform the Turners. By the start of World War II, for example, there was already a new national slogan in place, "Turnerism is Americanism," and the association's name went from *Nordamerikanischer Turnerbund* to the more Americanized "American Turners."[52]

The philosophy that physical fitness is critical to a person's mental and psychological health unites American Turners still today. It is embodied in the association's national motto ("A Sound Mind in a Sound Body") as well as in the athletic and scholastic offerings they sponsor at the club level. While membership is open to any ethnicity, most Turners claim German ancestry.[53]

While fostering a sense of group solidarity, community organizations like the ones described above also acted as shields, insulating members from their Anglo-American counterparts, other ethnic groups, and even from other German Americans. This separation, one might argue, added to nativist sentiment at the time, but not all German clubs and societies in nineteenth-century America were inward looking.[54] Take, for example, the Turners who, in addition to reforming select American institutions, helped German immigrants integrate into their new communities by offering English classes and encouraging their members to pursue U.S. citizenship.[55] They even promoted leisurely interaction between Germans and Americans:

> Sundays are spent in the same way as in the Fatherland, with dancing, singing, and music; or the older ones enjoy the pleasure of the young, over a good lager beer; and many Americans come out to those places on Sunday afternoon—young and old—to enjoy themselves; knowing that there they can drink a glass of beer in peace and harmony; hear a merry song, and see their German friends enjoy a dance. Sometimes a speech on morality, or other topics, is delivered.[56]

Fig. 6.3. Festival of the North American Turner Bund held in Wrights Grove in Chicago, 1869. From *Leslie's Illustrated Weekly*, August 28, 1869; courtesy Newberry Library.

To be sure, nothing drew Germans together quite like their love of beer halls (gardens, if set outside amid lawns and shady trees), picnics, and festivals; these were key features of many, if not most, German American clubs, regardless of the club's stated purpose. Intended for families, beer halls were spacious, well-lit places to gather and enjoy music, dancing, games, and, of course, lager beer. Unlike male-dominated, dimly lit American saloons, where patrons stood along a long bar, patrons at beer halls (and gardens) sat at long, shared tables that invited a spirit of *Gemütlichkeit*, a German word that connotes congeniality, belonging, and good-natured cheer. In other words, they promoted group cohesion among an otherwise heterogeneous German American

Fig. 6.4. Georg Bunsen. Courtesy Labor and Industry Museum of Belleville, Illinois.

Georg Bunsen

Georg Bunsen was one of the most admired educators in Illinois in the mid-1800s. He dedicated much of his time, including Saturdays, to instructing teachers in the Belleville vicinity where he and his family had settled. Renowned for his teaching methods, he followed the principles of Johann Heinrich Pestalozzi, known as the Father of Modern Education, whose theories and practices have informed elementary education as we know it today. His strong and dedicated following among both German and American teachers led to the establishment of the Belleville Teachers' Institute.

Bunsen also held a range of elected offices and, in so doing, was at the forefront of many developments in Illinois' education system. He was a proponent of the Free School Idea as a member of the Illinois Constitutional Committee in 1847.[1] In 1856 he was appointed by the governor to the state's first State Board of Education. In this capacity, he helped found Illinois State Normal School (now Illinois State University), the state's first teacher-education school and public institution of higher education. Never the slacker, Bunsen also dedicated himself to improving the public schools by serving as St. Clair County's superintendent from 1855 to 1859 and as Belleville's school board director from 1859 to 1872. The Bunsen School (now Nichols Community Center) was named in his honor.

community.[57] Similar to beer halls, picnics were cheerful, family-oriented affairs complete with social activity and entertainment. Clubs and churches frequently organized them, and, in cities, labor and political associations sometimes held them in working-class neighborhoods. In these latter cases, they were often accompanied by political speeches.[58]

Festivals were frequent, highly visible displays that included parades and performances as well as music, food, and beer. There wasn't much that Germans didn't celebrate; national holidays and anniversaries were occasions to unite just as Sunday afternoons were. They also adopted and adapted key American celebrations, like the Fourth of July and Washington's Birthday.[59] Festive culture not only brought greater personal meaning and satisfaction to their lives in America but also helped define German American identity.[60] "German Day" celebrations, which sprang up in the late nineteenth century, had the twin aims of promoting unity and heritage community bonding as well as showcasing conceptions of German American identity to other ethnic groups.

Of course, as Germans continued to arrive and filter into the state, a number of other organizations were formed, with many carrying out rather practical tasks, such as volunteer fire companies and aid societies. The German Aid Society of Chicago was undeniably one of the foremost aid societies. Through donations, it helped German speakers pay for necessities like clothing and healthcare as well as find work and evade common newcomer pitfalls. Other noncultural clubs, such as mutual support clubs, helped protect Germans from persecution and provided financial assistance.[61]

Theater, music, art, and literature featured strongly in Chicago's German culture.[62] There were many notable nineteenth-century poets from Chicago's German community, and German theaters regularly put on performances by local German American playwrights.[63] Germans were especially known for their music. German-born Theodor Thomas founded the Chicago Symphony Orchestra, and the symphony's ranks were mostly composed of Germans until World War I. German music festivals were held in Chicago in 1857, 1868, and 1881. The last two of these festivals were very large, with massive choirs and orchestras, featuring German singing clubs from throughout the United States and Germany.[64]

Though an interest in the arts was common among the upper and lower classes alike, by the late nineteenth century, working-class Germans in Chicago had developed their own distinct expression of this culture. They had their own newspapers, unions, singing societies, theaters, schools, picnics, and festivals, as well as their own literary traditions, which could be seen published in labor newspapers like the *Chicagoer Arbeiter-Zeitung*. Activities like gymnastics, boating, and shooting were also deeply ingrained in Chicago's German working-class culture.[65]

Illinois was quite possibly one of the best places in America for Germans and their descendants to live during the second half of the nineteenth century. Family, community, and organizational support led to a situation in which German language and culture thrived. Towns, streets, buildings, and organizations bore the names of important or prominent Germans; Illinois even elected its first German-born governor, John P. Altgeld, in 1893, and Chicago voted in its first German American mayor, Fred Busse, in 1907.[66]

Language

While Germans gradually shifted to English in the late nineteenth and early twentieth centuries, especially with second- and third-generation Germans identifying more and more as American, several generations still used German natively in the home as well as in a variety of social institutions. On Christmas eve in 1901, the *Quincy Journal* printed this profile on John Leonard Roeder, a man about to celebrate his 101st Christmas (emphasis ours):

> If the subject of this sketch, John Leonard Roeder, of 308 Payson Avenue, this city, lives till the 21st day of January 1902, less than a month hence, he will be 102 years of age. . . . Mr. Roeder was born in Rothenburg, Germany, and lived there, following the trade of a cobbler, until 1843, when he decided to come to America. . . . In Quincy Roeder again took up his trade and he remembers many of the prominent men for whom he made shoes. He recalls with pride that Gov. John Wood would never allow anyone else to make his boots. . . . WITH HIS FIFTY-SEVEN YEARS OF LIFE IN AMERICA HE HAS NEVER LEARNED THE ENGLISH LANGUAGE.

The American Midwest is rich in examples of people from all walks of life who didn't suffer economically or socially as a result of being unable to speak English.[67] So, while the swift learning of English has historically been considered *the* ticket to American success for earlier immigrants, with success being understood to mean economic and social mobility, conclusions from systematic studies on the historical patterns of learning English among immigrants cast doubt on this view.[68] Learning English in nineteenth-century America was neither quick nor effortless. Further, it wasn't uncommon for some Anglo-Americans in German-dominant communities to learn German.[69]

Ethnic Privilege and Pride

Turning back to the big picture, Illinois Germans entered the twentieth century comfortable in their chosen country and state. German trends were noticeable in the architectural landscape, as well as in local cuisine, music, and education.[70] Overall, they were largely accepted, favored even as an immigrant group, by the host culture. Meanwhile, the immense swell of new arrivals, like Slavs, Italians, and Russian Jews, prompted people, including reputable scholars, to draw sharp distinctions between "old" and "new" immigrants in ways that elevated Germans' status even further:

> It is obvious that the replacement of the German and English immigration by southern Italians, Poles, Russian Jews and Slovaks is a loss to the social organism of the United States. The congestion of foreigners in localities in our great cities, the increase in crime and pauperism are attributable to the poorer elements. All these are presented by this transformation of our immigration.[71]

> The entrance of such vast masses of peasantry degraded below our utmost conceptions, is a matter which no intelligent patriot can look upon without the gravest apprehension and alarm. They are beaten men from beaten races. They have none of the ideas and aptitudes such as belong to those who were descended from the tribes that met under the oak trees of old Germany to make laws and choose chiefs.[72]

The aversion toward "new" immigration found support in a line of thought in the social sciences that contended that some races—essentially those of Anglo-Saxon descent like the Germans—were biologically superior to all others.[73] It was the 1911 release of "scientific" evidence from the United States Immigration Commission, however, that gave these racial distinctions political currency.[74] The forty-one-volume empirical report on immigrants in America most notably concluded that arrivals from southern and eastern European nations were inferior (i.e., low-skill, low-wage, etc.) to those from northern and western European ones, so much so that their influx posed a threat to American standards of living.[75] The immigration restriction acts of the 1920s would be a direct result of this "scientific racism."[76]

The reaction among Germans was one of intensified national and ethnic pride. Efforts to preserve their culture and influence in America emerged in short order, oftentimes with hubris.[77] Publications appeared that recounted, for instance, the German immigrant experience and accomplishments, as did monuments of German cultural icons like Goethe and Schiller in public parks.[78] In Chicago, the German American Historical Society of Illinois was founded in 1900 to chronicle the contributions of German immigrants to the state of Illinois.[79] The great lengths they went to in order to write themselves into American history, Luebke observes, were not simply matters of "cultural chauvinism." They also represented an appeal for widespread American approval and recognition as well as a show of their own sense of patriotic citizenship and belonging.[80]

That Germany was well on its way to military and economic might was also cause for excitement. The scientific and industrial successes of the Fatherland as well as its reputation for world-class literature and music helped to reinforce Germans' sense of superiority in America. Trends in American taste in the arts and culture also worked to their advantage. German composers and artists were all the rage, and the children of wealthy Americans often studied abroad at German universities, which were acknowledged to be among the best.[81]

As the largest and most successful non-Anglo group in the state, Germans at the turn of the century enjoyed their prestige and acceptance. Predictably, that would change with the coming of World War I, when anything associated with "German" came to be viewed as unpatriotic. Efforts to conform Germans to Anglo-American ways became urgent and ugly, but anti-German persecution was hardly the death knell to German language and culture. The traditional narrative belies a more complex reality, one in which the turn of the century brought on internal and external changes to German cultural life and ethnic identity even before the outbreak of the war, and also one in which that culture survived—albeit changed—beyond the war's end.

On the Shift from German to English

Language shift occurs when speakers stop using one language in favor of another. In the American Midwest, several generations used German in the home as well as in a variety of social institutions—like churches, schools, and newspapers—before gradually transitioning to English during the late nineteenth and early twentieth centuries.[1] So, what event or set of events brought about German's decline?

The view that has been filtered through to the general public is that decreased immigration alongside increased integration, including increased proficiency of English among older immigrants and their descendants, led to the shift from German to English. While these and related factors, including the anti-German fervor during World War I, certainly helped exacerbate the process, a better understanding of the era suggests that the decline or, rather, shift from German to English was already under way as part of a broader reconfiguration of community structure referred to as "verticalization."[2] Built around Roland Warren's theory of "Great Change," verticalization occurs when locally organized institutions and structures in a community relinquish much of their autonomy. Policy decisions become centralized, with regional or national organizations outside the community assuming control. This paradigm shift is largely attributed to urbanization.[3]

Examples of verticalization can be found in a range of institutions. Take, for instance, church services. As Catholic churches began to proliferate in Chicago and elsewhere, disputes began to emerge among ethnic groups—particularly between the Catholic Irish and Catholic Germans—regarding the language of the service. German Catholic churches stressed the importance of maintaining services in the German language as a means of preserving German culture and, in consequence, the German Catholic faith. The motto of the German Catholic Church in America was "Language Keeps Faith," but church leaders did not always agree.[4] In 1886 Pope Leo XIII turned down German American requests for an ethnic diocese, which left it up to American bishops to create separate German churches. So, for example, while Chicago's first archbishop, the Reverend Patrick A. Feehan, supported the creation of German churches in the 1880s, as did Archbishop James Quigley in the early twentieth century, later leaders, such as George William

Mundelein, focused more on Americanization and a united church (as opposed to a multiethnic one), stressing the use of English in its parochial schools.[5] We see a fairly similar pattern in the Lutheran churches in the late nineteenth century and after; that is, leadership did not go out of their way to preserve programs of language or cultural maintenance, particularly if such a move would have political repercussions (though instances of churches in rural agricultural communities continuing the use of German until and through the early twentieth century are not uncommon).

Another example of the move toward centralization can be found in education. Schools in early Illinois were run autonomously, that is, by the local communities with little to no state or national oversight. Language diversity, then, was alive and well, and for communities heavily settled by Germans, students were taught subjects in German. This wasn't only because the make-up of the school district, including the pool of viable instructors, in these communities was soundly German but also that many parents preferred their native tongue over English as the language of instruction. It wasn't until the Edwards Law of 1889 that restrictive language legislation came about in Illinois. It stipulated that all parochial and public schools teach in English, a provision very much like Wisconsin's Bennett Act, which was passed that same year. Though both laws were repealed, the English-only movement was set in motion. It garnered support, in part, because of the 1883 Compulsory School Attendance Law, which was later amended in 1889, whereby Illinois mandated "attendance for a portion of the year at either a public or private school."[6] Most states enacted similar attendance legislation by the early 1900s, often out of a growing concern over child labor and exploitation, but it was largely advisory until after World War II. By the 1920s, teaching in German (or any other imported language) was mostly eradicated.[7]

A final example of an institution affected by external transformations is the German press. In the mid- to late nineteenth century, practically every town in the Midwest with a sizeable German population founded and supported its own German-language newspaper. Around the turn of the century, however, fewer publications were founded, and many of the existing ones either merged or died out in the face of economic pressures. While the circumstances surrounding the German-language press's demise are certainly more nuanced than that, this position, or downward trajectory of German (and other ethnic) newspapers, was not terribly different from that of nonethnic newspapers in this era.[8] Smaller papers simply gave way to larger, more metropolitan ones irrespective of the existing German American state of affairs.

The shift to English spanned a good century, a fact that ties into the larger narrative of social change in the early twentieth century, specifically the framework of verticalization. That transformation dealt the ultimate blow to German language and culture; the fallout from other events, such as World War I, scholarship insists, only sped its erosion. A counterexample offered by linguists and historians that correlates horizontal structures with language maintenance, the opposite of shift, is one where a minority language remains dominant, such as German among the Amish (and Mennonites) and Yiddish among the Hasidic Jews. Thanks to the highly localized social ties and networks, or horizontal structures, found in these communities, German and Yiddish continue to prosper.

7

WORLD WAR I AND ITS AFTERMATH

There was enormous tension in the pre–World War I years between the forces of assimilation and the need to preserve German culture and ideals. Take, for example, third-, fourth-, and fifth-generation German Americans. They naturally had weaker ties to Germany than those of the founding generation and their children, and though the late 1880s witnessed an uptick in immigration to America, those increases weren't coming from Germany. The majority of American newcomers by 1910 were emigrating from southern and eastern European nations.[1] That caused quite the national stir and outcry, which had a momentous, if not pivotal, effect on the perception and pursuits of German Americans.

Meanwhile, as cities grew and diversified, English began to replace German in many aspects of German American life.[2] In the schools, this came both as a natural progression and as a result of specific legislation requiring that elementary education be conducted in English. Churches, too, had begun to conduct services in English (Catholic more so than Lutheran). And German-language newspapers, though still quite numerous, had begun to decline by 1900, in part as a result of the 1893 recession. In fact, several of Chicago's newspapers had already ceased publication by the beginning of World War I.[3]

In rural communities, where people's lives orbited around conservative German Protestant and Catholic churches, German language and culture persisted, sometimes well into the mid-twentieth century. But this was an exception rather than the norm. Increasing numbers of German Americans were eager to shed their heritage and become "fully American," something that put German American leadership on edge.[4]

Fearing the loss of ethnic loyalty and cultural affinity among the younger generations, German American leaders worked hard to reinforce German Americanism as a cohesive ethnic identity with political might.[5] No group better captures the ambitions of unity and preservation quite like the 1901 formation of the National German-American Alliance. Founded in Philadelphia, it was the first organization claiming to represent the interests of all German Americans. With both a Chicago branch and a Missouri–Southern Illinois Division, the Alliance's primary efforts were spent on the promotion of German in schools and the other unifying issue among Germans: beer. To be sure, the main political focus was fighting prohibition up through the organization's demise in 1918.[6] While the issue of alcohol had always been a sore spot between Germans and temperance advocates, the growing possibility of a constitutional prohibition amendment—one that would compromise their lifestyle (and for those in the alcohol business, livelihood) in what was esteemed to be a pluralistic society—was defensibly much worse. In 1907, for example, the Missouri and Southern Illinois Division published an anti-prohibition pamphlet stating, "The campaign for prohibition . . . has assumed such an intolerant form, that it may well be defined as a menace to society."[7] In this sense, they perhaps saw themselves as better stewards of democratic ideals and personal liberties than Anti-Salooners.

As organizations like the Alliance increased their national political activity, they became easy targets for a growing nativist movement in the buildup to World War I. Cultural trends turned away from German art and music, for example, and German universities lost popularity.[8] The positive reputation enjoyed by many German Americans at the turn of the century soon began to sour. An organization that was so powerfully inclined to further the status of German Americans essentially undercut it, and this is doubly disturbing when you consider that the Alliance actually attracted little interest from everyday German Americans. Most members were second- and third-generation middle-class Protestants, hardly representative of all members of the community.

The real shift in attitude toward German Americans, however, came when Kaiser Wilhelm II rose to power and the German empire expanded. Americans viewed Germany and its monarch in an increasingly negative light, and many even harbored suspicions that German American organizations like the Alliance were secretly serving the Kaiser. Criticism of "hyphenism" became widespread, and those using the hyphen to denote their ethnic identity (German-American, Irish-American, etc.) were seen to still have one foot in their country of origin, and as such, were of dubious political allegiances.[9] While modern work on ethnic identity in diasporic settings has naturally problematized this sentiment, it was a pervasive one, with President Woodrow Wilson propounding in 1914, "Some Americans need hyphens in their names because only part of them have come over. But when the whole man has come over, heart and thought and all, the hyphen drops of its own weight out of his name."[10]

Far more damaging was that during the first three years of World War I, before U.S. involvement, many German American institutions, including the Alliance, did vocally support and defend Germany. In the beginning there were countless patriotic demonstrations supporting Germany in Chicago, for example, and some German Americans even signed up to fight for their ancestral homeland.[11] Also in 1914, the Alliance sponsored a protest in Chicago against the negative depictions of Germany in the press. The meeting resulted in a mass demonstration and march as well as letters of support to the Kaiser and pledges of financial support to Germany.[12] Indeed, in the early months of the war, many saw no reason *not* to support Germany, sending relief funds to Germans overseas and purchasing German war bonds.[13] Newspapers such as the *Chicago Abendpost* and the *Illinois Staats-Zeitung* even defended the claim that Germany's Kaiser was not at fault for the war's eruption; they viewed the conflict as a battle between Russian and Germanic cultures and blamed England, France, and Russia for the spate of violence.[14] All this didn't escape the public's notice, and, for a time, it created a cycle in which German American leaders defended their ethnicity and Germany while the Anglo population became more and more suspicious.[15]

Exacerbating this suspicion was the fact that in 1915–16, when the United States purported neutrality but was supplying arms to the Allies, there were multiple acts of sabotage committed on American soil by German agents trying to prevent the outflow of these munitions. The most famous of these were the July 30, 1916, explosions at the "Black Tom Island" munitions depot in New York Harbor, New Jersey. The depot stored munitions bound for Britain and France and, as it later came out, German agents led by the German ambassador to the United States had lit numerous fires at the storage site. This and other acts of sabotage fueled the growing anti-German sentiment during a period when many German Americans continued—somewhat obliviously—to vocally support their homeland.[16]

Despite the support of many German American leaders for Germany, Illinois' German American population overall exhibited a variety of positions on the war when it broke out, with the vast majority taking amazingly little notice of it (not unlike the American population as a whole). They had other, and to their mind, more pressing domestic and local issues to contend with, most crucially temperance and education.[17] Churches—at least the official organizations—tended to be politically neutral regarding the war. Acutely aware of the consequences of appearing to support the Kaiser, they concerned themselves instead with their ability to continue their cultural ways, which included conducting church life in German. Individual pastors and church members held a variety of viewpoints, of course, and many individual Catholics were indiscreet in their expression of support for Germany.[18] On the other hand, radicals like socialists and anarchists contested the war throughout as pacifists, which only brought them trouble. They were often seen as traitorous supporters of the Kaiser rather than ideologically opposed to warfare.[19]

As the United States entered World War I, the German-language press as well as many other German American organizations prudently declared their patriotism for America.[20] At the Lincoln (formerly Germania) Club's Chicago Centennial celebration on November 9, 1918, Ernest J. Kruetgen stated, "[J]ust as Lincoln called Americans of the North to fight against their brothers in the South to preserve the Union, so have Americans of German blood been called upon to take part in our country's struggle against the people of their own races."[21] And indeed, many German Americans had signed up to go overseas and fight "their brothers," including several German Americans from Quincy and Adams County who became the first from the area to be killed in the war.[22] Others retained their pro-German attitude, and still others—many churches, for example—simply tried to recede into the background as much as possible.[23]

Meanwhile, official engines of government had started working in concert with private patriotic organizations to whip up broad support for the war through the use of propaganda and social pressure. Organizations, such as the American Defense Society and the National Security League, played a powerful role in swaying the American public—which had favored neutrality all the way up to 1917—toward participation in the war, and their propaganda efforts included demonizing Germans and inflaming anti-German sentiment, often through unsubstantiated claims of atrocities committed by the "Huns" in Belgium.[24] In Chicago, a group called the Four Minute Men was founded in April 1917 to lecture on various aspects of patriotism and the war in movie theaters. Their name derived from the four minutes it took to change a film reel, as well as the obvious reference to the American Revolution.[25]

Once the United States had joined the war, arms of the federal government, such as the newly formed federal Committee on Public Information (CPI), took charge of these efforts to "sell the war" through posters, pamphlets, speeches, media campaigns, and films.[26] The United States was undertaking its most massive propaganda campaign ever. George Creel, the head of the CPI, adopted the Four Minute Men initiative in June 1917 and created groups of volunteer citizen-speakers across the country. The Four Minute Men eventually expanded beyond their original movie theater venues and spoke in an array of public spaces.[27]

This federal war propaganda continued to use Germany as the primary symbol of the enemy. As images of the Kaiser and his army paraded across the news headlines, the old stereotypes of Germans as hardworking and orderly morphed into a new stereotype of the Germans as rigidly efficient and militaristic.[28] It was a small step to apply these new anti-German images to German American communities at home. At a Baltimore Flag Day ceremony on June 14, 1917, for example, President Wilson had this to say:

> The military masters of Germany denied us the right to be neutral. They filled our unsuspecting communities with vicious spies and conspirators and sought to corrupt the opinion of our people in their own behalf. When they found they could not do that, their agents diligently spread sedition against us and sought to draw our own people from their allegiance . . .[29]

Ordinary German Americans were suddenly to be viewed with suspicion and malice, and government propaganda actively promoted the fear of a German American conspiracy against America.[30]

The fear of this conspiracy, real or imagined, led the government to pass numerous laws impacting the lives of German American citizens, German-born aliens (those born in Germany who had not been naturalized), and political radicals. In June 1917 Congress passed the Espionage Act, in which the postmaster general was given broad powers to prohibit the mailing of publications he considered "advocating or urging treason, insurrection, or forcible resistance to any law of the United States." The postmaster general at the time, Albert Burleson, used this law to target socialists and other political radicals as well as German Americans.[31] In the fall of 1917, the Trading with the Enemy Act expanded his powers and required that any foreign-language newspaper reporting on the war include an English-language translation for the local postmaster to review. This proved to be prohibitively expensive for most German-language newspapers, and many did not survive because of it.[32]

Also in the fall of 1917, the U.S. government began requiring all German-born aliens older than thirteen to register with the government. In addition, they were banned from places of "military importance," including railroad depots and boats, and they were required to obtain permission to travel within the United States or to relocate.[33] Finally, by spring of 1918, the Sedition Act passed, which stated in part:

> Whoever, when the United States is at war . . . shall willfully utter, print, write or publish any disloyal . . . language about the form of government of the United States or the Constitution of the United States . . . or shall willfully utter, print, write, or publish any language intended to incite . . . resistance to the United States, or to promote the cause of its enemies, or shall willfully display the flag of any foreign enemy . . . and whoever shall . . . support or favor the cause of any country with which the United States is at war . . . shall be punished by a fine of not more than $10,000 or the imprisonment for not more than twenty years, or both . . .[34]

In essence, what was once a simple show of pride in one's heritage—say, displaying a German flag—now amounted to near-treason. These federal wartime efforts to regulate the behavior of its citizens—both through propaganda and through the enactment of new laws—were disseminated in large part via state and local councils of defense. The Illinois State Council of Defense (SCD), which was created in May 1917, utilized press releases, pamphlets, and mass meetings to work up public sentiment. The SCD even ran a newspaper service distributing war news and propaganda. It also enlisted citizen-speakers like the Four Minute Men to disseminate their patriotic message; Illinois' Four Minute Men alone reached an estimated eight hundred thousand people per week.[35]

The Illinois SCD kept a close eye on the German American community, often measuring patriotism by the amount spent on Liberty bonds. Indeed, despite many Illinois Germans' display of patriotism at the onset of U.S. involvement in the war, they began to be perceived as showing lackluster support for the war as the months went by. State and local councils began pressuring these citizens to contribute to Liberty bond drives and other fundraising efforts, and social pressure from peers was extreme. German-language newspapers, the Lutheran Church, political radicals, and pacifists of all stripes were often targeted as insufficiently patriotic or even accused of treason.[36]

Several German American citizens, in a demonstration of patriotism, volunteered to work for the SCD to reach out to their communities, and the council regularly made "requests" of German American communities regarding patriotic behavior, including the purchase of bonds, as well as the expression of their culture and language.[37] The council's *Final Report* reads in part:

> The use of the German language, particularly in churches, schools, Sunday schools, etc., has been a constant source of agitation. . . . In dealing with this question we recognized that little had been done prior to the war in the way of discouraging the use of foreign languages. . . . We, therefore, urged that the use of the German language . . . wherever young children were concerned, should be given up as a voluntary patriotic act and as a concession to public opinion. We did not request churches to give up preaching in German, nor did we request the discontinuance . . . of German language newspapers and periodicals. We urged, however, that the German language in churches, newspapers, etc., should be used as an instrument for patriotic education and for the stimulating of a higher standard of American citizenship. As a result of this policy a number of churches voluntarily gave up the use of the German language in all their church exercises, and others discontinued its use in their parochial and Sunday schools.[38]

As the above quote indicates, the SCD methodically worked to eliminate the influence of German culture in Illinois, and these efforts often targeted the most obvious expression of it: language.[39] German was never overtly banned in Chicago, but it was generally dropped from everyday use, and in some cities and towns, such as Staunton and Steeleville, local city councils and local councils of defense passed ordinances and notices demanding that English be the only language spoken in public.[40] In addition, the Illinois civil service exam—which had included questions in the German language—was now English only, and German-born aliens were fired from state employment.[41]

Targeting the German language also meant targeting organizations where German was spoken and taught, and where German culture was disseminated: primarily schools, churches, clubs, and newspapers. As discussed elsewhere, many of these organizations were already in the process of adopting English as a result of broader societal changes, and many German communities were by this time considerably Americanized. That said, a number of churches—especially Lutheran churches—still conducted their services in German, and German was a major component of foreign-language education in public and parochial schools.[42] These churches and schools came under enormous pressure to eliminate all traces of German language and culture. Some complied, and some resisted. Resistance was met with threats of violence; when Lutheran parochial schools near Anchor and Colfax refused to eliminate German from their curriculum, a mob threatened to burn the buildings.[43] Mennonite churches (as well as a number of other buildings affiliated with the German American community) were vandalized with yellow paint to symbolize cowardice, and skulls and crossbones were painted over the doors.[44] In May 1918, a federation of German Catholic societies was scheduled to meet in Peoria; they were forced to cancel when the city "withdrew its hospitality."[45] German-language books were burned by mobs of patriots, German newspapers were burned as a project of the Boy Scouts, and public libraries in German strongholds such as Quincy were forced to eliminate German-language publications from their holdings.[46] Many Germans in the United States faced bigotry and persecution, but Chicago in particular experienced some of the more vehement anti-German activity.[47]

German musical culture was prominent in Illinois, and, as such, it became a target of anti-German activity. The Chicago

Fig. 7.1. Children standing beside an anti-German sign in Edison Park, Chicago, 1917.
Courtesy Chicago History Museum; DN-0069264, Chicago Daily News negatives collection.

Symphony Orchestra (formerly called the Theodore Thomas Orchestra, after its German founder), was almost entirely made up of Germans prior to World War I and had been celebrated as one of the best symphonies in the nation. Now its members' loyalty was questioned, and they were threatened with arrest. Four members were eventually expelled, and the conductor, Frederick Stock, was forced to temporarily resign as he sought to gain his citizenship.[48] Additionally, German musical compositions were banned from venues throughout the state.[49]

The attempt to eradicate all traces of German influence included not only cultural expression but place names and even food. There were efforts to rename "sauerkraut" as "liberty cabbage" (similar to "freedom fries" in the 2000s), and the "frankfurter" became the hot dog.[50] Some restaurants removed any evidence of the German language or the word "German" from their menus.[51] Out of 115 street names in Chicago, 82 were suddenly de-Germanized, including the long-lost streets of Berlin, Hamburg, Frankfurt, Coblentz, Lubeck, and Rhine. Additionally, the Bismarck School became the General Frederick Funston School.[52]

Many of these changes came at the demand of patriotic citizens, and as anti-German feelings quickly rose, acts against German Americans became a relatively common occurrence. By October 1917, wild stories of the mass infiltration of German and Austrian spies in America were being reported as fact in respected newspapers, and the public saw treason everywhere they looked.[53] Suspicion led to harassment of anyone with so much as a German name or a subscription to a German-language newspaper, and as the months went on, it escalated to violence. By March 1918, a Quincy newspaper was reporting, "Southern Illinois doesn't laugh when one says German spy. Instead Southern Illinois gets out tar and feathers, and her vigilance societies begin parading the town."[54] In Quincy and elsewhere, numerous individuals were arrested for refusing to buy Liberty bonds, making "disloyal statements," and behaving in any way—real or not—that could be interpreted as unpatriotic.[55] More than this, German Americans were forced by mobs to buy Liberty bonds, sing patriotic songs and kiss the flag, and other "patriotic" acts. German churches, schools, and homes were painted yellow to symbolize disloyalty, and individuals were indeed tarred and feathered.[56]

Rural Illinois in particular saw numerous incidents. In East Alton, a German American was threatened with hanging and forced to kiss the American flag because he refused to close his business during an event promoting Liberty bond sales. A farmer from Kenney was beaten for allegedly making pro-German comments. And John Rynders, a grocer in Athens, was made to kiss the flag and parade through town wearing a banner because he didn't contribute groceries to a bond drive dinner event. In Pocahontas, a man was even forced to kiss a flag from the walls of his own house.[57] In Nokomis, a mob pressed several suspected German sympathizers to kiss the flag, and some were severely beaten.[58]

German churches were also targeted. A seventy-five-year-old Lutheran pastor from a church near Pinkneyville was violently attacked and tarred for making allegedly unpatriotic comments during a sermon. He was admitted to the hospital for his injuries. A pastor near Maryville was harassed until he and his family moved to Kansas. Reverend J. D. Metzler of Edwardsville refused to follow daylight saving time and made ostensibly pro-German remarks. After hearing of a plot to tar and feather him, he went into hiding for three weeks, only to reappear and announce he was going on a leave of absence.[59]

Illinois' German communities responded by emphasizing their patriotism as well as their Americanness, contributing time and funds to the war effort, taking public loyalty oaths, and often voluntarily removing evidence of the German language from their organizational names—and sometimes even changing their surnames to something less German (like Schmidt becoming Smith). For example, in Bloomington, the Turners renamed themselves the Columbia Fraternal Society, and the Verein Vorwärts of New Athens changed its name to New Athens Singing Society. In Chicago, the Germania Club, Hotel Bismarck, and Hotel Kaiserhof became the Chicago Lincoln Club, Hotel Randolph, and Hotel Atlantic, respectively. Churches and clubs also began conducting their business in English if they hadn't been doing so already. Most German-language newspapers that didn't close down entirely converted to English only.[60]

All of this is to say that the trauma of World War I had a lasting and substantial impact on German communities in Illinois, and it amplified the assimilatory process. Census data point to the likelihood that some Germans denied their heritage in the 1920 census; the official data show a 25.3 percent reduction in the number of Germans between 1910 and 1920, despite immigration data showing an increase in immigrants. This discrepancy was especially dramatic in Illinois.[61]

Developments in the 1920s impacted Illinois German Americans as well. Prohibition quashed the lively culture of German saloons and beer gardens as well as Chicago's German-dominated brewing industry.[62] Owing to a number of pressure points, the German-language press never recovered, and the number of German-language newspapers continued to drop through the 1920s, with the influential *Illinois Staats-Zeitung* disappearing in 1922.[63] The number of churches conducting services in German also continued to decline after World War I.

At first glance, it might seem that all traces of German culture in Illinois were permanently erased by the traumas of World War I as well as by the other changes that came with the early twentieth century. As Melvin G. Holli states about Chicago, "Almost nowhere are German Americans as a group as visible as many smaller groups."[64] While this may be true, it does not necessarily follow that German culture ceased to exist after World War I. Indeed, much of the recent literature points to the fact that German American communities persisted, albeit changed, after the war. Many German Americans—particularly in rural areas heavily settled by Germans—adapted, rather than erased, their ethnic identity.[65] And as we will discuss in the next chapter, German American communities in areas such as St. Clair County persisted into the 1970s and 1980s.

So, while many German Americans became quieter in regards to their ethnic identity during the decade immediately following World War I, they did continue to express their German alliances at the ballot box and through charitable donations overseas. Chicago Germans had generally voted Democratic since the 1892 election that brought the German American John P. Altgeld to the governorship.[66] Now they turned away from that party—which had been the party of Wilson and World War I—and overwhelmingly voted Republican, in what Luebke termed, "the politics of revenge."[67] In the 1924 election, the community supported either the Republican ticket or the third-party candidate, Robert La Follette.[68] By 1928, German American leaders no longer emphasized the importance of the ballot box, and the community ceased to vote as a bloc.[69] The majority of Chicago Germans—as well as the rest of Chicago—was once again voting for Democrats by the 1930s.[70]

Illinois Germans expressed their ethnicity in other ways as well. Clubs and societies, though moderated, continued to play a role in German American cultural life, and German Day festivals returned in the 1920s, though the celebrations were small at first.[71] The Alliance reorganized as the German-American Citizens League, or the *Deutsch-Amerikanische Burgerbund*, in Chicago in 1920, and the Steuben Society of America was founded in 1919.[72] As for migration, the interwar years also saw a burst in German immigration, with 1924 cresting at 75,091 newcomers (see figure 7.2).[73]

By 1930 German culture in Illinois was once again visible, in the form of German-language classes in the schools, German Day celebrations, and German theater and music.[74] While many of the traditional German clubs were on the decline, there was a growing interest in German American ethnic heritage and history.[75] In 1938 folklorist Charles Neely wrote of Randolph and St. Clair Counties:

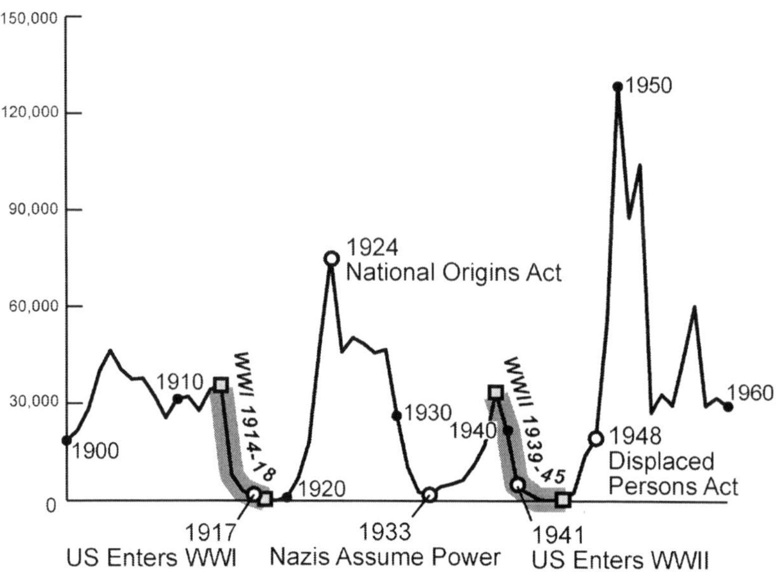

Fig. 7.2. German immigrants to the United States, 1900–1960. Statistics from International Migration and Naturalization, series C 89–119, "Immigrants, by Country: 1820 to 1970."

> Today that region seems more like a detached portion of Germany than a part of [Southern Illinois]. Many of the people are bilingual, speaking a broken English and a patois that is a strange compound of German and English words—a patois that is as incomprehensible to a master of literary German as it is to the English-speaking Southern Illinoisans. They keep their language alive in parochial schools, and they hand their folk heritage down from generation to generation. They tell German folk tales and sing German ballads and songs; they build houses that are decidedly German in architecture. . . . [76]

Neely's observations on the cultural and linguistic experiences of residents in southern Illinois find support among those who grew up in the region in decades that followed, with one gentleman, Steve Bense, sharing this about his bilingual upbringing in Millstadt in the 1960s and 1970s:

> I was raised in a household where my parents spoke both High and Low German, although I never learned to speak nor fully grasp the Low German vernacular. While German was spoken in our home, by the time I came along, English was

> the more dominant language being spoken—except during supper, when German was expected and even this was relaxed as years went by. My siblings and I—I am the youngest of five—only learned High German, and we learned it mostly in our local public school.[77]

The "patois" Neely describes was likely a combination of what linguists call codeswitching, which is when people—sometimes consciously but oftentimes not—shift in conversation between one or more languages, and lexical borrowing, that is, the adoption of words from one language into another. To be sure, German was clearly being displaced by English as the dominant language during this period, and considering that by this point Germans had been in the Midwest for a good century, it was a long time coming, strikingly so if compared to the speed at which contemporary immigrants, such as Spanish speakers, learn English (and abandon their first languages).[78] Of particular interest, and something we'll circle back to in the following chapter (see the side story on German effects on English in the Midwest), is that traces of that shift can be found in the regional variety of English spoken today, with even the most casual of observers noticing the distinct pronunciations, words, and structures unique to the Midwest.

When the Nazis assumed power in 1933, German immigration to the United States had dropped to the second lowest point in a century (see figure 7.2).[79] It wasn't until the immediate years leading up to World War II that the nation saw a small new wave of highly educated (mostly) Jewish refugees from Nazi Germany. Germany (and the rest of Europe) experienced a "brain drain" as a result, because this group included talented scholars and academics who went on to advance their fields and receive high recognition for their work here in the states. The majority, approximately one hundred thousand, came between 1939 and 1941, just as Hitler was ratcheting up anti-Semitic positions.[80] More had desired entry but were denied it due to restrictive immigration policies and, to varying degrees, concerns with regards to the economy and national security.[81] Tragically, many would-be immigrants died as a result in camps and ghettos during the Holocaust.[82] Immigration resumed in the wake of World War II, though it wasn't until 1948 that Congress introduced the Displaced Persons Act to resettle victims of Nazi persecution in the United States.[83]

With the Nazis in power, German culture once more became a source of embarrassment.[84] The German American Bund, originally known as the Free Society of Teutonia, was truly one of the most infamous (and humiliating) societies with German American ties in U.S. history. With roots in Chicago, it was established in 1924 long after mass migration had ceased. Anti-Semitic and anti-Communist, it had an ideology similar to that of Nazi Germany. With membership estimates at around twenty-five thousand and most—but not all—members of German descent, this ethno-nationalist organization advertised its causes in the form of publications, rallies, and youth camps.[85] Despite its propaganda, it never garnered broad appeal, with most Germans in America disapproving of its mission and activities. Having had limited impact, the German American Bund dissolved with incredible swiftness after the United States entered World War II.

Although very few German Americans were sympathetic to the Nazis, German American leadership did little to speak out against them either. Understandably, many German Americans, remembering the backlash against them during the First World War, had opposed U.S. involvement in this war. Other groups in Illinois, especially in the Chicago area, felt the same way, leading to a strong Chicago-led isolationist movement.[86] Germans in Illinois and elsewhere did not experience the recoil they had during World War I, however.[87] Admittedly, they were by now well enough adapted that they didn't stand out in the way they had twenty-five years earlier, and American hatred of the Germans was keenly focused directly on the Nazis in Germany this time.[88]

To be sure, and in conclusion, the world wars failed to effect any lasting damage on the reputation of German Americans. The nastiness German Americans had faced—while very real and at moments truly terrifying—was a blip in an otherwise favorable tenure in America.[89] The second half of the twentieth century therefore was one of continued integration and uninterrupted success, with the United States absorbing close to one million new arrivals from Germany between World War II and the end of the twentieth century.[90] In fact, in 1980 German Americans made up the largest ethnic group in Illinois as well as in the nation.[91] Assimilation didn't, however, result in the loss of German ethnic consciousness and identity in the Midwest.[92] With that, let's turn now to some major ways in which Germans have left their mark on Illinois.

Protecting English, Promoting Americanism: Better Speech Week

While it's fair to say that most of us have had experiences with language "purists," folks who enjoy exposing deviations from what's considered Standard English (*whom*, not *who!*), it's doubtful that anyone reading this book was either made to recite a pledge vowing to use proper language or court-martialed for poor English. And, yet, with origins in Chicago, that's just what happened about a century ago in some of the nation's schools.[1]

The "Better Speech Week," an initiative of the Chicago Women's Club (and directed by organizations like the National Council of Teachers of English and the General Federation of Women's Clubs, sponsored by the American Academy of Arts and Literature and the Society of Pure English), aggressively campaigned for speech improvement in schools from 1918 to 1930, using slogans such as these to draw attention to and concern for the cause, often tying national identity to language:

> **"American Speech Means American Loyalty"**
> **"Be a patriot, in thought, in deed, in speech"**
> **"The American Flag, The American Home, The American Language"**

Published in local newspapers or used on posters, such slogans readily imply that "good" English was considered a foundational aspect of being a "good" American. Though the United States has never had an official national language, similar views exist today but are being challenged by recent scholarship on language and immigration.[2]

The promotion of Americanism through language, spurred by the Americanization movement, which was particularly active during and after World War I, becomes even more apparent in the "Watch Your Speech Pledge," penned by Grace Williamson Willet of the Chicago Women's Club (see figure 7.3).[3] Many schoolchildren across America were required to recite this pledge, but language improvement wasn't just an individual effort. It was a collective—and punitive—one as well, meaning that if a child substituted a "foreign 'ya'" for a "good American 'yes,'" he could count on his peers to call him out on it. Indeed, acting as classroom detectives, schoolchildren recited the following, vowing to report any offenders of the English language: "I hereby pledge myself a secret service agent to protect the language of my country, to capture all spies of Bad-English and to keep my position secret."[4] Guilty verdicts of improper language use carried consequences. For example, "Bad-English spies" were often interned and forced to reflect on their errors through essays. In other cases, a culprit was required to wear "a tag denoting his error." Schools in Rockford, Illinois, even went so far as to capitalize on the better speech campaign, stating that "each offense involved a fine of one cent."

Better Speech Week fizzled out with the onset of the Great Depression but has recently found resurgence in the form of National Grammar Day. Established in 2008, its one-day-per-year campaign to "speak well, write well, and help others do the same" is about promoting standard, by-the-book grammar, not patriotism.[5] Whatever your views on language, at least National Grammar Day doesn't dole out punishments, fine you, or probe your American identity.

BETTER AMERICAN SPEECH WEEK

OCT. 27, to NOV. 2, 1918

ONE LANGUAGE FOR A UNITED PEOPLE

SPEAK THE LANGUAGE OF YOUR FLAG.

SLOVENLY SPEECH BESPEAKS A SLOVENLY MIND

WATCH YOUR SPEECH

PLEDGE:

I love the UNITED STATES OF AMERICA.

I love my country's LANGUAGE.

I PROMISE:

(1) that I will not dishonor my country's speech by leaving off the last syllables of words;

(2) that I will say a good American "yes" and "no" in place of an Indian grunt "um-hum" and "nup-um" or a foreign "ya" or "yeh" and "nope";

(3) that I will do my best to improve American speech by avoiding loud harsh tones, by enunciating distinctly and speaking pleasantly, clearly and sincerely;

(4) that I will try to make my country's language beautiful for the many boys and girls of foreign nations who come here to live;

(5) that I will learn to articulate correctly one word a day for one year.

Better American Speech Committee
Chicago Woman's Club
410 S. Michigan Ave.
Chairman
Katherine Knowles Robbins

Scanlan School Press

Fig. 7.3. Watch Your Speech Pledge for Children. Archives of the Chicago Women's Club, Chicago History Museum; ICHi-173528A.

The Hanging of Robert Prager

Fig. 7.4. Robert Paul Prager. Courtesy *St. Louis Post-Dispatch*.

Of all the incidents in which German Americans were targeted during World War I, perhaps the most hideous is the April 5, 1918, hanging of Robert Paul Prager in Collinsville, Illinois.[1] A native of Dresden, Germany, Prager immigrated to the United States in 1905. He was a drifter with limited education, but the 1917 entry of the United States into World War I stirred him. In a show of allegiance, he began the naturalization process and attempted to enlist in the navy that same year. It was in the following year, however, that Prager's tragic story began.

In 1918 he was living in Collinsville and working as a coal miner in Maryville. By many accounts a stubborn and quarrelsome character, Prager was also a vocal socialist. He was denied membership to the United Mine Workers of America due to his disagreeable personality, his political viewpoints, and conflicts with union leadership. Unfortunately for Prager, it didn't help that the union, which had recently been on strike, was divided over the issue of socialist politics, with politically radical Germans being targeted by more conservative union leadership. In addition, at the time of Prager's rejection from the union, there were coinciding rumors circulating about a German agent who was planning to blow up the mine in Maryville. As Prager was unappealing in both personality and appearance (he was blind in one eye) and as he espoused controversial political views, no one made for a likelier spy, or fall guy.

On April 3 Prager was accosted in Maryville by a group of miners and told to leave town. Later that same day, union leaders Moses Johnson and James Fornero informed him of the rejection of his union membership application. According to Johnson's account of the conversation (though keep in mind that Johnson would also later assert Prager's guilt as a spy), Prager expressed such sympathy for the German cause that they feared for his safety and escorted him back to Collinsville, asking the police to put him in "protective custody." The police refused, and Prager returned to his home.

Incensed at the union officials' attempt to arrest him, Prager returned to Maryville the next day to defend himself. He brought with him a document he had written asserting his loyalty to the United States and attacking the union for denying him membership. He posted this document in public spaces in Maryville. That night in Collinsville, events went from bad to worse for Prager in stunningly rapid succession.

A group of drunken Maryville miners appeared at Prager's door around 9:30 P.M. They stripped him, wrapped him in a U.S. flag, and then dragged him through the streets barefoot, forcing him to sing patriotic songs. The police interrupted the scene and took Prager into protective custody. The mayor of Collinsville, John H. Siegel, arrived at the police station and urged the crowd outside to disperse. Prager's life was almost spared, save for what happened next.

An ex-soldier and former miner of German ancestry named Joseph Riegel approached the mayor and demanded entry to the jail. The mayor stepped aside to let Riegel in, and the mob swarmed through the doorway. After a thorough search of the jail, the mob discovered where Prager was hiding and dragged him outside, where they continued to force him to kiss the flag and sing patriotic songs. At this point, terrified for their own lives, the police and mayor did nothing to stop them.

The mob marched Prager outside the city limits, and Riegel and a handful of others made ready to hang him. Prager asked for a moment to write a letter before dying, and he wrote a brief note to his parents in Dresden. He then knelt and said a prayer in German before walking of his own accord back to the noose that had been prepared for him. Robert Paul Prager died at 12:30 A.M. on April 5, 1918.

The nation reacted to Prager's murder mostly with shock and horror. Newspapers close to the event tended to be more ambivalent, however, as were local authorities. The Collinsville chief of police even went on record saying that the hanging was a good thing in that if Prager hadn't been killed, "I believe a mob would have vented its rage by hanging two or three Collinsville persons . . ."[2] Mayor Siegel deflected blame in a more palatable way by accusing the U.S. government of being too lenient on disloyal citizens and thus provoking citizens to take matters into their own hands. This was a common response to anti-German violence.

State authorities, on the other hand, came down hard on Collinsville, with Governor Frank O. Lowden personally vowing to bring the mob leaders to justice. Some in the federal government also condemned the mob violence, notably Attorney General Thomas Gregory, who sent representatives to Illinois to investigate the situation there. Disturbed by a climate of hysteria and vigilantism, he urged President Wilson to use his influence to calm the nation. But Wilson hardly batted an eye, only issuing a proclamation against mob rule several months later.

The crime was investigated with varying degrees of enthusiasm. The governor and state's attorney worked to identify participants in the crime, but Collinsville officials refused to cooperate. The coroner of Madison County was helpful, however, and some of the most incriminating testimony was heard by the coroner's jury—including a confession from Joseph Riegel.[3] On April 25, twelve participants were indicted for murder, as well as four Collinsville police officers for omission of duty and malfeasance in office. Over seven hundred individuals were interviewed for the murder trial's jury panel by the time they found twelve who were acceptable. The trial itself was very brief. The defense mainly argued that it was impossible to identify with certainty who had participated, as arguments that Prager was unpatriotic or disloyal were deemed irrelevant by the judge (though the defense did close its case with statements that Prager was a suspected spy).

The jury took less than an hour to return their verdict of not guilty.[4] The prosecution had failed to prove guilt beyond a reasonable doubt, in their opinion. Several days later, the charges against the Collinsville police officers were dropped, due to concerns that an impartial jury would be impossible to find.

Prager's murder was no doubt a shocking climax in a series of violent and humiliating attacks on German Americans, and for many years it was regarded as stemming almost exclusively from the fact that he was German. Recent scholarship, however, has focused on the fact that Prager's socialism probably played just as much of a role in his persecution; in fact, World War I brought with it the persecution of socialists and pacifists along with German Americans.[5] Additionally, the community of Collinsville had a large population of German Americans, and no doubt the fear of being accused of disloyalty contributed to the mob mentality. Riegel himself, a German and one of the ringleaders in the hanging, had been accused of disloyalty less than a year before the event. As one witness to the event stated, "most of the Germans . . . were saying you're either pro or you're anti, and they had to be anti . . ."[6]

8

HERITAGE AND LINGUISTIC LANDSCAPE TODAY

Considering that Germans made up one of the largest immigrant groups in Illinois as well as in other Midwestern states for most of the nineteenth century, they have no doubt left their mark on the region today. Driving through Illinois, one can find numerous towns and landmarks with German names. Some communities in southwestern Illinois whose names have German origins (and often strong German-heritage roots that continue to this day) are Maeystown, Johannisburg Township, Wartburg, New Hanover, New Baden, Darmstadt, and Millstadt.[1] Elsewhere in the state, communities with German-based names include Schaumburg, Venedy, Teutopolis, Hecker (after Friedrich Hecker), Bismarck, Bremen, DeKalb, Freeburg, Hanover, Hamberg, New Berlin, and Sigel.[2] In Chicago, many streets and other place names still bear German names, including Altgeld Street, Germania Place, Goethe Street (and Goethe Elementary School), Hirsch Street, Humboldt Park, Kruger Avenue, Lehmann Court, Lieb Avenue, Schiller Street, Von Steuben High School, and Wolfram Street, despite the extensive renaming of German place names during World War I.[3] And if you wander the city's streets and parks, you can still find a plethora of German statues and monuments, such as that of Goethe in Lincoln Park.

Along with place names, architecture is one of the earliest and most visible artifacts of German influence. Early immigrants to southwestern Illinois often built traditional brick cottages, designing and building their homes much like they would have back in Germany. These houses were small, basic, and box-like, with tiny front yards and large gardens in the back. They proved practical for both town and country living, so most Illinois Germans in the region saw little reason to vary style or floorplan.[4] Many of these homes continue to populate the landscape in Belleville and other communities in southwestern Illinois, and historical groups are working to preserve this heritage for posterity (see figure 8.1).[5] Historic neighborhoods in Belleville and West Belleville are already on the National Register of Historic Places—precisely for their abundance of historic German architecture.[6]

Fig. 8.1. Historic German American house, East Van Buren Street, Belleville, 2011. Courtesy Belleville Historical Society, bellevillehistoricalsociety.org.

Chicago's architecture, transformed by the fire of 1871, is no less a product of its German forebears. Because many nineteenth-century German immigrants worked in the building trades, they played a large role in rebuilding the city after the fire.[7] So, German craftsmen and laborers literally had a hand in the city's reconstruction, while prominent German American architects have strongly influenced the look of Chicago up through the modern day. Individuals like Dankmar Adler and Ludwig Mies van der Rohe left an unmistakable imprint on Chicago's distinctive architecture. Adler partnered with the famous Louis Sullivan to form the "Chicago School" of architecture, and together they shaped the look of the city in the postfire years. Van der Rohe, equally illustrious, was a leader in the New Bauhaus school, which moved wholesale from Germany to Chicago in the buildup to World War II. This resulted in an explosion of German-influenced modern architecture in the city's downtown during the mid-twentieth century. Numerous other German Americans have also contributed to Chicago's landscape, including Helmut Jahn, Charles Wacker, and many others.[8] All of this is to say, of course, that anyone touring Chicago's architectural landmarks will inevitably experience the designs of numerous German architects and planners.

Food is another recognizable remnant of German America. German-themed restaurants, taverns, and specialty shops are not unusual in Illinois; at the time of this writing, traditional German restaurants in Illinois numbered about twenty, and there were about thirty specialty food shops in Illinois selling German food.[9] And there are several foods of German origin that have simply become a part of everyday Illinois culture. Hot dogs, potato salad, sauerkraut, pretzels, and, of course, beer are enjoyed by all, not just those of German ancestry. Other Illinois staples also have German roots; for example, restaurants in heavily German towns and cities like Quincy commonly feature menu items such as pork tenderloins, or "Lendenstuck" as they are known in German.[10]

German culture continues to be celebrated by German American clubs in cities and towns all over Illinois, most notably in the Chicago area, where approximately ten thousand individuals participate in German heritage and cultural organizations.[11] While some of Chicago's nineteenth-century German clubs survive to this day, other organizations have formed more recently, either in response to a particular influx of German immigrants or simply to celebrate German culture or ancestral heritage. The famous Germania Club dissolved in 1986, but the Women's Germania Club continues to this day, as does the Chicago Columbia Club, a women's club focusing on educational programming. Chicago's Northwest Turner club (formed with the 1956 merger of the three Chicago-area Turner societies) continues to be active as a gymnastics club in Schiller Park.[12] And the Schwaben Verein, which performs charitable work and holds an annual German-American Summerfest (also known as the Cannstatter Volksfest), recently celebrated its 138th anniversary.[13] The Donauschwaben Society of Chicago, which has a small library and museum, and the American Aid Society of German Descendants, a charity organization, both formed to support East Germans fleeing Communism in the wake of World War II.[14] In 1959, the Deutsch Amerikanischer National Kongress, or DANK, was founded as the first national German American organization since World War II. The North Chicago chapter quickly formed, and it continues today in the form of Dankhaus, a German American cultural center located in the historically German Lincoln Park. The organization not only provides German-language classes and German movie nights but also boasts a museum, library, and art gallery, all dedicated to preserving German and German American culture in Chicago.[15] Additionally, the Goethe Institute of Chicago offers language and culture classes as well as events.[16] German American clubs are active elsewhere in Illinois, too, in cities like Peoria and Rockford.[17]

As they did back in their heyday, nearly all of the German clubs hold or participate in German-themed festivals and events throughout the year. These include Mayfest; Cannstatter Volksfest, held in August; the German-American Fest and von Steuben parade, held in September in Chicago; and, of course, Oktoberfest.[18] Appealing to a wide variety of people, these festivals typically include German-themed music, dancing, food, and drink. Chicago, Belleville, Quincy, and Naperville also hold a Christkindlmarkt each year.[19]

Even as German American culture was at a time very heterogeneous, the most visible twenty-first-century expressions of German American cultural identity in Illinois—and throughout America—are fairly homogenized. Celebrations like Oktoberfest, along with other Bavarian traditions such as lederhosen, lager beer, and oompah bands typify for many what it means to be German American.[20] In reality, of course, other regions of Germany have their own distinct cultures and traditions, and many German immigrants to Illinois came from regions other than Bavaria.[21] Conversely, in some communities, traditions are identified as German when it might be more accurate to say that they are broadly European—polka dancing and sausages, for example, are common traditions among German and Polish communities (and others as well), while many German Christmas traditions are similar to other European Christmas traditions. While today there is less conflict around some of the more commodified and homogenized expressions of German American heritage, as recently as the 1980s, Illinois Germans practicing the old culture often looked with distain on the newer, more commercial celebrations, considering them inauthentic.[22]

These transformations point to a larger truth: that German American identity itself has changed over the years, with the most recognizable signs and expressions today being largely symbolic. This is something Herbert Gans terms "symbolic ethnicity."[23] This is when aspects of ethnic identity are transformed into symbolic expressions, evoking "a love for and a pride in a tradition that can be felt without having to be incorporated in everyday behavior."[24] In this way, German American identity has become predominantly a heritage identity, one that is voluntary and flexible, that is, not lived in the day-to-day.

The German American community has always taken an active role in the construction of its own ethnic identity.[25] Even prior to the 1871 unification of Germany, there were efforts among German American political leaders to bring countrymen together under one umbrella.[26] This was a monumental task, and one at which they were only partially successful given the broad diversity among German immigrants and their descendants. And as markers of "Germanness" converged into mainstream American society, efforts to recapture and promote ethnic distinctiveness and solidarity intensified, resulting in the "exaltation of a sort of homogenized German culture": "Celebration, singing societies and beer were the few things that nearly all Germans could relate to, and it is not surprising that these played a major role in attempts to mold a German unity in the 1890s."[27]

Most German Americans today are generations away from their immigrant ancestors, and, as we have explored, German American institutions experienced a decline in the early twentieth century while many German Americans downplayed their ethnic and cultural heritage during the world wars. The surge in interest in genealogy and "roots" in the 1970s brought with it an increase in German heritage activity, with millions of later-generation Americans rediscovering—and redefining—their German ancestry. New heritage organizations formed, and old ones found new purpose. Heritage tourism, genealogy, and the study of German American history have grown over the years and contributed to the transformation of German American ethnic identity. A number of cities and towns have developed sister-city programs with German communities. Belleville, Belvidere, Chicago, Columbia, Dixon, Millstadt, Peoria, Quincy, Schaumburg, Tinley Park, Waterloo, and West Chicago all have sister cities in Germany.[28] Chicago, though host to fewer German Americans than in decades past, continues to be a center of German American culture, hosting countless German clubs, and, until recently, the largest German-language newspaper in the United States, the *Amerika-Woche*.[29]

While Illinois is clearly one of the most German states in terms of its settlement history, with many communities continuing to represent themselves as "German" places, it has become much

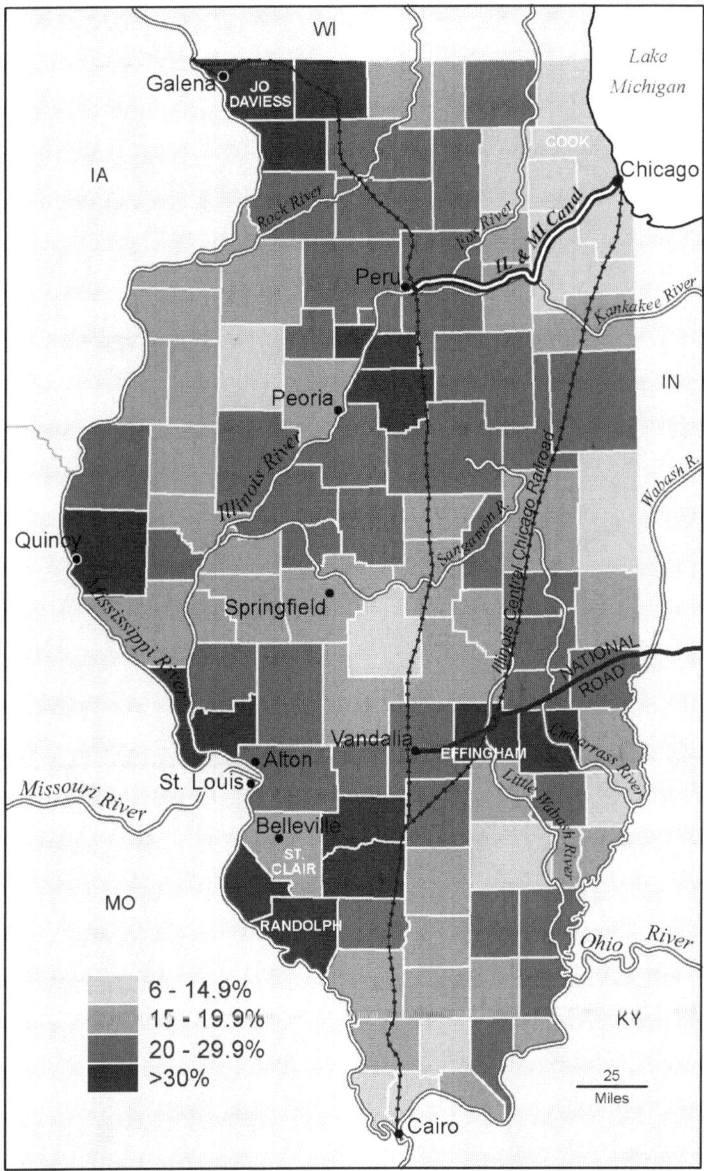

Fig. 8.2. German ancestry in Illinois, by county, 2013. Data from the American Community Survey, 2009–2013, five-year estimates, table B04001, "First Ancestry Reported."

more variegated in recent years. Federal census data and related community surveys point to a recent and sustained influx of newcomer groups, though some counties in Illinois remain German strongholds. In the 2013 American Community Survey, 13.5 percent of Illinoisans claimed German as first ancestry, with that number as high as 38 percent, 37 percent, and 33 percent in counties with historical German influence like Effingham, Jo Daviess, and Randolph Counties, respectively (see figure 8.2). In St. Clair County, 19.5 percent of residents identified as German American, a drop from previous years but still higher than the state overall.[30] What we see in these counties isn't surprising given that this region is a German heritage center where large numbers of Germans had settled, formed community-based institutions, and maintained the use of German.[31] Through the 1980s, speech varieties, like "High German" and "Low German," continued to be used to denote heritage.[32] This isn't particularly big news to natives of southwestern Illinois who, based on our experiences, show a great deal of pride in and affection for their ethnic roots:

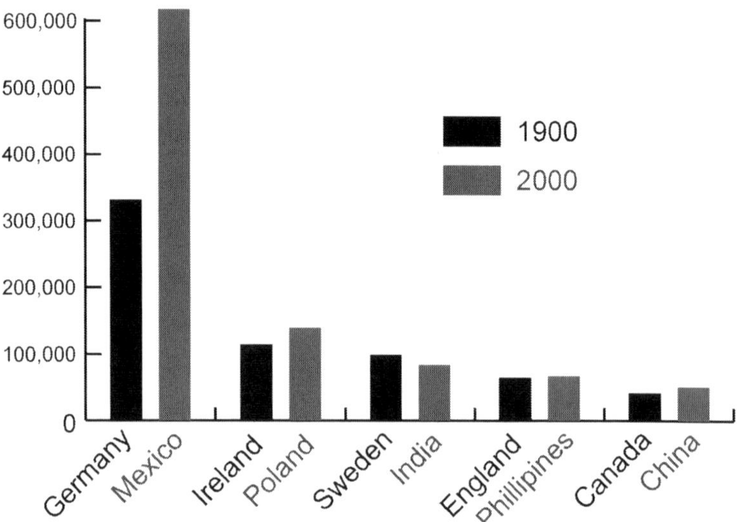

Fig. 8.3. Top five countries of birth among Illinois' foreign-born, 1900 versus 2000. Data from 1900 U.S. census, table 33, "Foreign Born Population, Distributed According to Country of Birth, by States and Territories," and from 2000 U.S. census, summary file 3, table QT-P15, "Region and Country or Area of Birth of the Foreign-Born Population."

> I am very proud of the profoundly German community [Millstadt] where I was raised. We had a saying in my hometown: 'It was so German, even the dogs barked in German!' Even in the 1960s and 1970s, before I left to join the service [in 1974 at seventeen years of age], one could walk into a local tavern, restaurant, or store, and hear the German accents, if not actual German being spoken.[33]

While you'd be hard-pressed to find German heritage speakers in the community today, local and regional English dialects in the Midwest bear markers of immigrant languages like German. They have, however, since transcended other ethnic groups, becoming regional—rather than ethnic—markers of identity and belonging, something we treat separately in this chapter (see the side story on German effects on English in the Midwest).

What does surprise in figure 8.2, however, is that only 6 percent of Cook County's population claimed German ancestry (compared with 25 percent in 1900).[34] The county's drop in percentage of those identifying with this ancestry over time might be explained by the fact that Chicago and the surrounding area has experienced a good amount of population growth since the days when Germans were immigrating in large numbers, resulting

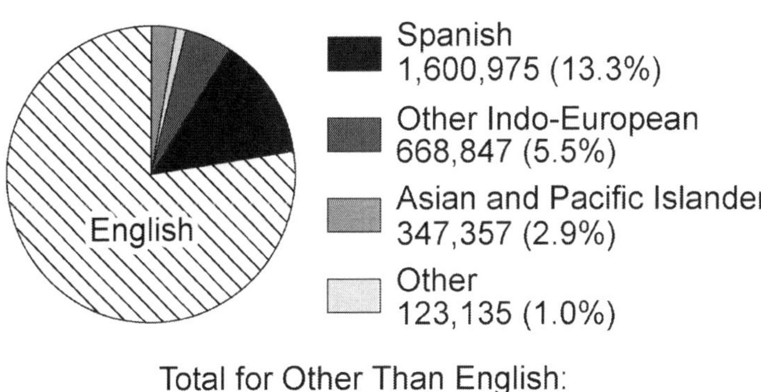

Fig. 8.4. Languages other than English spoken at home in Illinois, 2015. Other Indo-European languages include Germanic and Slavic languages; Asian languages include Chinese and Korean; other languages include Arabic, Finnish, and Native American languages. Data from the American Community Survey, 2011–2015, five-year estimates, table S1601, "Language Spoken at Home."

in more demographic changes than smaller communities have experienced. Even by 1920, Germans were no longer the biggest ethnic group immigrating to Chicago (figure 8.3 shows a comparison of leading foreign-born nationalities in Illinois in 1900 as compared to 2000).[35]

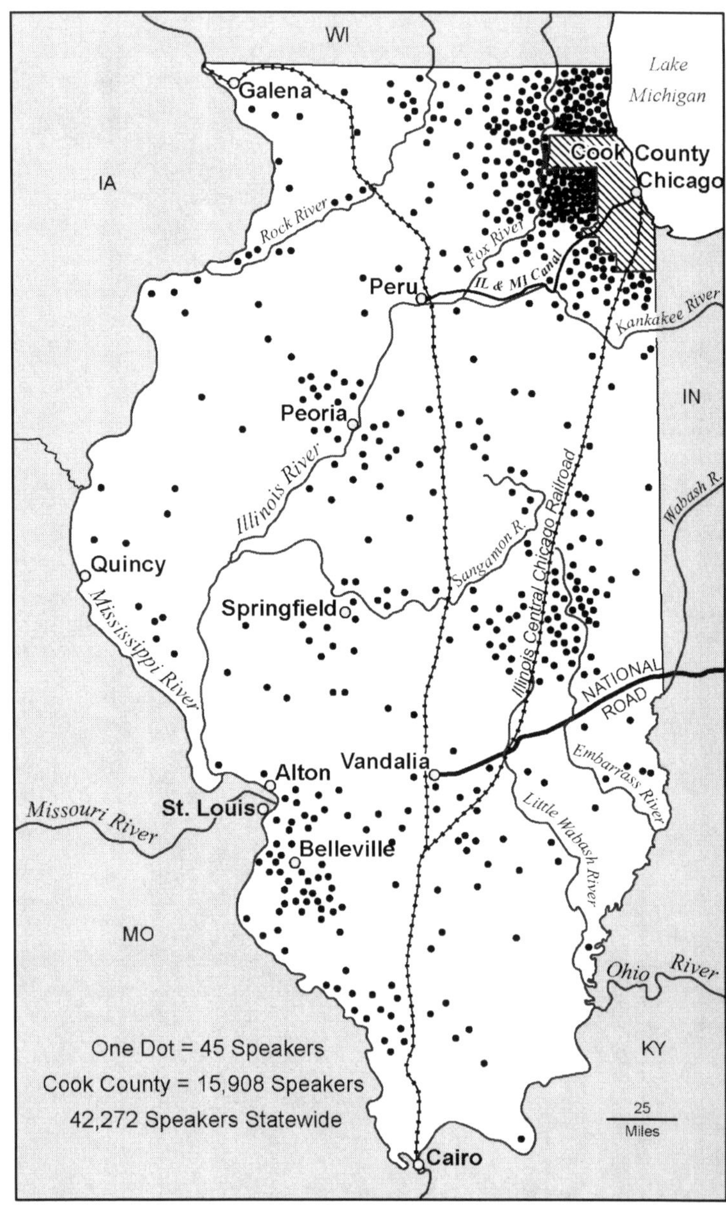

Fig. 8.5. German spoken at home in Illinois, by county, 2015. Data from the American Community Survey, 2011–2015, five-year estimates, table B16001, "Language Spoken at Home by Ability to Speak English for the Population 5 Years and Over."

As Illinois, especially Chicago, absorbs in great numbers newer immigrants, the state's cultural and linguistic landscape will continue to evolve—just as it has since its first settlers. It's hard to predict in precisely what ways, but the notable increase in Spanish speakers, for instance, is sure to have an effect on ways of speaking and cultural perspectives as well as regional identity. Already, Spanish speakers easily make up Chicago's largest proportion of inhabitants who speak a language other than English (see figure 8.4), with the state also showing a steady loss in the number of German speakers over the years. In 1980, German ranked third as a foreign language spoken in the home (though all other languages were, even then, far behind that of Spanish), with 97,804 speakers.[36] By 2015, this number had been reduced by about half to 42,272, ranking tenth for languages other than English spoken at home (see figure 8.5).[37]

In conclusion, the history of Illinois reminds us that Germans, whose mass migration to the state began in the 1840s and extended over a period of roughly fifty years, have a long tradition here, leaving footprints of their history, language, and culture. Even as the state grows in its ethnic diversity, it continues to celebrate and promote a "German" place image. Festivals and parades, for example, have become central to conceptions of German American identity (though participation is not exclusive to, nor necessarily even dominated by, those with ancestral ties to Germany). The importance of German heritage to Illinois' identity is also expressed through heritage tourism in communities heavily settled by Germans. While there doesn't appear to be any resistance to this image at present, we can't help but wonder whether and, if so, how the state's sense of place and identity will shift and converge as new (non-German) groups make their home in Illinois and younger generations redefine what it means to be from Illinois and, indeed, what it means to be an American.

German Effects on English in the Midwest

All words originate somewhere, and most in English go back to an old Germanic source. We know the verb *to tell* is related to Dutch *tellen* and German *zählen*. Both of these verbs mean *to count*, which explains where uses like *bank teller* (or *bank counter*) or *to tell time* (or *to count time*) in English came from. There are countless other words in English with etymological ties to Germanic languages, but they aren't always obvious to non-linguists. Words that do have an obvious connection to German in the popular mind, however, are oftentimes *loanwords*. These are words that users of one language—in this case, English—have appropriated from another—in this case, German.[1]

Loanwords are typically borrowed because no equivalent can be found in the host language; they add precision and nuance to a language. Many German words have become such a natural part of our American English vocabulary that everyone, everywhere uses them. Examples include terms like *kindergarten*, *dachshund, wunderkind, fest, sauerkraut*, *kaput*, *doppelgänger, blitzkrieg, angst, schadenfreude,* and *ersatz*. A contemporary structural borrowing is the prefix *uber* (from German *über*, a preposition which means over, about, or beyond), as in *ubercritical* (very or super critical) or *uberhelpful* (very or super helpful). Its use in English denotes superlative status to the word it affixes, and because its pronunciation in English doesn't approximate the native pronunciation in German, we know that this prefix came to us via writing.[2]

Other loanwords are used in specific disciplines, such as *zeitgeist* (in literature and across the historical sciences), *gestalt* (in psychology), and *übermensch* (in philosophy), or in areas known for heavy German settlement. In the Midwest, including large swaths of Illinois, German-sourced words for food and drink abound, as evidenced by *stollen*, *kuchen*, *pumpernickel*, *wurst*, *frankfurter*, *krapfel*, *strudel*, *pfeffernüsse* cookies, *kaffee klatsch, schmierkäse, schnapps, bock* beer, and *prosit*.

Beyond loanwords, German has "imposed" some features onto regional varieties of English, such as those found in the Midwest.[3] *Imposition*, like borrowing, is a result of language contact, which is when two or more languages, such as German and English, are used concurrently within a community. It is, however, the product of imperfect second-language acquisition, whereby well-established parts of one language work their way into the "native" structure of another. As German slowly gave way to English in the Midwest, some of its features were transferred to the local variety, resulting in pronunciations, words, and structures that are regionally unique today.[4]

Chicago stereotypes like those made famous by the iconic *Saturday Night Live* radio talk show skit "Bill Swerski's Superfans" provide distinct pronunciation examples, such as in the signature line, "Da Bears!"[5] The "th" sound is pronounced as "d" in *the,* and the final "s" sound is devoiced from the standard "z" to "s" pronunciation in *bears*. These examples are not unique to Chicago; speakers in other parts of the Upper Midwest, where many early settlements were also homogenously German, make the same marked sounds.[6]

What makes the "Bill Swerski's Superfans" skit intriguing is that its humor relies on a national awareness of accent, one that attributes these particular sounds to Chicagoans, specifically working-class men. Linguists have for some time known that the trajectory of recognizable features is heavily influenced by social factors. Males have been shown to make the "d" sound to a much higher degree than females. In these examples, the former (i.e., "d" in *the*) is often stigmatized and receding in use while the latter (i.e., devoicing) is spreading, even resurging.[7]

Illinois shares many linguistic regionalisms with its neighbor states, owing to common social history and demographic patterns. In scholarship, a lot has been published on the effects German has had on Wisconsin English. Far less has been written about the effects German has had on the English spoken in Illinois, with two exceptions known to us. The first is a 1948 article on German language influences in St. Clair County in which the author, Jesse W. Harris, discusses place names, vocabulary (often with a connection to eating and drinking, like the examples provided earlier), expletives like *dummkopf* (blockhead), formulaic greetings as in *wie geht's* (how are you), names of social organizations (such as the *Liederkranz* [choral society]), and "the order of words in the sentence, with the uses of certain words, and with pronunciation."[8] Nearly forty years later, in 1986, and as part of a large-scale survey on the construction and negotiation of German ethnicity in southwestern Illinois, another piece came out that included similar, though more nuanced, observations on German-language traces in and around St. Clair County.[9] In it, and among much else, folklorist John M. Coggeshall wrote that although the German language had all but disappeared, German Americans in the region—and in some cases non-Germans too—still spoke with an identifiably "Dutchy" accent as informed by distinct sounds, words, expressions, and grammatical constructions, with speakers native to the area asserting, "Outsiders say that an accent exists, 'but we don't notice it,' a woman from eastern St. Clair County commented. 'We call it "Dutchiness" about the way they talk, the way they express certain things, the way their voice tone rises and falls,' a retired brewery worker explained."[10] Examples provided in both articles tie in nicely with those in much more recent studies on German imposition on Wisconsin English, five of which include:[11]

1. "these" and "those" pronounced as "diz" and "doz"
2. "cut one's hairs"
3. A. Give me the knife *once*.
   B. Just pick it up *once*.
4. He even works on Sunday *yet*.
5. A. Come to see us Sunday, *ain't it*?
   B. That's a real old house, *ain't it yet*?

For those raised in the Midwest, these uses may not seem all that peculiar or even raise eyebrows. But for those born and bred elsewhere, they are linguistically distinctive. The first example concerns pronunciation (and relates back to the television skit discussed just moments ago), denoting the substitution of a "d" sound for a "th" sound, something German speakers past and present reliably do when speaking English. Because "d" for "th" has become socially stigmatized in recent years, it's likely that some younger Illinoisans today have only heard it as parody. Next, whereas in English we talk about our heads as having "hair," in German they have "hairs" (from *Haare*), owing to the fact that the noun "hair" in German is countable (unlike in English). In the third example, *once* mirrors the use of *mal*, a discourse marking that works in German to soften commands. "Just give me the knife, won't you," makes for a standard equivalent, but the English translation of that word performs that function in the above case. The fourth example is adverbial in nature. In German, *noch* can mean both *still* and *yet*, which explains the use of *yet* in the above instance in place of *still*. The tag question, *ain't it* (or *ainna*), as evidenced in the final example, comes from German *nicht wahr* (isn't that so)?

Why these specific features (and others not discussed here) have been retained in the English spoken in parts of Illinois and the Upper Midwest today while others have been lost is not fully understood.[12] What is known, however, is that the vast majority of children and grandchildren born to German immigrants in these states grew up speaking German natively, increasingly alongside English. That German-rich input, which was supported in a range of institutions for years, even decades, helped set the stage for the development of a regional pattern that crosses state lines.

Notes

Select Annotated Bibliography

Index

NOTES

1. Introduction

1. Nearly one thousand French settlers colonized the Bottomlands of present-day southwestern Illinois in the 1700s. Kaskaskia, which was located at the intersection of the Kaskaskia and Mississippi Rivers, was the epicenter of French Illinois. Under French rule, some Germans even immigrated to the region, along with other Europeans, to work in the French military. A few stayed after their tour was complete, fully integrating into French colonial life. Roger Biles, *Illinois: A History of the Land and Its People* (DeKalb: Northern Illinois University Press, 2005), 12–15.

2. While land was being sold in 1796 at a mere two dollars an acre, the minimum lot size the government would allow for purchase was 640 acres. This effectively priced out most of the population. Additionally, the federal government would not allow the sale of land until previous claims to the land had been settled; and large amounts had been fraudulently acquired by speculators, leaving it unclear as to who legally owned the property. Early Illinois settlers often risked potential legal difficulties regarding ownership of land. Biles, *Illinois*, 33.

3. Actual figures vary, with upward of thirty-eight thousand reported in Biles, *Illinois*, 62. Total population of Illinois in 1850 from U.S. Census Bureau, "Resident Population and Apportionment of the US House of Representatives: Illinois," 2001, accessed August 1, 2017, https://www.census.gov/dmd/www/resapport/states/illinois.pdf.

4. Howard B. Furer, *The Germans in America, 1607–1970: A Chronology & Fact Book* (Dobbs Ferry, NY: Oceana Publications, 1973), 49.

5. Ibid., 65; U.S. Census Bureau, "Resident Population and Apportionment."

6. Maldwyn A. Jones, *American Immigration*, 2nd ed. (Chicago: University of Chicago Press, 1992), 178.

7. Frederick C. Luebke, *Bonds of Loyalty: German-Americans and World War I* (DeKalb: Northern Illinois University Press, 1974), 30.

8. Anglo-American, or Yankee, refers to residents born in the United States with English and Scots-Irish ancestry.

9. That said, there were more positive perceptions of Germans as compared to other immigrant groups during much of this era, a point we make in later chapters.

10. Frederick C. Luebke, *Germans in the New World: Essays in the History of Immigration*, Statue of Liberty–Ellis Island Centennial Series (Urbana: University of Illinois Press, 1990), 180.

11. Karl A Sinnhuber, *Germany: Its Geography and Growth*, 2nd ed. (London: J. Murray, 1970), 14.

12. If they weren't secularized or unaffiliated, they were largely Reform Jews (especially by the last decades of the nineteenth century) who considered Judaism a religion, not a nationality. Irving Cutler, "The Jews of Chicago: From Shtetl to Suburb," in *Ethnic Chicago: A Multicultural Portrait*, ed. Peter d'Alroy Jones and Melvin G. Holli (Grand Rapids, MI: W. B. Eerdmans Pub. Co., 1995), 146–47. In contrast, the 1880s Yiddish-speaking Jews of eastern European origins (e.g., Russia, Poland, Romania, and so on), were heavily Orthodox. They clung to Old World traditions and beliefs. They experienced difficulties adapting to life in America and stood out in ways that German Jews who had come before them had not.

13. To say that their migrations in the midcentury era were structurally similar is not intended to distract from their differences. For a thoroughgoing account of German Jewish migration in the nineteenth century, see work by historian and researcher Avraham Barkai: "German-Jewish Migration in the Nineteenth Century," in *Migration across Time and Nations: Population Mobility in Historical Contexts*, ed. Ira A. Glazier, Luigi De Rosa, and International Economic History Congress (New York: Holmes & Meier, 1986); *Branching Out: German-Jewish Immigration to the United States, 1820–1914*, Ellis Island Series, 3rd ed. (New York: Holmes & Meier, 2001). Other sources to consult are Naomi W. Cohen, *Encounter with Emancipation: The German Jews in the United States, 1830–1914* (Philadelphia: Jewish Publication Society, 1984); Rudolf Glanz, *Studies in Judaica Americana* (New York: Ktav, 1970); and Rudolph Glanz, "German Jewish Mass Immigration 1820–1880," in *American Jewish Archives Journal* 22, no. 1 (1970), Jacob Rader Marcus Center of the American Jewish Archives, accessed August 1, 2017, http://americanjewisharchives.org/publications/journal/PDF/1970_22_01_00_glanz.pdf. For further reading on Jewish communities in Chicago, refer to Irving Cutler, *Chicago's Jewish West Side* (Mount Pleasant, SC: Arcadia Publishing, 2009); Irving Cutler, "Jews," *The Electronic Encyclopedia of Chicago* (Chicago: Chicago Historical Society, 2005), accessed February 15, 2018, http://www.encyclopedia.chicagohistory.org/pages/671.html; and Walter Roth, *Looking Backward: True Stories from Chicago's Jewish Past* (Chicago: Chicago Review Press, 2005).

14. Luebke, *Germans in the New World*, 88.

2. Nineteenth-Century German Immigration and Settlement

1. Migration to the New World is almost always linked in the popular mind to the United States, though other popular destinations for Germans in the nineteenth century included Brazil, Canada, and Argentina.

2. The Napoleonic emancipation of Jews was largely reversed following the results of the Congress of Vienna. The Edict of 1812, however, preserved some civil liberties for Prussian Jews.

3. In most parts of Germany, land went to the eldest son, meaning that it couldn't be divided among multiple heirs (i.e., impartible inheritance). However, in southwestern Germany as well as later in Rhineland Prussia and in much of Hesse, where many immigrants came from in the first half of the nineteenth century, it was possible to distribute inherited land among multiple heirs (i.e., partible inheritance). Walter D. Kamphoefner, "At the Crossroads of Economic Development: Background Factors Affecting Emigration from Nineteenth-Century Germany," in *Migration across Time and Nations: Population Mobility in Historical Contexts*, ed. Ira A. Glazier, Luigi De Rosa, and International Economic History Congress (New York: Holmes & Meier, 1986), 175. In Prussia, seemingly progressive land reforms were not particularly favorable to struggling farmers either. The Stein-Hardenberg reforms mandated that peasants could own land, which ultimately did more harm than good though because the nobles—as the main beneficiaries—weren't forgiving of crop failures or bad harvests. Peasants were indebted to them for any income lost on crops, and if debts went unpaid, they became the burden of heirs who were forced to make good on them. Another problem was that many farmers, with serfdom abolished, took advantage of the opportunity to become landowners, which resulted in tiny allotments and, consequently, insufficient yields across the board for farmers and their families. In order to make ends meet, many farmers had to work additionally as day laborers.

4. Stanley Nadel, *Little Germany: Ethnicity, Religion, and Class in New York City; 1845–80* (Urbana: University of Illinois Press, 1990), 16. Another fifteen thousand or so immigrated to Russia (ibid., 16). More had attempted to emigrate but didn't have the means to pay transatlantic passage. They returned to the communities more destitute than when they had left and without legal claim. Mack Walker, *Germany and the Emigration: 1816–1885* (Cambridge, MA: Harvard University Press, 1964), 30–31.

5. Originating in England, industrialization seized Europe in advance of other regions, including the United States.

6. As a result, scores of children were born outside of wedlock. A central contribution on the topic of nineteenth-century German marriage laws, including their connection to population growth and illegitimacy rates at the time, has been made by John Knodel, in "Law, Marriage and Illegitimacy in Nineteenth-Century Germany," *Population Studies* 20, no. 3 (1967): 279–94, http://www.jstor.org/stable/2172673, and "Malthus Amiss: Marriage Restrictions in 19th Century Germany," *Social Science* 47, no. 1 (1972): 40–45, http://www.jstor.org/stable/41959553.

7. While most Germans emigrated as families, German Jews tended to send one family member (e.g., a grown son) with the idea to earn money, typically as a peddler or craftsman, which could then be used to bring the rest of the family over to the United States.

8. Walker, *Germany and the Emigration*, 46.

9. Ibid., 79.

10. Mark Wyman, *Immigrants in the Valley: Irish, Germans, and Americans in the Upper Mississippi Country, 1830–1860* (Chicago: Nelson-Hall, 1984), 53–54; Douglas K. Meyer, *Making the Heartland Quilt: A Geographical History of Settlement and Migration in Early Nineteenth-Century Illinois* (Carbondale: Southern Illinois University Press, 2000), 236.

11. Other notables who fled to Illinois include Georg Bunsen, who later became St. Clair's superintendent of schools (a sidebar on him can be found in chapter 6), Gustav Bunsen, and Theodore Engelmann. Engelmann established two German-language newspapers in Belleville, *Der Freiheitsbote für Illinois* and *Belleviller Beobachter*.

12. Observers differ slightly in their start and end dates for each of the three waves.

13. Attitudes about and governmental response to emigration in Germany varied by sender state as well as by period of emigration. For more on this, as well as conditions for permission to emigrate, see Walker, *Germany and the Emigration*.

14. Hans Joachim Hahn, *The 1848 Revolutions in German-Speaking Europe* (New York: Routledge, 2013), 38.

15. Walker, *Germany and the Emigration*, 47.

16. Jacob Gross, "A German Family in Chicago: 1856," *Chicago History* 4, no. 10 (1956): 315.

17. For further detail on the Revolution of 1848, including a chronology of events preceding and following, see Mary Fulbrook, *A Concise History of Germany*, 2nd ed. (Cambridge: Cambridge University Press, 2004), chapter 5. Another excellent source is Hahn, *1848 Revolutions*.

18. German Jewish immigration to America increased during these years as well because German Jews had identified with (and participated in) the revolutionary movement, one that would have emancipated them had it been successful.

19. The year 1854 was one in which German immigration peaked, with 215,000 new arrivals. Frederick C. Luebke, *Bonds of Loyalty: German-Americans and World War I* (DeKalb: Northern Illinois University Press, 1974), 28.

20. Walker, *Germany and the Emigration*, 159. The *Allgemeine Auswanderungszeitung*, published from 1846 to 1871, was one newspaper written specifically for German emigrants. Its supplement, "Der Pilot," ran from 1855 to 1864 and provided advice in the form of testimonials and letters. The newspaper has been digitized by the Universal Multimedia Electronic Library of Thuringia University and State Library: http://zs.thulb.uni-jena.de/receive/jportal_jpjournal_00000025. An article (in German) featuring Illinois can be found here: http://zs.thulb.uni-jena.de/receive/jportal_jpvolume_00033465.

21. Rudolf A. Hofmeister, *The Germans of Chicago* (Champaign, IL: Stipes Pub. Co., 1976), 14; Walter D. Kamphoefner, Wolfgang Helbich, and Ulrike Sommer, *News from the Land of Freedom: German Immigrants Write Home*, Documents in American Social History, trans. Susan Carter Vogel (Ithaca, NY: Cornell University Press, 1991), 17.

22. Kamphoefner et al., *News from the Land of Freedom*, 10.

23. While emigration continued in the south and west, it had slowed by this time and never returned to the rates of 1854. Walker, *Germany and the Emigration*, 184.

24. John B. Jentz and Richard Schneirov, *Chicago in the Age of Capital: Class, Politics, and Democracy during the Civil War and Reconstruction* (Urbana: University of Illinois Press, 2012), 120.

25. They tended to be "single or unaccompanied by family members," ibid., 119; Hartmut Keil and John B. Jentz, *German Workers in Chicago: A Documentary History of Working-Class Culture from 1850 to World War I* (Urbana: University of Illinois Press, 1988), 3–4.

26. Frederick C. Luebke, *Germans in the New World: Essays in the History of Immigration*, Statue of Liberty–Ellis Island Centennial Series (Urbana: University of Illinois Press, 1990), 163; Hofmeister, *Germans of Chicago*, 13. For a conflicting numerical report, see Avraham Barkai, "German-Jewish Migration in the Nineteenth Century," in *Migration across Time and Nations: Population Mobility in Historical Contexts*, ed. Ira A. Glazier, Luigi De Rosa, and International Economic History Congress (New York: Holmes & Meier, 1986), 206.

27. Howard B. Furer, *The Germans in America, 1607–1970: A Chronology & Fact Book* (Dobbs Ferry, NY: Oceana Publications, 1973), 66.

28. Under the new Imperial Constitution, Germany's Jewish residents were at last afforded equal rights and citizenship.

29. Luebke, *Germans in the New World*, 163.

30. U.S. Department of State Bureau of Statistics et al., *Special Consular Reports*, v. 30–32 (Washington, DC: Government Printing Office, 1904), x, accessed May 21, 2014, http://books.google.com/books/about/Special_consular_reports.html?id=wIdJAAAAMAAJ.

31. By 1787, the United States passed the Northwest Ordinance, creating the Northwest Territory, which included present-day Illinois, Indiana, Ohio, Michigan, and Wisconsin; Roger Biles, *Illinois: A History of the Land and Its People* (DeKalb: Northern Illinois University Press, 2005), 28; Lois Carrier, *Illinois: Crossroads of a Continent* (Urbana: University of Illinois Press, 1998), 32. Twelve years later, in 1800, Congress passed a bill to form the Indiana Territory, which included both present-day Indiana and Illinois. Although slavery was prohibited in the Northwest Territory, in 1807 the government of the Indiana Territory passed indenture laws designed to effectively re-enslave blacks. These laws enraged some segments of the population in the eastern portion of the territory, and they rallied to join Ohio, a free territory. This motivated politicians to work together to divide the Indiana Territory in two, and on March 1, 1809, the Illinois Territory was created; Kaskaskia was its capital (Biles, *Illinois*, 33–34).

32. The only other state that had similarly liberal voting laws was Texas, at least until 1846. That's partly why Texas, like Illinois, was settled heavily by Germans in the 1830s and 1840s.

33. Illinois, *Constitution of the State of Illinois*, 1848, Article VI, accessed June 29, 2016, http://www.idaillinois.org/cdm/ref/collection/isl2/id/211.

34. See Meyer, *Making the Heartland Quilt*, chapter 1 ("Frontier Illinois Place Images") for a discussion of Illinois boosters and salient place images.

35. Wyman, *Immigrants in the Valley*, 101–2.

36. Paul W. Gates, *The Illinois Central Railroad and Its Colonization Work* (Cambridge, MA: Harvard University Press, 1934), 198–99. The original publication can be viewed online: Johann Georg Kohl, *Reisen im Nordwesten der Vereinigten Staaten* (New York: D. Appleton and Co., 1857), accessed August 17, 2017, https://archive.org/stream/reisenimnordwes00kohlgoog#page/n11/mode/2up.

37. Gates, *Illinois Central Railroad*, 103–5; Hofmeister, *Germans of Chicago*, 23; Stewart H. Holbrook, *The Story of American Railroads: From the Iron Horse to the Diesel Locomotive* (Mineola, NY: Dover Publications, 2016), 108.

38. The development of the ICR lands can be found in "A Table Comparing the Number of Residents, Homes, Institutions, and Businesses in 1850 with 1856," in Frederick Gerhard, *Illinois as It Is* (Chicago: Keen and Lee, 1857), 417–18, accessed August 1, 2017, http://quod.lib.umich.edu/m/moa/afk4275.0001.001/428?page=root;size=100;view=image.

39. Ferdinand Ernst was the first German to write an account of Illinois in German. Raymond Jürgen Spahn, *German Accounts of Early Nineteenth Century Life in Illinois* (Edwardsville: Southern Illinois University at Edwardsville, 1978), 477–78.

40. Steven W. Rowan, "Gustav Korner Attacks Gottfried Duden in 1834: Illinois against Missouri?" (presented at the 33rd Annual Symposium of the Society for German-American Studies, New Ulm, MN, April 17, 2009), accessed May 24, 2014, http://www.gustavekoerner.org/FINAL%20Rowan%20New%20Ulm%20paper%20.pdf.

41. The greater the expectation is, the stronger the disappointment will be. Living in the western states wasn't what it was cracked up to be, at least according to some immigrants who began referring to Duden's book as "Duden's Eden." See a convenient summary of the struggles immigrants faced in Gottfried Duden, "Introduction," *Report of a Journey to the Western States of North America, and a Stay of Several Years along the Missouri (During the Years 1824, 1825, 1826, and 1827)*, gen. ed. James W. Goodrich; ed. and trans. George H. Kellner, Elsa Nagel, Adolf E. Schroeder, and W. M. Senner (Columbia: University of Missouri Press, 1980), xx.

42. Wyman, *Immigrants in the Valley*, 58–59. See Spahn, *German Accounts*, for a discussion of other German-language publications, including works of fiction and natural science set in the United States, commissioned by European governments to provide a description of conditions in America for potential emigrants. This last category was often less idyllic in its descriptions of American life in order to counter the vast literature that blatantly promoted it. *Allgemeine Auswanderungszeitung* is available digitally at http://zs.thulb.uni-jena.de/receive/jportal_jpjournal_00000025.

43. Linda Schelbitzki Pickle, *Contented among Strangers: Rural German-Speaking Women and Their Families in the Nineteenth-Century Midwest* (Urbana: University of Illinois Press, 1996), 47–48.

44. Wyman, *Immigrants in the Valley*, 27–32.

45. As printed in Kamphoefner et al., *News from the Land of Freedom*, 154–55.

46. Wyman, *Immigrants in the Valley*, 50.

47. Michael K. Brinkman, *Quincy, Illinois, Immigrants from Münsterland, Westphalia, Germany* (Westminster, MD: Heritage Books, 2010), 192; see also Walter D. Kamphoefner, *The Westfalians: From Germany to Missouri*. Princeton, NJ: Princeton University Press, 2014.

48. Wyman, *Immigrants in the Valley*, 63.

49. "Latin" settlements existed in Texas, too, given the highly educated Germans who had immigrated there.

50. Robert W. Frizzell, "Migration Chains to Illinois: The Evidence from German-American Church Records," *Journal of American Ethnic History* 7, no. 1 (University of Illinois Press, 1987): 59–73, http://www.jstor.org/stable/27500562, 62–63.

51. Wyman, *Immigrants in the Valley*, 67.

52. Hofmeister, *Germans in Chicago*, 201.

53. Wyman, *Immigrants in the Valley*, 107–8.

54. Meyer, *Making the Heartland Quilt*, 33. By 1840, the Galena land office was replaced by Dixon on the Rock River in Lee County.

55. Kent P. Slack, *The Germans and the Gem City: A Study of the Impact of German Immigrants on the Growth of Adams County and the City of Quincy, Illinois, from 1830 to 1890* (master's thesis, Illinois State University, 1994).

56. Regarding boosterism and real estate, see Hofmeister, *Germans of Chicago*, 23.

57. Hartmut Keil and John B. Jentz, "German Working Class Culture in Chicago," *Gulliver*, no. 9 (1981): 134; Christiane Harzig, "Creating a Community: German-American Women in Chicago," in *Peasant Maids—City Women: From the European Countryside to Urban America*, ed. Christiane Harzig (Ithaca, NY: Cornell University Press, 1997), 187.

58. Melvin G. Holli, "German-American Ethnic Identity from 1890 Onward," *Ethnic Chicago: A Multicultural Portrait*, ed. Peter d'Alroy Jones and Melvin G. Holli (Grand Rapids, MI: W. B. Eerdmans Pub. Co, 1981), 94; Keil and Jentz, *German Workers in Chicago*, 3.

59. Irving Cutler, *Chicago: Metropolis of the Mid-Continent* (Carbondale: Southern Illinois University Press, 2006), 65. Cook County in 1850 comprised the largest concentration of adult male Germans in the state at 17.9 percent. Meyer, *Making the Heartland Quilt*, 234.

60. Cutler, *Chicago*, 67; Hartmut Keil, "Chicago's German Working Class in 1900," in *German Workers in Industrial Chicago: A Comparative Perspective*, ed. Hartmut Keil and John B. Jentz (DeKalb: Northern Illinois University Press, 1983), 20–21.

61. And at the same time, less than one-third of the workforce was involved in agricultural pursuits. Biles, *Illinois*, 124.

62. Cutler, *Chicago*, 81.

63. Keil, "Chicago's German Working Class," 30; Harzig, "Creating a Community," 190; Hofmeister, *Germans of Chicago*, 48, 50.

GRAYS VS. GREENS

1. Fast-forward some thirty years, and the generational and political divisions repeat themselves. "The Greens" of the 1848 era became "the Grays" of the 1880s as new immigrants arrived: "By the 1880s, the 'Grey' Forty-eighter generation had long shed its revolutionary image and now saw itself as a group of ambitious middle-class citizens in contrast to the newly arrived proletarians from industrializing Germany who challenged their beliefs in free enterprise and American economic freedom with the ideas of European socialism." Dorothee Schneider, *Trade Unions and Community* (Urbana: University of Illinois Press, 1994), 8.

2. Ernest Bruncken, "German Political Refugees in the United States during the Period from 1815–1860," *Deutsch-Amerikanische Geschichtsblätter* 3, no. 3 (1903): 43.

3. Susanne Martha Schick, *"For God, Mac, and Country": The Political Worlds of Midwestern Germans during the Civil War* (Ann Arbor, MI: UMI, 1994), 12.

A GERMAN STATE IN THE UPPER MISSISSIPPI VALLEY

1. Gottfried Duden and James W. Goodrich, *Report on a Journey to the Western States of North America and a Stay of Several Years along the Missouri (during the Years 1824, 1825, 1826, and 1827)*, gen. ed. James W. Goodrich; ed. and trans. George H. Kellner, Elsa Nagel, Adolf E. Schroeder, and W. M. Senner (Columbia: State Historical Society of Missouri, 1980).

2. "The 1833 Call for Emigration: The Giessen Emigration Society," *Utopia: Revisiting a German State in America*, accessed June 2, 2014, http://mo-germans.com/exhibits/a-call-for-emigration-the-giessen-emigration-society/.

3. Adolf Schroeder, "German Folklore and Traditional Practices in the Mississippi Valley," in *French and Germans in the Mississippi Valley: Landscape and Cultural Traditions*, ed. Michael Roark (Cape Girardeau, MO: Center for Regional History and Cultural Heritage, Southeast Missouri State University, 1988), 157.

4. Ibid.

GUSTAV KÖRNER

1. See Thomas Nipperdey, *Germany from Napoleon to Bismarck: 1800–1866*, trans. Daniel Nolan (Princeton, NJ: Princeton University Press, 1996), chapter 3, "Restoration and Vormärz, 1815–48," for an in-depth examination of events preceding and following this popular uprising.

2. The spelling of "Gustav" varies, sometimes appearing as "Gustave." As for "Koerner," the "e" is inserted in the absence of an umlauted "o." The information for this piece primarily came from the following sources: Cynthia Fuener, "A Naturalized Politician: The Life of Gustave Koerner," *Historic Illinois* 27, no. 5 (February 2005), reprinted by the Gustave Koerner House Restoration Committee, Belleville, Illinois, accessed August

13, 2017, https://gustavekoerner.org/wp-content/uploads/2016/03/histil.pdf; Gustave Philipp Körner, *Memoirs of Gustave Koerner, 1809–1896: Life-Sketches Written at the Suggestion of His Children*, ed. Thomas J. McCormack, 2 vols. (Cedar Rapids, IA: Torch Press, 1909), accessed August 1, 2017, https://archive.org/details/memoirsofgustave01kr and https://archive.org/details/memgustave02khorrich; Christopher Stratton, *Gustave Koerner House National Historic Register Application*, 2004, prepared by Fever River Research, Springfield, Illinois, for the Gustave Koerner House Restoration Committee, accessed June 1, 2014, http://www.gustavekoerner.org/nhr.pdf.

3. Körner, *Memoirs of Gustave Koerner*, 1:156.

4. Here's the full route Körner and his companions took: From New York, they traveled upstream on the Hudson River to connect with the Erie Canal to reach Buffalo. From Buffalo, they crossed Lake Erie to arrive in Cleveland. From there, they journeyed along the Ohio and Erie Canal to Portsmouth. They then traveled downstream on the Ohio River to Louisville where they caught a steamboat bound for St. Louis on the Mississippi River. Source of route: ibid., 1:266–86.

5. Ibid., 1:284. On page 296, Körner describes another offensive scene in which "a young slave girl" is lashed "with a cow hide" in St. Louis.

3. The Journey to Illinois

1. There were three options for nineteenth-century emigration from Germany, namely: emigration with consent, emigration with a passport, or illegal emigration. Michael K. Brinkman, *Quincy, Illinois, Immigrants from Münsterland, Westphalia, Germany* (Westminster, MD: Heritage Books, 2010), 1:21.

2. Mark Wyman, *Immigrants in the Valley: Irish, Germans, and Americans in the Upper Mississippi Country, 1830–1860* (Chicago: Nelson-Hall, 1984), 49.

3. German immigrants departing from Hamburg were also regularly routed through Liverpool (in England), which carries the distinction of being "the cheapest and most unpleasant way to America." Mack Walker, *Germany and the Emigration, 1816–1885* (Cambridge, MA: Harvard University Press, 1964), 161.

4. An important turning point in steamship travel, one that made ocean crossings far more efficient and viable, was the invention of the screw propeller (which replaced paddle propulsion).

5. Rudolf A. Hofmeister, *The Germans of Chicago* (Champaign, IL: Stipes Pub. Co., 1976), 14; Walter D. Kamphoefner, Wolfgang Helbich, and Ulrike Sommer, *News from the Land of Freedom: German Immigrants Write Home*, Documents in American Social History, trans. Susan Carter Vogel (Ithaca, NY: Cornell University Press, 1991), 36.

6. Though the requirement was often violated, Congress also insisted upon companies providing "proper food and ventilation during the long trip." Hofmeister, *Germans of Chicago*, 35. The American passenger laws of 1847, aimed at reducing disease and unhygienic conditions onboard, preceded the Carriage of Passengers Act of 1855.

7. Howard B. Furer, *The Germans in America, 1607–1970: A Chronology & Fact Book* (Dobbs Ferry, NY: Oceana Publications, 1973), 48.

8. Kent P. Slack, *The Germans and the Gem City: A Study of the Impact of German Immigrants on the Growth of Adams County and the City of Quincy, Illinois, from 1830 to 1890* (master's thesis, Illinois State University, 1994), 15.

9. *Let's Go to America!: The Path of Emigrants from Eastern Westphalia to the USA*, trans. William George (Löhne: H. Brackmann, 1986), 42–43; Slack, *Germans and the Gem City*, 16–17.

10. Hartmut Keil and John B. Jentz, *German Workers in Chicago: A Documentary History of Working-Class Culture from 1850 to World War I* (Urbana: University of Illinois Press, 1988), 10, 34.

11. Douglas K. Meyer, *Making the Heartland Quilt: A Geographical History of Settlement and Migration in Early Nineteenth-Century Illinois* (Carbondale: Southern Illinois University Press, 2000), 231; Walker, *Germany and the Emigration*, 171.

12. It was New York's Castle Garden, which opened in 1855, that received the major inflow of German immigrants in the nineteenth century (as the all-familiar Ellis Island didn't open until 1892).

13. Wyman, *Immigrants in the Valley*, 5–6.

14. Ibid., 58; Hofmeister, *Germans of Chicago*, 24; Roger Biles, *Illinois: A History of the Land and Its People* (DeKalb: Northern Illinois University Press, 2005), 59. The canal was also its own draw for farmers, merchants, and anyone else needing to ship large quantities of goods back to the East Coast.

15. Wyman, *Immigrants in the Valley*, 6.

16. Paul W. Gates, *The Illinois Central Railroad and Its Colonization Work* (Cambridge, MA: Harvard University Press, 1934), 88–89.

17. "Major U.S. Immigration Ports," Ancestry.com, 2016, accessed August 12, 2017, https://www.ancestrycdn.com/support/us/2016/11/majorusports.pdf.

18. Ibid., 45–46; Hofmeister, *Germans of Chicago*, 42–43.

19. Thomas Adam, *Germany and the Americas: O–Z* (Santa Barbara, CA: ABC-CLIO, 2005), 232. In Hofmeister's *Germans of Chicago*, the founding date provided is spring of 1853 (p. 116).

CORNELIUS SCHUBERT: DIARY OF A JOURNEY

1. Cornelius Schubert, "The Diary of Cornelius Schubert," translated from German by Mrs. Henry Klump Sr. and Miss Mary Klump 1937, Folder 6, Schubert Family papers, C3005, The State Historical Society of Missouri Manuscript Collection. Please note that the punctuation and spelling in the provided excerpts has been maintained from the original translation.

2. *Selected Passenger and Crew Lists and Manifests*, National Archives, Washington, DC, digital image, Ancestry.com, accessed October 21, 2018, http://ancestry.com.

1868 NEW YORK IMMIGRATION COMMISSION REPORT ON THE LEIBNITZ

1. Hofmeister, *Germans of Chicago*, 36–39, as reproduced from Frederich Kapp, *Immigration and the Commissioners of Emigration of the State of New York* (New York: The Nation Press, 1870), 189.

4. Rural and Urban Living

1. Saint Clair County, Illinois, *History of St. Clair County, Illinois: With Illustrations . . . and Biographical Sketches, Etc.* (Philadelphia: Brink, McDonough & Co., 1881), 64.

2. Michael K. Brinkman, *Quincy, Illinois, Immigrants from Münsterland, Westphalia, Germany* (Westminster, MD: Heritage Books, 2010), 165.

3. United States, National Archives, "Homestead Act (1862) Document Info," OurDocuments.gov, accessed February 3, 2016, http://www.ourdocuments.gov/doc.php?flash=true&doc=31.

4. Walter D. Kamphoefner, Wolfgang Johannes Helbich, and Ulrike Sommer, *News from the Land of Freedom: German Immigrants Write Home*, Documents in American Social History, trans. Susan Carter Vogel (Ithaca, NY: Cornell University Press, 1991), 52.

5. Paul W. Gates, *The Illinois Central Railroad and Its Colonization Work* (Cambridge, MA: Harvard University Press, 1934), 233.

6. Illinois Central Railroad Company, *A Guide to the Illinois Central Railroad Lands: The Illinois Central Railroad Company, Offer for Sale over 1,400,000 Acres of Selected Prairie and Wood Lands, in Tracts of Forty Acres and Upwards, Suitable for Farms, on Long Credits and Low Prices, Situated on Each Side of Their Railroad, Extending through the State of Illinois* (Chicago: Illinois Central Railroad Office, 1859), 14, accessed February 9, 2016, http://hdl.handle.net/2027/uiuo.ark:/13960/t42r3qq67.

7. Ibid., 16.

8. The description was prepared as an advertisement to sell the farm, but the farm never sold and remained in the family for generations to come. Letter #344, from Frank J. Reiss, Summer 1889, published in Stephen W. Reiss, *It Takes a Matriarch: 780 Family Letters from 1852 to 1888 Including Civil War, Farming in Illinois, Life in St. Louis, Life in Sacramento, Life in the Theater, Wagon Making in Davenport, and the Lost Family Fortune* (Bloomington, IN: AuthorHouse, 2009), 257–58.

9. Kamphoefner et al., *News from the Land of Freedom*, 61.

10. Illinois farmers embraced mechanization to a much higher degree than did their counterparts in Germany during the latter half of the nineteenth century. Ibid., 56–60.

11. Linda Schelbitzki Pickle, *Contented among Strangers: Rural German-Speaking Women and Their Families in the Nineteenth-Century Midwest* (Urbana: University of Illinois Press: 1996).

12. Ibid., 74. Letter from Wiemer Stommel, letter of June 24, 1850, Bochum Emigrant Letter Collection, Ruhr University, Bochum, Germany.

13. Ibid., 74. In Yankee marriages, the husband and wife dynamic was more democratic, owing to a meshing of culturally derived beliefs about farming resources and processes, a point Salamon lays out in detail in chapter 5 of her book. Sonya Salamon, *Prairie Patrimony: Family, Farming, and Community in the Midwest* (Chapel Hill: University of North Carolina Press: 1995).

14. Pickle, *Contented among Strangers*, 90.

15. Salamon, *Prairie Patrimony*, 124.

16. Walter D. Kamphoefner, "German Americans: Paradoxes of a 'Model Minority,'" in *Origins and Destinies: Immigration, Race, and Ethnicity in America*, ed. Silvia Pedraza and Rubén G. Rumbaut (Belmont, CA: Wadsworth, 1996), 153; Hartmut Keil and John B. Jentz, *German Workers in Chicago: A Documentary History of Working-Class Culture from 1850 to World War I* (Urbana: University of Illinois Press, 1988), 4.

17. Farming practices included crop rotation and the use of fertilizers. Walter D. Kamphoefner, *The Westfalians: from Germany to Missouri* (Princeton, NJ: Princeton University Press, 1987), 126.

18. Look no further than the 1980 census for evidence of their stewardship. In it, German Americans were revealed to be the largest ethnic group involved in agriculture, accounting for approximately "one third of all American farmers." Kamphoefner et al., *News from the Land of Freedom*, 60–61.

19. Ibid., 166.

20. Sonya Salamon terms the German cultural pattern "yeoman" and the Yankee one "entrepreneur" (Salamon, *Prairie Patrimony*, 7). Her analysis of German and Yankee ethnic types in relationship to farming beliefs and practices in Midwestern communities was particularly helpful in writing this description. See table 4.1 ("Typology of Midwestern Farming Patterns") on page 93 for a cursory breakdown.

21. Coming from a yeoman farmer tradition, one that views farming as a way of life and family endeavor, today's "save the family farm" movements have been ascribed to German-immigrant influence. Kathleen Neils Conzen, "Phantom Landscapes of Colonization: Germans in the Making of Pluralist America," in *The German-American Encounter: Conflict and Cooperation between Two Cultures, 1800–2000*, ed. Frank Trommler and Elliott Shore (New York: Berghahn Books, 2001), 16.

22. Hamlin Garland, "Creamery Man," in *Main-Travelled roads* (New York: Harper, 1899), accessed July 1, 2016, http://www.gutenberg.org/cache/epub/2809/pg2809-images.html. Note that the lines for German characters (or characters of German descent) were penned with "broken English" in mind. This is evident in phrasings like "Vot was Bill fightding apoudt," among many others.

23. Many Anglo-Americans viewed the Germans as "clannish" and exclusive due to their tight-knit communities. Frederick C. Luebke, *Bonds of Loyalty: German-Americans and World War I* (DeKalb: Northern Illinois University Press, 1974), 60.

24. Kamphoefner et al., *News from the Land of Freedom*, 53. In his book, Michael K. Brinkman provides a well-documented and quite exhaustive list of the occupations held by Münsterland immigrants who settled in Quincy, Illinois. Like other towns and cities in Illinois at the time, Quincy provided a situation that allowed immigrants to pursue the same occupations they had back in Germany. Brinkman, *Quincy, Illinois, Immigrants*, 158.

25. Keil and Jentz, *German Workers in Chicago*, 7.

26. Luebke, *Bonds of Loyalty*, 60.

27. Pickle, *Contented among Strangers*, 57.

28. Hartmut Keil and John B. Jentz, "German Working-Class Culture in Chicago," *Gulliver* 9 (1981): 138.

29. Jacob Gross, "A German Family in Chicago: 1856," *Chicago History* 4, no. 10 (1956): 316.

30. Carl Smith, "Prologue," *Dramas of the Haymarket* (Chicago Historical Society and Northwestern University, 2000), accessed February 3, 2016, http://www.chicagohistoryresources.org/dramas/prologue/prologue.htm.

31. As mentioned elsewhere, Illinois' railway system grew from 110 to 2,867 miles of track between 1850 and 1860. Gates, *Illinois Central Railroad*, 88–89; John B. Jentz and Richard Schneirov, *Chicago in the Age of Capital: Class, Politics, and Democracy during the Civil War and Reconstruction* (Urbana: University of Illinois Press, 2012), 13–15.

32. Theodore J. Karamanski, "Civil War," *The Electronic Encyclopedia of Chicago* (Chicago: Chicago Historical Society, 2005), accessed May 27, 2017, http://www.encyclopedia.chicagohistory.org/pages/2379.html.

33. Karen Sawislak, "Chicago Fire," *The Electronic Encyclopedia of Chicago* (Chicago: Chicago Historical Society, 2005), accessed May 28, 2017, http://www.encyclopedia.chicagohistory.org/pages/1740.html; Roger Biles, *Illinois: A History of the Land and Its People* (DeKalb: Northern Illinois University Press, 2005), 126–28.

34. Smith, "Prologue"; Biles, *Illinois*, 124–29.

35. U.S. Census Bureau, "1870 Census, Volume 1: The Statistics of the Population of the United States" (Washington, DC: U.S. Department of Commerce, Economics, and Statistics Administration, U.S. Census Bureau, 1872), 339, 389, accessed June 11, 2017, https://www2.census.gov/library/publications/decennial/1870/population/1870a-36.pdf; U.S. Census Bureau, "Eleventh Census—Volume 1 (Part I & Part II): Report on Population of the United States" (Washington, DC: U.S. Department of Commerce, Economics, and Statistics Administration, U.S. Census Bureau, 1895), 607, 671, accessed June 11, 2017, ftp://ftp2.census.gov/library/publications/decennial/1890/volume-1/1890a_v1-16.pdf.

36. Biles, *Illinois*, 130.

37. Although this number remained relatively stable, what changed was the proportion of second-generation Germans who outnumbered first-generation Germans even during the large immigrant wave of the 1880s. Hartmut Keil, "Chicago's German

Working Class in 1900," in *German Workers in Industrial Chicago: A Comparative Perspective*, ed. Hartmut Keil and John B. Jentz (DeKalb: Northern Illinois University Press, 1983), 20–21.

38. Christiane Harzig, "Creating a Community: German-American Women in Chicago," in *Peasant Maids and City Women: From the European Countryside to Urban America*, ed. Christiane Harzig (Ithaca, NY: Cornell University Press, 1997), 186.

39. Jentz and Schneirov, *Chicago in the Age of Capital*, 16–17; Biles, *Illinois*, 124–29.

40. Biles, *Illinois*, 138–40.

41. Keil and Jentz, "German Working-Class Culture," 144; Keil, "Chicago's German Working Class," 26.

42. Christiane Harzig, "Introduction: Women Move from the European Countryside to Urban America," in *Peasant Maids, City Women: From the European Countryside to Urban America*, ed. Christiane Harzig (Ithaca, NY: Cornell University Press, 1997), 15; Harzig, "Creating a Community," 185, 189–90; Keil and Jentz, *German Workers in Chicago*, 10; Keil and Jentz, "German Working-Class Culture," 138–39.

43. Keil and Jentz, *German Workers in Chicago*, 10.

44. Keil, "Chicago's German Working Class," 34; Keil and Jentz, "German Working-Class Culture," 142–43; Harzig, "Creating a Community," 188.

45. Christiane Harzig, "Chicago's German North Side, 1880–1900: The Structure of a Gilded Age Ethnic Neighborhood," in *German Workers in Industrial Chicago: A Comparative Perspective* ed. Hartmut Keil and John B. Jentz (DeKalb: Northern Illinois University Press, 1983), 129.

46. Harzig, "Chicago's German North Side," 138; Keil and Jentz, *German Workers in Chicago*, 5; Keil, "Chicago's German Working Class," 33; Harzig, "Creating a Community," 195–96.

47. Keil, "Chicago's German Working Class," 33.

48. Harzig, "Chicago's German North Side," 129.

49. Keil and Jentz, *German Workers in Chicago*, 127–28.

50. Keil, "Chicago's German Working Class," 30–33; Harzig, "Chicago's German North Side," 133.

51. Keil and Jentz, "German Working-Class Culture," 143, 145; Keil, "Chicago's German Working Class," 31–33.

52. Keil and Jentz, "German Working-Class Culture," 135; John B. Jentz, "Skilled Workers and Industrialization: Chicago's German Cabinetmakers and Machinists, 1880–1900," in *German Workers in Industrial Chicago: A Comparative Perspective* ed. Hartmut Keil and John B. Jentz (DeKalb: Northern Illinois University Press, 1983), 75–79.

53. Jentz, "Skilled Workers and Industrialization," 74.

54. Harzig, "Creating a Community," 196–97.

55. Keil and Jentz, "German Working-Class Culture," 138.

56. Irving Cutler, *Chicago: Metropolis of the Mid-Continent* (Carbondale: Southern Illinois Univ. Press, 2006), 82.

57. Keil and Jentz, *German Workers in Chicago*, 151; Keil and Jentz, "German Working-Class Culture," 34; Harzig, "Chicago's German North Side," 131.

58. Rudolf A. Hofmeister, *The Germans of Chicago* (Champaign, IL: Stipes Pub. Co., 1976), 129–36.

59. Biles, *Illinois*, 127. Born Moritz Beisinger, his emigration date is debatable, with Hirschler having it at 1856 (Eric E. Hirschler, "Jews from Germany in the United States," in *Jews from Germany in the United States*, ed. Eric E. Hirschler [New York: Farrar, Straus and Cudahy, 1955], 39), and the Encyclopedia of Chicago listing it as 1854, just to name a few.

60. Biles, *Illinois*, 127. Starting out in the stockyards at five dollars a month, he put his money in pigs whose legs had been broken in shipment. Hirschler, *Jews from Germany*, 39. An interesting biography on him can be found in the Spring 2008 issue of *Chicago Jewish History*, the publication of the Chicago Jewish Historical Society, available at http://chicagojewishhistory.org/pdf/2008/CJH_2_2008-web.pdf.

61. Keil and Jentz, *German Workers in Chicago*, 2, 6.

62. Luebke, *Bonds of Loyalty*, 59.

OBSERVATIONS OF INDUSTRIAL WORKING CONDITIONS

1. Alfred Kolb, *Als Arbeiter in Amerika: Unter deutsch-amerikanischen Großstadt-Proletariern*, trans. Burt Weinshanker, 5th rev. ed. (Berlin: K. Siegismund, 1909), 41–69, 74–79, 83–85, as it appears in Hartmut Keil and John B. Jentz, *German Workers in Chicago: A Documentary History of Working-Class Culture from 1850 to World War I* (Urbana: University of Illinois Press, 1988), 88–99. Translation, including footnotes, reprinted with permission from University of Illinois Press.

2. In the German text this quotation is in Bavarian dialect. *Altötting* is a Bavarian religious shrine.

3. The original text refers to the use of both first names and the familiar form of the pronoun *you*.

4. "R" stands for Réaumur, a temperature scale that registers the boiling point of water at eighty degrees and the freezing point at zero.

5. Children sprout up amidst misery like mushrooms on a dung heap. (Footnote in the original text.)

CHICAGO'S BREWING INDUSTRY

1. Bob Skilnik, *Beer: A History of Brewing in Chicago* (Fort Lee, NJ: Barricade Books, 2006), 3–4.

2. Ibid., 6.

3. Gregg Smith, *Beer in America: The Early Years, 1587–1840: Beer's Role in the Settling of America and the Birth of a Nation* (Boulder, CO: Siris Books, 1998), 175.

4. Skilnik, *Beer*, 22.

5. Ibid., 25.

6. Ibid., 37.

7. Siebel Institute, "Our History," accessed February 2, 2016, https://www.siebelinstitute.com/focus-and-history/.

8. Skilnik, *Beer*, 6–7.

9. For a listing, see Rudolf A. Hofmeister, *The Germans of Chicago* (Champaign, IL: Stipes Pub. Co., 1976), 137–38.

5. Nativism, Politics, and the Civil War

1. Roger Biles, *Illinois: A History of the Land and Its People* (DeKalb: Northern Illinois University Press, 2005), 131.

2. Germans were viewed in a more positive light than the Irish by the Reformers, but their religious practices were nevertheless seen as overly raucous, and nativists felt an urgent need to "Americanize" these immigrants.

3. Mark Wyman, *Immigrants in the Valley: Irish, Germans, and Americans in the Upper Mississippi Country, 1830–1860* (Chicago: Nelson-Hall, 1984), 149–52.

4. Frederick C. Luebke, *Bonds of Loyalty: German-Americans and World War I* (DeKalb: Northern Illinois University Press, 1974), 61.

5. Thirty-dollar fees are given as the amount in Gerald Gems, "The German Turners and the Taming of Radicalism in Chicago," *International Journal of the History of Sport* 26 (2009): 1928; most other sources give the amount as fifty dollars. For example, Rudolf A. Hofmeister, *The Germans of Chicago* (Champaign, IL: Stipes Pub. Co., 1976), 56.

6. By comparison, Anglo-American taverns were quite strictly locales for alcohol consumption; the idea of women and children as patrons was not just baffling but nonsensical.

7. Even as their voting numbers were growing, the Germans made up a relatively small electorate. In Illinois, for example, they only counted for one-sixth of the total population. Sabine Freitag, *Friedrich Hecker: Two Lives for Liberty*, ed. and trans. by Steven W. Rowan (St. Louis, MO: St. Louis Mercantile Library, 2006), 208.

8. Other issues that Germans monolithically opposed were education legislation that restricted parochial schools and women's suffrage.

9. Shifting German votes from the Democratic to the Republican Party is one of the Forty-Eighters' enduring political impacts. For more on the free-soil movement and ideology, see Bruce Levine, *The Spirit of 1848: German Immigrants, Labor Conflict, and the Coming of the Civil War* (Urbana: University of Illinois Press, 1992). Considered a classic on this political ideology is Eric Foner, *Free Soil, Free Labor, Free Men: The Ideology of the Republican Party before the Civil War* (New York: Oxford University Press, 1970), republished in 1995 with a new introduction.

10. Christian B. Keller, *Chancellorsville and the Germans: Nativism, Ethnicity, and Civil War Memory* (New York: Fordham University Press, 2007), 14. For more on Germans in the 1860 election, see Frederick C. Luebke, ed., *Ethnic Voters and the Election of Lincoln* (Lincoln: University of Nebraska Press, 1971); consult also Levine, *Spirit of 1848*, 249–53.

11. Thomas J. Craughwell, "History of the Catholic Vote," *OSV Newsweekly* (October 24, 2012), accessed February 5, 2016, https://www.osv.com/OSVNewsweekly/ByIssue/Article/TabId/735/ArtMID/13636/ArticleID/3933/History-of-the-Catholic-Vote.aspx.

12. Howard B. Furer, *The Germans in America, 1607–1970: A Chronology & Fact Book* (Dobbs Ferry, NY: Oceana Publications, 1973), 50–51; Freitag, *Friedrich Hecker*, 208; Walter D. Kamphoefner, "German-Americans and Civil War Politics: A Reconsideration of the Ethnocultural Thesis," *Civil War History* 37, no. 3 (1991): 244.

13. J. H. A. Lacher, "Francis A. Hoffmann of Illinois and Hans Buschbauer of Wisconsin," *Wisconsin Magazine of History* 13, no. 4 (1929–1930): 333–47, accessed February 10, 2016, http://content.wisconsinhistory.org/cdm/ref/collection/wmh/id/28767.

14. Paul Selby, "George Schneider," *Papers in Illinois History and Transactions* (Springfield: Illinois State Historical Society, 1906), 331–33, accessed February 10, 2016, https://books.google.com/books?id=-9VLAQAAMAAJ&lpg=PA331&dq.

15. Frank Baron, *Abraham Lincoln and the German Immigrants: Turners and Forty-Eighters*, Yearbook of German-American Studies, supplemental issue, vol. 4 (Lawrence: Published at the University of Kansas by the Society for German-American Studies, 2012), 6, 96. He bought a half share in 1859 but sold it once elected. Alison Clark Efford, "Abraham Lincoln, German-Born Republicans, and American Citizenship," *Marquette Law Review* 93, no. 4 (2010): http://scholarship.law.marquette.edu/mulr/vo193/iss4/37.

16. The same cannot be said of Illinois' Anglo-Americans, many of whom had roots in Tennessee, Kentucky, Virginia, and other southern states. They were not consistently antislavery. Mark Voss-Hubbard, *Illinois's War: The Civil War in Documents* (Athens: Ohio University Press, 2013), 1–2.

17. Wilhelm Hense-Jensen and Ernest Bruncken, *Wisconsin's Deutsch-Amerikaner bis zum Schluss des 19. Jahrhunderts*, vol. 2 (Milwaukee: Die Deutsche Gesellschaft, 1902), 117, accessed October 22, 2018, https://babel.hathitrust.org/cgi/pt?id=wu.89045898087;view=1up;seq=9.

18. Joseph R. Reinhart, *Yankee Dutchmen under Fire: Civil War Letters from the 82nd Illinois Infantry* (Kent, OH: The Kent State University Press, 2013), 1.

19. Walter D. Kamphoefner and Wolfgang Johannes Helbich, *Germans in the Civil War: The Letters They Wrote Home* (Chapel Hill: University of North Carolina Press, 2006), preface. Other sources point to two hundred thousand Germans or more. Among them, Hofmeister, *Germans of Chicago*, 87; Wolfgang Helbich, "German Immigrants in the American Civil War," in *Die deutsche Präsenz in den USA = The German presence in the U.S.A.*, ed. Josef Raab and Jan Wirrer (Berlin: Lit., 2008), 166. Noteworthy here, too, is that a large contingent of Illinois Germans fought in Missouri German regiments. They not only formed more quickly, with Kamphoefner reminding us that "of the five three-month regiments recruited at the outbreak of the war, four and one-half were Germans," but fighting "mit Sigel," a Missouri German of high repute who organized in support of the Union cause in St. Louis, was noble and honorable (Kamphoefner, "German-Americans and Civil War Politics," 246).

20. Letter from Otto Balck, August 12, 1862, as printed in Reinhart, *Yankee Dutchmen under Fire*, 22.

21. Reinhart, *Yankee Dutchmen under Fire*, 2.

22. Appointing the German-born to high-ranking positions to command fellow Germans was a strategic move on the part of Lincoln, one that was made to solicit greater participation among Germans in the war.

23. One qualification is that other ethnic groups, especially the Scandinavians, were known to join "all-German" regiments, though their number was relatively small. The Twenty-Fourth Illinois also had three companies of Hungarians (Reinhart, *Yankee Dutchmen under Fire*, 33).

24. Letter from Otto Balck, August 12, 1862, as printed in Reinhart, *Yankee Dutchmen under Fire*, 22.

25. Letter from Wilhelm Loeb, September 2, 1862, as printed in Reinhart, *Yankee Dutchmen under Fire*, 36.

26. Letter from Beta, August 28, 1862, as printed in Reinhart, *Yankee Dutchmen under Fire*, 35.

27. Letter from Wilhelm Loeb, September 2, 1862, as printed in Reinhart, *Yankee Dutchmen under Fire*, 36–37.

28. Keller, *Chancellorsville and the Germans*, 32–33.

29. Reinhart, *Yankee Dutchmen under Fire*, 2.

30. Losses for the Eighty-Second were high at 155. Victor Hicken, *Illinois in the Civil War* (Urbana: University of Illinois Press, 1966), 333.

31. A front-page article published on May 5, 1863, in the *New York Times* ("The Great Battle of Sunday") is a prime example of such backbiting. Accessed June 10, 2016, http://www.nytimes.com/1863/05/05/news/the-great-battle-of-sunday.html.

32. Biles, *Illinois*, 111.

33. James M. Bergquist, "The Forty-Eighters: Catalysts of German-American Politics," in *The German-American Encounter: Conflict and Cooperation between Two Cultures, 1800–2000*, ed. Frank Trommler and Elliott Shore (New York: Berghahn Books, 2001), 32–33; Levine, *Spirit of 1848*, 264–65. For more on the movement, see Richard Allen Gerber, "The Liberal Republicans of 1872 in Historiographical Perspective," *Journal of American History* 62 (1975): 40–75; and from Jörg Nagler on German participation and perspective, see "Die Deutschamerikaner und das Liberal Republican Movement von 1872," *American Studies* 33 (1988): 415–38.

34. Biles, *Illinois*, 132–33.

35. The People's Party, with Anton Hesing as one of the leaders, was a populist party organized around anti-prohibition issues shortly before the Panic of 1873. Though the party was German in its origins, Hesing and others took care to broaden its scope to represent other ethnicities in the city. The party won overwhelmingly in the 1873 Chicago election. The Workingmen's Party, on the other hand, developed out of a massive unemployed workers' demonstration in late 1873 and organized in early 1874. It

was socialist in nature and worked in opposition to the more moderate People's Party. The party, active in organizing unemployed workers throughout the 1870s depression, eventually became part of the Socialist Labor Party. Daniel A. Graff, "Socialist Parties," *The Electronic Encyclopedia of Chicago* (Chicago: Chicago Historical Society, 2005), accessed May 27, 2017, http://www.encyclopedia.chicagohistory.org/pages/1161.html; Joseph B. Jentz and Richard Schneirov, *Chicago in the Age of Capital: Class, Politics, and Democracy during the Civil War and Reconstruction* (Urbana: University of Illinois Press, 2012), 146–64; Hartmut Keil and John B. Jentz, *German Workers in Chicago: A Documentary History of Working-Class Culture from 1850 to World War I* (Urbana: University of Illinois Press, 1988), 100.

36. Biles, *Illinois*, 133; Carl Smith, "Prologue," *Dramas of the Haymarket* (Chicago: Chicago Historical Society and Northwestern University, 2000), accessed October 22, 2018, http://www.chicagohistoryresources.org/dramas/prologue/prologue.htm.

37. Keil and Jentz, *German Workers in Chicago*, 100.

38. Ibid., 7; Hofmeister, *Germans of Chicago*, 142–43.

39. Keil and Jentz, *German Workers in Chicago*, 7; Hofmeister, *Germans of Chicago*, 142–43; Walter D. Kamphoefner, Wolfgang Johannes Helbich, and Ulrike Sommer, *News from the Land of Freedom: German Immigrants Write Home*, Documents in American Social History, trans. Susan Carter Vogel (Ithaca, NY: Cornell University Press, 1991), 296.

40. Hofmeister, *Germans of Chicago*, 145.

41. Kamphoefner et al., *News from the Land of Freedom*, 294. German members of the Socialist Labor Party also helped finance English-language socialist papers, like the *Chicago Socialist*, the *Leader*, and the *Workmen's Advocate*. Hartmut Keil, "German Working-Class Radicalism after the Civil War," in *The German-American Encounter: Conflict and Cooperation between Two Cultures, 1800–2000*, ed. Frank Trommler, and Elliot Shore (New York: Berghahn Books, 2001), 41.

42. Keil and Jentz, *German Workers in Chicago*, 134.

43. Hofmeister, *Germans of Chicago*, 143–44.

44. Ibid., 143. The German American policeman Michael Schaack even described the Haymarket incident from an anti-labor perspective in his book, *Anarchy and Anarchists*. Hofmeister, *Germans of Chicago*, 148.

45. Frederick C. Luebke, "German Immigrants and American Politics: Problems of Leadership, Parties, and Issues," in *Germans in America: Retrospect and Prospect; Tricentennial Lectures Delivered at the German Society of Pennsylvania in 1983*, ed. Randall M. Miller (Philadelphia: The German Society of Pennsylvania, 1984), 58–59; accessed August 14, 2017, http://digitalcommons.unl.edu/cgi/viewcontent.cgi?article=1157&context=historyfacpub.

46. Eric E. Hirschler, "Jews from Germany in the United States," in *Jews from Germany in the United States*, ed. Eric E. Hirschler (New York: Farrar, Straus and Cudahy, 1955), 51. A biographical sketch of Felsenthal, who lived from 1822 to 1908, as well as the extended quote can be found in the January 7, 1922, issue of *The Reform Advocate* (no. 22).

47. *Allgemeine Amerikanisch-deutsche Katholiken-Versammlung: Verhandlungen der ersten allgemeinen amerikanisch-deutschen Katholiken-Versammlung zu Chicago, Ill.* (Cincinnati: Rosenthal & Co, 1887), 27.

FRIEDRICH HECKER

1. One of the most thoroughly grounded accounts of Friedrich Hecker's life and exploits—and the one chiefly consulted here—is Sabine Freitag's *Friedrich Hecker: Two Lives for Liberty*, ed. and trans. by Steven W. Rowan (St. Louis, MO: St. Louis Mercantile Library, 2006).

2. Ibid., 220.

3. Joseph R. Reinhart, *Yankee Dutchmen under Fire: Civil War Letters from the 82nd Illinois Infantry* (Kent, OH: The Kent State University Press, 2013), 47. Excerpts from the letters printed on pages 28, 30, and 36 bear witness to his discipline, fairness, and exacting standards.

LINCOLN, LIBERTY, AND THE KNOW NOTHINGS

1. Walter D. Kamphoefner, Wolfgang Johannes Helbich and Ulrike Sommer, *News from the Land of Freedom: German Immigrants Write Home*, Documents in American Social History, trans. Susan Carter Vogel (Ithaca, NY: Cornell University Press, 1991), 159.

2. Abraham Lincoln, letter to Joshua Speed, August 24, 1855, Abraham Lincoln Online, accessed February 5, 2016, http://www.abrahamlincolnonline.org/lincoln/speeches/speed.htm.

3. Lincoln had been a member of the Whig Party, which was known for having a nativist faction, before its disintegration. Because of this, Democrats accused him during his political career of having nativist sympathies.

4. Abraham Lincoln, "Speech at Chicago, Illinois," July 10, 1858, *Collected Works of Abraham Lincoln*, vol. 2, 500–501, accessed November 2, 2018, https://quod.lib.umich.edu/l/lincoln/lincoln2/1:526?rgn=div1;view=fulltext.

5. Abraham Lincoln, "Letter to Theodore Canisius, Springfield, May 17, 1859," *Collected Works of Abraham Lincoln*, vol. 3 (Ann Arbor: University of Michigan Digital Library Production Services, 2001), accessed October 22, 2018, https://quod.lib.umich.edu/l/lincoln/lincoln3/1:107?rgn=div1;view=fulltext.

6. The fourteenth declaration specifically stated, "That the Republican party is opposed to any change in our naturalization laws, or any state legislation by which the rights of citizens hitherto accorded to immigrants from foreign lands shall be abridged or impaired; and in favor of giving all and efficient protection to the rights of all classes of citizens, whether native or naturalized, both at home or abroad." Republican Party Platform of 1860, in "Political Party Platforms," The American Presidency Project, accessed June 30, 2016, http://www.presidency.ucsb.edu/ws/?pid=29620; Bruce Levine, "'The Vital Element of the Republican Party': Antislavery, Nativism, and Abraham Lincoln," *Journal of the Civil War Era* 1 no. 4 (2011): Kindle location, 954.

THE HAYMARKET AFFAIR

1. "Final Salutations: The Five Victims of Their Humanity Are Accompanied on Their Final Journey," *Chicagoer Arbeiter-Zeitung*, November 14, 1887, in Hartmut Keil and John B. Jentz, *German Workers in Chicago: A Documentary History of Working-Class Culture from 1850 to World War I* (Urbana: University of Illinois Press, 1988), 191.

2. Secondary sources consulted include Roger Biles, *Illinois: A History of the Land and Its People* (DeKalb: Northern Illinois University Press, 2005), 134–36; Carl Smith, *Dramas of the Haymarket* (Chicago: Chicago Historical Society and Northwestern University, 2000), accessed October 22, 2018, http://www.chicagohistoryresources.org/dramas/overview/over.htm ; Rudolf A. Hofmeister, *The Germans of Chicago* (Champaign, IL: Stipes Pub. Co., 1976), 146–48; Keil and Jentz, *German Workers in Chicago*, 191.

6. Cultural and Institutional Life

1. Stephen Joseph Shaw, *The Catholic Parish as a Way-Station of Ethnicity and Americanization: Chicago's Germans and Italians, 1903–1939* (Brooklyn, NY: Carlson Pub., 1991), 16, 43; Sabine Freitag, *Friedrich Hecker: Two Lives for Liberty*, ed. and trans. by Steven W. Rowan (St. Louis, MO: St. Louis Mercantile Library, 2006), 160.

2. We use "Evangelical" here to refer to a particular form of German Protestantism and not to modern-day forms of evangelism.

3. Mark Wyman, *Immigrants in the Valley: Irish, Germans, and Americans in the Upper Mississippi Country, 1830–1860* (Chicago: Nelson-Hall, 1984), 67.

4. Free Thinkers were carriers of Enlightenment principles, as were a great number of German Jews.

5. Wyman, *Immigrants in the Valley*, 54.

6. Frederick C. Luebke, *Bonds of Loyalty: German-Americans and World War I* (DeKalb: Northern Illinois University Press, 1974), 34.

7. Ibid., 35–39.

8. Ibid., 38.

9. John Bodnar, *The Transplanted: A History of Immigrants in Urban America* (Bloomington: Indiana University Press, 2008), 147; Luebke, *Bonds of Loyalty*, 38–39.

10. Luebke, *Bonds of Loyalty*, 41.

11. Scott Holl, "Brief History of the Evangelical Synod of North America," Eden Theological Seminary, 2008, 1, accessed July 13, 2016, http://library.webster.edu/luhr_library/guides/images/esna%20brief%20history.pdf.

12. Luebke, *Bonds of Loyalty*, 39.

13. Ibid., 42.

14. Bodnar, *Transplanted*, 148. In 1825, an early group of German Lutherans in Union County requested ministers from the North Carolina Synod to send men who were competent in both German and English so that German schools could be created "and the German language be retained." In the absence of German teachers,

they "foresaw dire consequences 'to them and their children.'" Wyman, *Immigrants in the Valley*, 160.

15. Walter D. Kamphoefner, Wolfgang Helbich, and Ulrike Sommer, *News from the Land of Freedom: German Immigrants Write Home,* Documents in American Social History, trans. Susan Carter Vogel (Ithaca, NY: Cornell University Press, 1991), 21.

16. Ibid., 165.

17. Peter d'Alroy Jones and Melvin G. Holli, *Ethnic Chicago* (Grand Rapids, MI: W. B. Eerdmans Pub. Co, 1995), 101; Other immigrant groups in Chicago paled by comparison, with Russians and Yugoslavs measuring around 60 percent and Italians, Lithuanians, and Ruthenians around 50 percent. For illiteracy rates, see Luebke, *Bonds of Loyalty*, 65.

18. For more on German-sourced influence on American education, we highly recommend Daniel Fallon, "German Influences on American Education," in *The German-American Encounter: Conflict and Cooperation between Two Cultures, 1800–2000*, ed. Frank Trommler and Elliott Shore (New York: Berghahn Books, 2001), 77–87.

19. Formal schooling was secondary to farming in some peasant families where children were central to the sustenance and succession of the family farm, a point we also make in chapter 4.

20. Exceptions to this pattern have occurred.

21. German began to lose its status as the language of science after World War I. German and Austrian scientists were barred from attending conferences and publishing in Western European journals while newly created organizations like the International Union of Pure and Applied Chemistry began using English and French as the language of communication and correspondence. Nina Porzucki, "Nobel Prize: How English Beat German as Language of Science," *BBC News Magazine*, BBC News, October 11, 2014, accessed July 14, 2016, http://www.bbc.com/news/magazine-29543708.

22. Germans throughout the state founded many private libraries and heavily contributed to the development of public ones in order to preserve works by German and German American authors. Don Heinrich Tolzmann, *Illinois' German Heritage* (Milford, OH: Little Miami Pub. Co., 2005), 132.

23. Wyman, *Immigrants in the Valley*, 160.

24. Rudolf A. Hofmeister, *The Germans of Chicago* (Champaign, IL: Stipes Pub. Co., 1976), 179.

25. The *Illinois Teacher* reproduced the dissenting report in its entirety, which includes other arguments on German's inexpediency and undesirability in the public school system. Illinois Education Association, *Illinois Teacher: Devoted to Education, Science and Free Schools* (Peoria, IL: N. C. Nason, 1860), 6:460, accessed July 13, 2016, https://books.google.com/books?id=j-gcAQAAMAAJ&dq.

26. *Du Page County Observer*, Naperville, Illinois, March 8, 1854, as cited in Ellen T. Eslinger, *Cultural Heritages of Naperville, Illinois The Pennsylvania Germans* (paper presented at the Fifth Illinois History Symposium, Springfield, IL, November

30–December 1, 1984), 22, accessed July 13, 2016, http://www.idaillinois.org/cdm/ref/collection/npl/id/11538; Other examples include teachers who sought out English instruction themselves. See Michael K. Brinkman, *Quincy, Illinois, Immigrants from Münsterland, Westphalia, Germany* (Westminster, MD: Heritage Books, 2010), 2:127. A lack in English proficiency among teachers was prevalent across the American Midwest. For Wisconsin, see Joseph Schafer's classic work *Four Wisconsin Counties* (Madison: State Historical Society of Wisconsin, 1927).

27. "German-Language Education in America," Max Kade Institute for German-American Studies, accessed July 13, 2016, http://mki.wisc.edu/research/culture_traditions/german-language-education-america.

28. Check out the following link for some fun converting between *Fraktur*, *Kurrent*, and *Sütterlin* (a later form of *Kurrent* used by schoolchildren in Germany in the early to mid-1900s): http://stevemorse.org/german/germanprintcurs.html?casing=upper&font=cursive&script=kurrent&leftposition=2&rightposition=2&german.

29. Antje Petty, "Immigrant Languages and Education: Wisconsin's German Schools," in *Wisconsin Talk: Linguistic Diversity in the Badger State*, ed. Thomas C. Purnell, Eric Raimy, and Joe Salmons (Madison: University of Wisconsin Press, 2013), 49–50.

30. Gerald R. Gems, "The German Turners and the Taming of Radicalism in Chicago," *International Journal of the History of Sport* 26, no. 13 (2009): 1929.

31. Howard B. Furer, *The Germans in America, 1607–1970: A Chronology & Fact Book* (Dobbs Ferry, NY: Oceana Publications, 1973), 64.

32. Carl Frederick Wittke, *The German-Language Press in America* (Lexington: University of Kentucky Press, 1957), 2.

33. Tolzmann, *Illinois' German Heritage*, 134; as also found in Karl Arndt, John Richard, and May E. Olson, *The German Language Press of the Americas* (Munich: Verlag Dokumentation, 1973).

34. Wittke, *German-Language Press in America*, 7.

35. As discussed in the previous chapter, however, there was a significant German presence in the labor and radical press; these papers were often at odds with the more moderate mainstream newspapers.

36. Luebke, *Bonds of Loyalty*, 61–63.

37. Robert Ezra Park, *The Immigrant Press and Its Control* (New York: Harper & Brothers, 1922), 310, accessed July 13, 2016, http://hdl.handle.net/10111/UIUCOCA:immigrantpressitsoopark.

38. Park's *Immigrant Press and Its Control* claims 46 percent (p. 312), as does Wittke's *German-Language Press in America* (p. 208).

39. Dorothee Schneider, *Trade Unions and Community: The German Working Class in New York City, 1870–1900* (Urbana: University of Illinois Press, 1994), 26–29.

40. Hofmeister, *Germans of Chicago*, 124.

41. Ibid., 191, 120–22.

42. Ibid., 122.

43. Already in 1858, an advertisement in the *Quincy Whig* for a "Grand Singing Festival" reported "some twenty singing clubs, at different towns in Missouri and Illinois, belonging to the Union, and it is supposed that not less than three hundred singers from abroad, will take an active part in the festival. This will be a rare treat to our citizens, who are music-appreciating people, and will, no doubt, unite with our German friends, to make this a general public demonstration." "Grand Singing Festival," *Quincy Daily Whig and Republican*, April 15, 1858, p. 3, accessed July 13, 2015, http://archive.quincylibrary.org.

44. Andreas Reichstein, *German Pioneers on the American Frontier: The Wagners in Texas and Illinois* (Denton: University of North Texas Press, 2001), 126.

45. *Sokol* was a similar movement among Czechs to promote nationalism and ethnic consciousness.

46. Hofmeister, *Germans of Chicago*, 176.

47. Reichstein, *German Pioneers on the American Frontier*, 128.

48. Furer, *Germans in America*, 40.

49. Annette R. Hoffman, "The American Turners: Their Past and Present," *Revista Brasileira De Ciências Do Esporte* 37, no. 2 (2015): 123.

50. It also distinguished them from their less radical counterparts back in Germany. To explain, the outbreak of the 1848 revolution split the German Turners into two factions. One, the *Deutscher Turnerbund* (German Gymnastic Union), supported a constitutional monarchy, while the other, the *Demokratischer Turnerbund* (Democratic Gymnastic Union), favored a German republic. The latter group of Turners, known today as the Forty-Eighters, were the ones who transformed German nationalism into a mass movement, resulting in the Revolution of 1848.

51. Gems, "German Turners," 2009; Gerald R. Gems and Gertrud Pfister, *Understanding American Sports* (London: Routledge, 2009), 71.

52. Hoffman, "American Turners," 123.

53. At the time of writing this manuscript, the association's national website reports fifty-three active clubs (accessed August, 15, 2017, http://www.americanturners.com/). A 2011 estimate reports 13,500 members—from Joseph R. Reinhart, *Yankee Dutchmen under Fire: Civil War Letters from the 82nd Illinois Infantry* (Kent, OH: The Kent State University Press, 2013), 200.

54. At the very least, pride in ethnic identity was misconstrued by some in mainstream American society as cliquish. Luebke, *Bonds of Loyalty*, 60.

55. Hoffman, "American Turners," 122.

56. "The Turner Association," *Quincy Herald*, February 2, 1857, as cited in Brinkman, *Quincy, Illinois, Immigrants*, 214–15.

57. Beer halls were especially important to Chicago's German working-class culture as they provided public spaces for union members and other political groups to meet and discuss local politics and working conditions. Hartmut Keil and John B. Jentz, "German Working-Class Culture in Chicago," *Gulliver* 9 (1981): 139; Christiane

Harzig, "Chicago's German North Side, 1880–1900: Structure of a Gilded Age Ethnic Neighborhood," in *German Workers in Industrial Chicago: A Comparative Perspective*, ed. Hartmut Keil and John B. Jentz (DeKalb: Northern Illinois University Press, 1983), 141.

58. Hartmut Keil and John B. Jentz, *German Workers in Chicago: A Documentary History of Working-Class Culture from 1850 to World War I* (Urbana: University of Illinois Press, 1988), 11.

59. Heike Bungert, "Regional Diversity in Celebrating Regional Origin," in *Regionalism in the Age of Globalism*, vol. 2, *Forms of Regionalism*, ed. Lothar Hönnighausen, Anke Ortlepp, James Peacock, and Niklaus Steiner (Madison, WI: Center for the Study of Upper Midwestern Cultures, 2005), 96. See also Steve Hoelscher, *Heritage on Stage: The Invention of Ethnic Place in America's Little Switzerland* (Madison: University of Wisconsin Press, 1998).

60. On the centrality of celebration in creating German American ethnicity, see Kathleen N. Conzen, "Ethnicity as Festive Culture: Nineteenth-Century German America on Parade," in *The Invention of Ethnicity*, ed. Werner Sollors (New York: Oxford University Press, 1989), 44–76.

61. Hofmeister, *Germans of Chicago*, 123.

62. Klaus Ensslen and Heinz Ickstadt, "German Working-Class Culture in Chicago: Continuity and Change in the Decade from 1900–1910," in Keil and Jentz, *German Workers in Industrial Chicago*, 245.

63. Hofmeister, *Germans of Chicago*, 227–39.

64. Ibid., 218–19.

65. Klaus Ensslen and Heinz Ickstadt, "German Working-Class Culture in Chicago," 242–45; Keil and Jentz, "German Working-Class Culture," 137; Hartmut Keil and John B. Jentz, "Introduction," in Keil and Jentz, *German Workers in Industrial Chicago*, 1.

66. Jones and Holli, *Ethnic Chicago*, 98; Hofmeister, *Germans of Chicago*, 108.

67. See Miranda E. Wilkerson and Joseph Salmons, "Linguistic Marginalities: Becoming American without Learning English," *Journal of Transnational American Studies* 4, no. 2 (2012): http://www. escholarship.org/uc/item/5vn092kk.

68. See, for example, Miranda E. Wilkerson and Joseph Salmons, "'Good Old Immigrants of Yesteryear' Who Didn't Learn English: Germans in Wisconsin," *American Speech* 83 (2008): 259–83; Teresa G. Labov, "English Acquisition by Immigrants to the United States at the Beginning of the Twentieth Century," *American Speech* 73 (1998); Walter Kamphoefner, "German American Bilingualism: Cui Malo? Mother Tongue and Socioeconomic Status among the Second Generation in 1940," *International Migration Review* 28 (1994).

69. See primary-source examples of this as found on page 15 of Wilkerson and Salmons, "Linguistic Marginalities"; and Brinkman, *Quincy, Illinois, Immigrants*, 102–3.

70. Brinkman, *Quincy, Illinois, Immigrants*, 256.

71. Frederick Jackson Turner, 1901, as quoted in Ben Wattenberg, "The New Immigrants, Head Shapes, and the Melting Pot: Franz Boas vs. Scientific Racism," The

First Measured Century Program Segments (PBS), accessed July 13, 2016, http://www.pbs.org/fmc/segments/progseg2.htm.

72. Francis Walker, "Restriction of Immigration," *Atlantic Monthly* 77 (June 1896): 828–29.

73. For a historical overview of white racial identity and how its definition has been informed by German and other immigrant groups, see chapter 5, "Fractured Whiteness," in Russell A. Kazal, *Becoming Old Stock: The Paradox of German-American Identity* (Princeton, NJ: Princeton University Press, 2004). Of particular interest in this chapter is the positioning of Germans as "old-stock" Americans, owing to their shared northwest European ancestry with Anglo-Americans, in direct response to "new" immigration.

74. More commonly known as the Dillingham Commission after its chairman, this body was sanctioned by Congress in 1907 to review U.S. immigration policy in light of the extraordinary escalation in immigration to America, particularly to its urban centers. For popular and "scientifically grounded" views toward race and ethnicity during this era, including how Germans fared, see chapter 3, "The Sauerkraut Question," in Luebke, *Bonds of Loyalty.*

75. Though support for this conclusion was based on a range of factors and statistical analyses, the report failed to control for recency of immigration, an omission that sorely disadvantaged new arrivals in comparison to older ones (who had had decades to adapt); John Powell, "Dillingham Commission," *Encyclopedia of North American Immigration* (New York: Facts on File, 2005), 78. Moreover, the commission's report (see vol. 5: *Dictionary of Races and Peoples*) was not immune to the trending and emerging schools of thought in the social sciences and eugenics, respectively, including the "scientific" racial typology of Europeans propagated by William Z. Ripley in his 1899 book, *The Races of Europe.*

76. Parallels between the societal racism and nativism experienced by southern and eastern European immigrants at the turn of the nineteenth century can easily be drawn to earlier as well as to contemporary immigrants. The fact is, newcomers to this country deemed too foreign or "un-American" have reliably battled nativism, oftentimes masked as nationalism. In colonial Pennsylvania, that was true even for the Germans, whose "whiteness" was most famously contested by Benjamin Franklin who had feared large-scale German immigration in much the same way people feared the influx of southern and eastern European immigrants well over a century later. Describing them as being "generally of what we call a swarthy complexion," and therefore not among the "purely white people of the world," he mused, "Why should Pennsylvania, founded by the *English*, become a Colony of Aliens, who will shortly be so numerous as to Germanize us instead of our Anglifying them, and will never adopt our Language or Customs, any more than they can acquire our Complexion." Benjamin Franklin, "Observations Concerning the Increasing of Mankind, Peopling of Countries, &c." (Boston: S. Kneeland, 1755), accessed July 14, 2016, http://www.digitalhistory.uh.edu

/disp_textbook.cfm?smtID=3&psid=85. Fast-forward to today, and though less explicitly race based, similar rhetoric and anxieties about the incommensurability and undesirability of contemporary immigrants from Latin America, Asia, and the Middle East abound in public discussion and debate as well as in political discourse. English-only activism, which is a direct outgrowth of the immigration restriction movement, makes for a good example. On the makings and basic tenets of the English-Only Movement, see James Crawford, "Anatomy of the English-Only Movement: Social and Ideological Sources of Language Restrictionism in the United States," *At War with Diversity: U.S. Language Policy in an Age of Anxiety* (Clevedon: Multilingual Matters, 2000).

77. Efforts were also made by German Jews (or those of German Jewish descent), who were at this time quite well established, to hurry the assimilatory process of Eastern European Jews for fears of being conflated with them (and thus being subject to discrimination).

78. Luebke, *Bonds of Loyalty*, 67–68

79. "The Meeting of the German-American Historical Society," *Illinois Staats-Zeitung*, May 24, 1900, The Newberry: Foreign Language Press Survey, accessed October 22, 2018, http://flps.newberry.org/article/5418474_8_0414/.

80. Luebke, *Bonds of Loyalty*, 49–50.

81. Christine Totten, "Elusive Affinities: Acceptance and Rejection of the German-Americans," in *America and the Germans: An Assessment of a Three-Hundred-Year History*, ed. Frank Trommler and Joseph McVeigh (Philadelphia: University of Pennsylvania Press, 1985), 2:193; Luebke, *Bonds of Loyalty*, 58–59. Göttingen and Berlin were the top universities that Americans studied at in Germany. Fallon, "German Influences on American Education," 84.

GEORG BUNSEN

1. Three times the size of the 1818 Constitution, which was drafted when Illinois was still a frontier state, the 1848 Constitution was written in response to Illinois' burgeoning growth. Frank Kopecky and Mary Sherman Harris, Understanding the Illinois Constitution (Springfield: Illinois LEARN Program, 2001), 3–4, accessed July 15, 2016, https://www.isba.org/sites/default/files/teachers/publications/constbook.pdf.

ON THE SHIFT FROM GERMAN TO ENGLISH

1. An exception is the Old Order Amish and Old Order Mennonites, well-established groups who continue to use Pennsylvania Dutch (alongside English) and pass it on to their children. As an aside, most scholars prefer the term "Pennsylvania German," which better connotes the Palatine dialects from which the language emerged over two centuries ago.

2. For a strong academic treatment of language shift as linked to community and regional structure, see Joseph Salmons, "Community, Region, and Language Shift in

German-Speaking Wisconsin," in *Regionalism in the Age of Globalism*, vol. 2: *Forms of Regionalism*, ed. Lothar Hönnighausen, Anke Ortlepp, James Peacock, and Niklaus Steiner (Madison, WI: Center for the Study of Upper Midwestern Cultures, 2005), 133–44. Two dissertations have also treated this topic. See Benjamin Frey, *Towards a General Theory of Language Shift: A Case Study in Wisconsin German and North Carolina Cherokee* (PhD diss., University of Wisconsin, 2013); and Felecia Lucht, *Language Variation in a German-American Community: A Diachronic Study of the Spectrum of Language Use in Lebanon, Wisconsin* (PhD diss., University of Wisconsin-Madison, 2007).

3. Roland L. Warren, *The Community in America*, 3rd ed. (Chicago: Rand-McNally, 1978).

4. For Lutherans, a similarly close connection between language and faith was expressed. German was, in their words, *die Sprache Luthers* ("the language of Luther"). Georg von Bosse, *Das deutsche Element in den Vereinigten Staaten under besonderer Berücksichtigung seines politischen, ethnischen, sozialen, und erzieherischen Einflusses* (New York: E. Steiger & Co., 1908), 457, accessed November 3, 2018, https://books.google.com/books?id=tmwaAQAAIAAJ&dq; Georg von Bosse, *Ein Kampf um Glauben und Volkstum* (Stuttgart: C. Belsersche Verlagsbuchhandlung, 1920), 19, accessed July 15, 2016, https://ia902701.us.archive.org/22/items/einkampfumglaubeoobossiala/einkampfumglaubeoobossiala.pdf

5. Stephen Joseph Shaw, *The Catholic Parish as a Way-Station of Ethnicity and Americanization: Chicago's Germans and Italians, 1903–1939* (Brooklyn, NY: Carlson Pub., 1991), 13–28.

6. John Williston Cook, *The Educational History of Illinois: Growth and Progress in Educational Affairs of the State from the Earliest Day to the Present* (Chicago: The Henry O. Shepard Company, 1912), 156. To clarify, the amendment in 1889 lowered the age to seven (from eight) and extended the school year to sixteen (from twelve) weeks.

7. Interestingly, and as an interethnic grab for power, smaller ethnic groups were known to support language restriction measures because they would help "block German, America's most commonly spoken non-English language until the 1950s." Slavs, for example, voted against foreign language instruction in *any* language, in order to prevent German from being taught in the schools. Germans, several years later, blocked Slavs from teaching their own languages in the schools. Jonathon Zimmerman, "Ethnics against Ethnicity: European Immigrants and Foreign-Language Instruction, 1890–1940" *Journal of American History* 88, no. 4 (2002): 1386.

8. An analysis of these circumstances, including how they square with the historical record, can be found in Joseph Salmons, "The Shift from German to English, World War I and the German-Language Press in Wisconsin," in *Menschen zwischen zwei Welten: Auswanderung, Ansiedlung, Akkulturation*, ed. by Walter G. Rödel and Helmut Schmahl (Trier: Wissenschaftlicher Verlag Trier, 2002), 179–93. While the quantitative data provided are specific to Wisconsin, the conclusions are not. Chapters 13 and 14 of Carl Wittke's *The German Language Press in America* (Lexington: University of Kentucky Press, 1957) provide historical context as well.

7. World War I and Its Aftermath

1. Statistics from *International Migration and Naturalization*, Series C, "Immigrants by Country: 1820–1970," confirm as much.

2. Gerald Gems, "The German Turners and the Taming of Radicalism in Chicago," *International Journal of the History of Sport* 26 no. 13 (October 2009): 1935; Michael K. Brinkman, *Quincy, Illinois, immigrants from Münsterland, Westphalia, Germany* (Westminster, MD: Heritage Books, 2010), 256.

3. Walter D. Kamphoefner, "The German-American Experience in World War I: A Centennial Assessment," *Yearbook of German-American Studies* 49 (2014): 19; Rudolph A. Hofmeister, *The Germans of Chicago* (Champaign, IL: Stipes Pub. Co., 1976), 164.

4. La Vern J. Rippley, "Ameliorated Americanization: The Effect of World War I on German-Americans in the 1920s," in *America and the Germans: An Assessment of a Three-Hundred-Year History*, ed. Frank Trommler and Joseph McVeigh (Philadelphia: University of Pennsylvania Press, 1985), 2:217–20; Christine Harzig, "Germans," Electronic Encyclopedia of Chicago, Chicago Historical Society, 2005, accessed July 1, 2016, http://www.encyclopedia.chicagohistory.org/pages/512.html; Melvin G. Holli, "German-American Ethnic Identity from 1890 Onward," *Ethnic Chicago: A Multicultural Portrait*, ed. Peter d'Alroy Jones and Melvin G. Holli (Grand Rapids, MI: W. B. Eerdmans Pub. Co., 1981), 96–97.

5. Frederick C. Luebke, *Bonds of Loyalty: German-Americans and World War I* (DeKalb: Northern Illinois University Press, 1974), 45–46; Russell A. Kazal, *Becoming Old Stock: The Paradox of German-American Identity* (Princeton, NJ: Princeton University Press, 2004), 130–34.

6. Rippley, "Ameliorated Americanization," 220–22; Carl Frederick Wittke, *German-Americans and the World War (with Special Emphasis on Ohio's German-Language Press)* (Columbus: Ohio State Archaeological and Historical Society, 1936), 163–67; Luebke, *Bonds of Loyalty*, 98; Charles T. Johnson, "National German-American Alliance," *Germany and the Americas: Culture, Politics, and History*, ed. Thomas Adam (Santa Barbara, CA: ABC-CLIO, 2005).

7. National German-American Alliance, *Effect of Prohibition: An Argument on the Errors of Prohibition* (St. Louis, MO: The Alliance, 1908), 1, accessed April 20, 2016, http://iiif.lib.harvard.edu/manifests/view/drs:5198169$1i.

8. Christine Totten, "Elusive Affinities: Acceptance and Rejection of the German-Americans," in *America and the Germans: An Assessment of a Three-Hundred-Year History*, ed. Frank Trommler and Joseph McVeigh (Philadelphia: University of Pennsylvania Press, 1985), 2:193; Luebke, *Bonds of Loyalty*, 58–59.

9. Luebke, *Bonds of Loyalty*, 68–71.

10. "Wilson Condemns Foreign Alliances," *New York Times*, May 17, 1914, 19; Similar rhetoric can be found even today among politicians and media pundits (see, e.g., Eugene Scott, "Sarah Palin: Black Lives Matter Is a 'Farce,'" CNN, July 9, 2016, accessed

July 16, 2016, http://www.cnn.com/2016/07/08/politics/sarah-palin-black-lives-matter/index.html).

11. Hofmeister, *Germans of Chicago*, 60–61, 91–92.

12. Wittke, *German-Americans*, 27–28.

13. Ibid., 30; Luebke, *Bonds of Loyalty*, 93.

14. Wittke, *German-Americans*, 6–7.

15. Luebke, *Bonds of Loyalty*, 87–89.

16. Michael Warner, "The Kaiser Sows Destruction: Protecting the Homeland the First Time Around," *Studies in Intelligence* 46, no. 1 (2002): accessed April 1, 2018, https://www.cia.gov/library/center-for-the-study-of-intelligence/csi-publications/csi-studies/studies/vol46no1/article02.html. For a complete history of the Black Tom incident, see Jules Witcover, *Sabotage at Black Tom: Imperial Germany's Secret in America, 1914–1917* (Chapel Hill, NC: Algonquin Books, 1989).

17. Wittke, *German-Americans*, 4–5; Luebke, *Bonds of Loyalty*, 88–89.

18. Luebke, *Bonds of Loyalty*, 101–7.

19. Ibid., 101, 232; Wittke, *German-Americans*, 5–6.

20. Luebke, *Bonds of Loyalty*, 228–31; Wittke, *German-Americans*, 172.

21. Hofmeister, *Germans of Chicago*, 92.

22. Ibid.; Kamphoefner, "German-American Experience," 8.

23. Luebke, *Bonds of Loyalty*, 225–27.

24. Tina Stewart Brakebill, "From 'German Days' to '100 Percent Americanism': McLean County, Illinois 1913–1918; German Americans, World War One, and One Community's Reaction," *Journal of the Illinois State Historical Society (1998–)* 95, no. 2 (2002): 156–57; Luebke, *Bonds of Loyalty*, 235.

25. Lisa Mastrangelo, "World War I, Public Intellectuals, and the Four Minute Men: Convergent Ideals of Public Speaking and Civic Participation," *Rhetoric & Public Affairs* 12, no. 4 (2009): 608–9, accessed July 12, 2016, https://muse.jhu.edu/; United States, Committee on Public Information, Division of Four Minute Men, Chicago Branch, *The Four Minute Men of Chicago* (Chicago: History Committee of the Four Minute Men of Chicago, 1919), 7, accessed July 12, 2016, http://books.google.com/books?id=SvQ-AQAAMAAJ.

26. The Library of Congress has a large collection of World War I propaganda posters available online here: http://www.loc.gov/pictures/collection/wwipos/.

27. Mastrangelo, "World War I," 608–9; Brakebill, "From 'German Days,'" 156–58; Robert A. Wells, "Propaganda at Home (USA)," *1914–1918 Online: International Encyclopedia of the First World War*, accessed July 12, 2016, http://encyclopedia.1914-1918-online.net/article/propaganda_at_home_usa; United States, *Four Minute Men*, 7.

28. Luebke, *Bonds of Loyalty*, 84–86.

29. United States, President (1913–1921: Wilson), *Americanism: Woodrow Wilson's Speeches on the War—Why He Made Them and What They Have Done: The President's Principal Utterances in the First Year of War; with Notes, Comments and War Dates, Giving*

Them Their Historical Setting, Significance and Consequences, and with Brief Quotations from Earlier Speeches and Papers / Compiled, Edited and Annotated by Oliver Marble Gale (Chicago: Baldwin Syndicate, n.d.), 56, accessed July 12, 2016, http://hdl.handle.net/2027/uc2.ark:/13960/t16m35z59.

30. Brakebill, "From 'German Days,'" 150.

31. Brenda Roth, "Burleson, Albert Sidney (1863–1937)," in *The United States in the First World War: An Encyclopedia*, ed. Anne Cipriano Venzon (New York: Garland Pub., 1995), 114–15.

32. Brakebill, "From 'German Days,'" 156–57; Luebke, *Bonds of Loyalty*, 241–42.

33. Luebke, *Bonds of Loyalty*, 255–56.

34. United States, "A Portion of the Amendment to Section 3 of the Espionage Act of June 15, 1917," *Statutes at Large* (Washington, DC, 1918), 40:553, accessed July 12, 2016, http://www.gwpda.org/1918/usspy.html.

35. Roger Biles, *Illinois: A History of the Land and Its People* (DeKalb: Northern Illinois University Press, 2005), 188–89; Brakebill, "From 'German Days,'" 158.

36. Luebke, *Bonds of Loyalty*, 235–40; Biles, *Illinois*, 193.

37. Brakebill, "From 'German Days,'" 158–62; Illinois War Council, and Samuel Insull, *Final Report of the State Council of Defense of Illinois, 1917–1918–1919: An Official Body Created by an Act of the General Assembly Approved by the Governor May 2, 1917* (1919), 93, accessed July 12, 2016, http://www.idaillinois.org/cdm/ref/collection/isl8/id/1887.

38. Illinois War Council, *Final Report*, 93.

39. Brakebill, "From 'German Days,'" 150.

40. Hofmeister, *Germans of Chicago*, 73; Wittke, *German-Americans*, 186; Luebke, *Bonds of Loyalty*, 16.

41. Brinkman, *Quincy, Illinois, Immigrants*, 272–73.

42. Luebke, *Bonds of Loyalty*, 36–38.

43. Brakebill, "From 'German Days,'" 164–66.

44. Wittke, *German-Americans*, 191.

45. Luebke, *Bonds of Loyalty*, 15–16.

46. Wittke, *German-Americans*, 178–79, 189; Brinkman, *Quincy, Illinois, Immigrants*, 266–69.

47. Kamphoefner, "German-American Experience," 17.

48. Hofmeister, *Germans of Chicago*, 74–78; Holli, "German-American Ethnic Identity," 98–101, 104.

49. For example, the Tri-City Symphony Orchestra was forced to cut the German piece "Pilgrim's Chorus" from its program, and the Chicago Opera Company was banned from performing German-language operas. Wittke, *German-Americans*, 183.

50. Holli, "German-American Ethnic Identity," 104.

51. Brinkman, *Quincy, Illinois, Immigrants*, 264.

52. Hofmeister, *Germans of Chicago*, 75–76; Wittke, *German-Americans*, 184; Kamphoefner, "German-American Experience," 18.

53. Luebke, *Bonds of Loyalty*, 243–44.

54. "You Can Help Fight the German Spy Propaganda," *Quincy Herald*, March 30, 1918, microfilm. As quoted in Brinkman, *Quincy, Illinois, Immigrants*, 277.

55. Brinkman, *Quincy, Illinois, Immigrants*, 278–82.

56. Luebke, *Bonds of Loyalty*, 247; Wittke, *German-Americans*, 193.

57. Luebke, *Bonds of Loyalty*, 14.

58. Brinkman, *Quincy, Illinois, Immigrants*, 283.

59. Luebke, *Bonds of Loyalty*, 15.

60. Brakebill, "From 'German Days,'" 163; Ülkü Güney, "German Ethnic Identity in Chicago Before and During the First World War," *Journal of Faculty of Letters* 32, no. 1 (Ankara: Hacettepe University, 2015): 160; Luebke, *Bonds of Loyalty*, 18–19; Hofmeister, *Germans of Chicago*, 74; Wittke, *German-Americans*, 176.

61. Rippley, "Ameliorated Americanization," 224.

62. Brinkman, *Quincy, Illinois, Immigrants*, 261–62; Harzig, "Germans"; Biles, *Illinois*, 204.

63. Hofmeister, *Germans of Chicago*, 164; Frederick C. Luebke, *Germans in the New World: Essays in the History of Immigration* (Urbana: University of Illinois Press, 1990), 69–70; United States, Library of Congress, "About Illinois Staats-zeitung. (Chicago, Ill.) 1848–1922," Chronicling America, accessed July 12, 2016, http://chroniclingamerica.loc.gov/lccn/sn85033492/.

64. Holli, "German-American Ethnic Identity," 93.

65. Peter C. Weber, "Ethnic Identity during War: The Case of German American Societies during World War I," *Nonprofit and Voluntary Sector Quarterly*, no. 1 (2014): 185, HeinOnline, EBSCOhost, accessed August 19, 2017.

66. Harzig, "Germans."

67. Luebke, *Germans in the New World*, 88.

68. Rippley, "Ameliorated Americanization," 225; Holli, "German-American Ethnic Identity," 107.

69. Luebke, *Germans in the New World*, xvii.

70. Harzig, "Germans."

71. Luebke, *Germans in the New World*, 57.

72. Ibid., 58–62.

73. Statistics from *International Migration and Naturalization*, Series C, 105, "Immigrants by Country: 1820 to 1970."

74. Holli, "German-American Ethnic Identity," 108; Hofmeister, *Germans of Chicago*, 125, 225.

75. Organizations such as the Carl Schurz Memorial Foundation, the Goethe Society of America, and the German-American Conference were primarily run by second- and third-generation German Americans, while new immigrants in the 1920s were much less interested in maintaining a common ethnic bond than their predecessors had been. Luebke, *Germans in the New World*, 69–70.

76. Charles Neely and John Webster Spargo, *Tales and Songs of Southern Illinois* (1938; Carbondale: Southern Illinois University Press, 1989), 5.

77. Steve Bense, email communication, July 21, 2016.

78. Similar reports of the era point to the centrality of the postwar years in the German-to-English shift. A curricular program, for example, for German-language Lutheran schools in the Midwest in 1930 stated,

> If we compare the current state of the German language in our circles with that of a decade ago, we find that in most areas, a significant change has taken place. English has displaced German. One sees that in our schools too. While earlier beginners mostly could still speak or at least understand German, the situation is now the opposite. The language of the land has become the language of our children. There are still language islands where the old order still holds, but this situation will change in such places with time. (From German: Vergleichen wir den gegenwärtigen Stand der deutschen Sprache in unsern Kreisen mit dem vor einem Jahrzehnt, so finden wir, dass sich in den meisten Gegenden ein bedeutender Umschwung vollzogen hat. Die englische Sprache hat die deutsche verdrängt. Das sieht man auch in unsern Schulen. Während früher die Anfänger zum großen Teil die deutsche Sprache sprechen oder doch verstehen konnten, so ist jetzt das Gegenteil der Fall. Die Landessprache ist die Muttersprache der Kinder geworden. Es gibt allerdings noch Sprachinseln, in denen die alte Ordnung herrscht, doch wird dieser Zustand an solchen Orten sich mit der Zeit ändern. (Source: E. Ebert and H. M. Zurstadt, *Lehrplan für den Unterricht in der deutschen Sprache in den lutherischen Elementarschulen und Anleitung für den Gebrauch desselben: Verabfaszt im Auftrage des Lehrplankomitees der Allgemeinen Schulbehörde der Synode von Missouri, Ohio und andern Staaten* [St. Louis, MO: Concordia Publishing House, 1930], 2.)

For more on the shift from German to English in the early twentieth century, with sharp focus on the sociohistorical context of contact-induced change, see Miranda Wilkerson, Mark Livengood, and Joseph Salmons, "The Socio-Historical Context of Imposition in Substrate Effects," *Journal of English Linguistics* 42 (2014): 1–23. On the learning of English among immigrants, see, for example, Alejandro Portes and Richard Schauffler, "Language Acquisition and Loss among Children of Immigrants," in *Origins and Destinies: Immigration, Race, and Ethnicity in America*, ed. Silvia Pedrazza and Ruben G. Rumbaut (Belmont, CA: Wadsworth, 1996), 432–43; Calvin Veltman, "The Status of the Spanish Language in the United States at the Beginning of the 21st Century," *International Migration Review* 24, no. 1 (1990): 108–23.

79. The absolute lowest period of immigration was during World War I.

80. Luebke, *Germans in the New World*, 173.

81. The United States had no official refugee policy in place at the time. Building off the 1921 Emergency Quota Act, the National Origins Act of 1924 had reduced immigration to the United States through a national origins quota (a system that wasn't abolished until 1965). While that quota favored immigrants from northern and western European nations, with Germany having one of the highest allotments under the act, the sheer number of German Jews fleeing Nazi persecution exceeded the limit. But that's not all. Statistics show that the authorized quota for Germany remained unfilled between the years 1933 and 1939, with only 74,130 (out of an authorized allotment of 183,112) German Jews receiving visas (Barbara L. Bailin, *The Influence of Anti-Semitism on United States Immigration Policy with respect to German Jews during 1933–1939* [master's thesis, City University of New York, 2011], 4, accessed August 16, 2017, http://academicworks.cuny.edu/cgi/viewcontent.cgi?article=1261&context=cc_etds_theses). Bureaucratic red tape exacerbated by Jewish antipathy and the fact that public opinion didn't favor increased immigration for fears that refugees would bring economic competition, promote communism, or be undercover Nazi agents were contributing factors. See Richard Breitman and Alan M. Kraut, *American Refugee Policy and European Jewry, 1933–1945* (Bloomington: Indiana University Press, 1987), 9; Richard Breitman and Alan M. Kraut, "Anti-Semitism in the State Department, 1933–44: Four Case Studies," in *Anti-Semitism in American History*, ed. David A. Gerber (Urbana: University of Illinois Press, 1986).

82. Parallels drawn between Europe's Jewish refugee crisis of the 1930s and early 1940s and subsequent humanitarian crises of the early twenty-first century are not without merit. As of the publishing of this book, the number of displaced persons is the highest since World War II. For contemporary discussions and historical comparisons of anti-refugee hysteria, see, for example, any of the following: Laura Tavares, "Text to Text: Comparing Jewish Refugees of the 1930s with Syrian Refugees of Today," *New York Times* Lesson Plans, accessed August 16, 2017, https://www.nytimes.com/2017/01/04/learning/lesson-plans/text-to-text-comparing-jewish-refugees-of-the-1930s-with-syrian-refugees-today.html?_r=0); Daniel Victor, "Comparing Jewish Refugees of the 1930s with Syrians Today," *New York Times*, November 19, 2015, accessed August 16, 2017, https://www.nytimes.com/2015/11/20/us/comparing-jewish-refugees-of-the-1930s-with-syrians-today.html; Ishaan Tharoor, "What Americans Thought of Jewish Refugees on the Eve of World War II," *Washington Post*, November 17, 2015, accessed August 16, 2017, https://www.washingtonpost.com/news/worldviews/wp/2015/11/17/what-americans-thought-of-jewish-refugees-on-the-eve-of-world-war-ii/?tid=sm_fb&utm_term=.53eac8ac142f.

83. While the groundwork for this legislation was laid by President Harry Truman (see his December 22, 1945, "Statement and Directive by the President on Immigration to the United States of Certain Displaced Persons and Refugees in Europe"), he signed it with reluctance, urging that "a fairer, more humane bill be passed" for concerns that this one had provisions that rendered many Jewish refugees (as well as others) ineligible for resettlement. The act was amended in 1950 to be more inclusive. Harry S. Truman,

"Statement by the President upon Signing the Displaced Persons Act," June 25, 1948, online by Gerhard Peters and John T. Woolley, The American Presidency Project, accessed August 16, 2017, http://www.presidency.ucsb.edu/ws/?pid=12942.

84. Holli, "German-American Ethnic Identity," 108.

85. "German American Bund," Holocaust Encyclopedia (Washington, DC: United States Holocaust Memorial Museum, 2016), accessed July 12, 2016, http://www.ushmm.org/wlc/en/article.php?ModuleId=10005684.

86. Biles, *Illinois*, 229.

87. While some resident aliens were targeted and a portion detained, the true victims of U.S. persecution during World War II were Japanese Americans.

88. Biles, *Illinois*, 231.

89. Compared to other ethnic groups in the nation's history, such as native people, enslaved Africans, Chinese, Mexicans, and so on, Germans were treated remarkably well and had an overall easy go at it in American society.

90. Willi Paul Adams, La Vern J. Rippley, and Eberhard Reichmann, *The German-Americans: An Ethnic Experience* (Indianapolis: Max Kade German-American Center, Indiana University–Purdue University at Indianapolis, 1993), accessed July 16, 2016, https://www.researchgate.net/publication/265201857_The_German-Americans_An_Ethnic_Experience.

91. Edward W. Fernandez, Nancy S. Sweet, Michael J. Levin, and Arthur R. Cresce, *Ancestry of the Population by State, 1980: 1980 Census of Population; Supplementary Report* (Washington, DC: U.S. Department of Commerce, Bureau of the Census, 1983), 15–32, accessed July 16, 2016, https://www.census.gov/population/www/censusdata/files/pc80-s1-10/tab03.pdf.

92. In regions like the mid-Atlantic, where eighteenth-century German immigrants largely settled, assimilation seemed to erase manifestations of German ethnic identity. See Kazal, *Becoming Old Stock.*

PROTECTING ENGLISH, PROMOTING AMERICANISM: BETTER SPEECH WEEK

1. For the scope of this section, important sources are Dennis Baron's blog post "National Grammar Day in Wartime" on the Web of Language, March 3, 2013, as found here: https://illinois.edu/blog/view/25/89120; H. G. Paul, "A Report on Better Speech Week," *The English Journal* 9, no. 4 (1920): 194–200; and *Primary Education* 27 (Boston: Educational Pub. Co., 1919): 604, accessed July 15, 2015, https://books.google.com/books?id=mWIVAAAAIAAJ&dq.

2. See, for example, Miranda E. Wilkerson and Joseph Salmons, "'Good Old Immigrants of Yesteryear' Who Didn't Learn English: Germans in Wisconsin," *American Speech* 83 (2008).

3. For more on that movement, see Elena Vesselinov, "Americanization," in *The Encyclopedia of Social Problems*, ed. Vincent N. Parrillo (Thousand Oaks, CA: Sage Publications), 44–45.

4. Chicago Women's Club Records, Chicago History Museum.

5. "A Brief History of National Grammar Day," *Grammarly*, accessed July 15, 2016, https://www.grammarly.com/blog/a-brief-history-of-national-grammar-day/?AT3572=3.

THE HANGING OF ROBERT PRAGER

1. This story has been covered elsewhere and much more substantively. The main sources we consulted while writing this piece were Frederick C. Luebke, *Bonds of Loyalty: German-Americans and World War I* (DeKalb: Northern Illinois University Press, 1974), chapter 1, and E. A. Schwartz, "The Lynching of Robert Prager, the United Mine Workers, and the Problems of Patriotism in 1918," *Journal of the Illinois State Historical Society (1998–)* 95, no. 4 (University of Illinois Press, 2002): 414–37, accessed August 16, 2017, http://www.jstor.org/stable/40193598.

2. Luebke, *Bonds of Loyalty*, 11.

3. Riegel changed his testimony after it was recommended that he be charged with murder. Luebke, *Bonds of Loyalty*, 20.

4. According to Luebke, it took forty-five minutes; according to others, twenty-five—Schwartz, "Lynching of Robert Prager," 417.

5. Peter C. Weber, "Ethnic Identity during War: The Case of German American Societies during World War I," *Nonprofit and Voluntary Sector Quarterly* 43, no. 1 (February 2014): 199.

6. Schwartz, "Lynching of Robert Prager," 422.

8. Heritage and Linguistic Landscape Today

1. John M. Coggeshall "'One of Those Intangibles': The Manifestation of Ethnic Identity in Southwestern Illinois," *Journal of American Folklore: Journal of the American Folklore Society* 99, no. 392 (1986): 203.

2. Edward Callery, *Place Names of Illinois* (Urbana: University of Illinois Press, 2009), eBook Academic Collection (EBSCOhost), EBSCOhost, accessed July 4, 2016.

3. Rudolph A. Hofmeister, *The Germans of Chicago* (Champaign, IL: Stipes Pub. Co., 1976), 5.

4. Douglas K. Meyer, "German Cottage Structure-Types in Southwestern Illinois," in *French and Germans in the Mississippi Valley: Landscape and Cultural Traditions*, ed. Michael Roark (Cape Girardeau, MO: Center for Regional History and Cultural Heritage, Southeast Missouri State University, 1988), 191–98; Coggeshall "One of Those Intangibles," 195.

5. The Belleville Historical Society in particular is working to restore historically significant architecture in Belleville. For images of still-standing German cottages, see http://bellevillehistoricalsociety.org/photos/.

6. Town of West Belleville and National Register of Historic Places, *National Register of Historic Places Registration Form: Town of West Belleville*, 2014, accessed July 5, 2016, https://www.nps.gov/nr/feature/places/pdfs/14000111.pdf; City of Belleville and National Register of Historic Places, *National Register of Historic Places Nomination*

Form: Belleville Historic District, 1974, accessed July 5, 2016, http://gis.hpa.state.il.us/pdfs/200698.pdf.

7. Melvin G. Holli, "German-American Ethnic Identity from 1890 Onward," *Ethnic Chicago: A Multicultural Portrait*, ed. Peter d'Alroy Jones and Melvin G. Holli (Grand Rapids, MI: W. B. Eerdmans Pub. Co., 1981), 94.

8. Hofmeister, *Germans of Chicago,* 251–59.

9. "German Restaurants: Illinois," germanfoods.org, accessed August 1, 2016, http://germanfoods.org/find/german-restaurants-illinois/. Many of these specialty food shops cater to recent immigrants from Europe more broadly rather than to an exclusively German population.

10. Steve Eighinger, "German Roots Run Deep in Quincy's History," *Quincy Herald-Whig*, June 27, 2015, accessed August 1, 2016, http://www.whig.com/story/29423683/german-roots-run-deep-in-quincys-history#.

11. "Chicago/Ill: The German Newspaper 'Amerika-Woche,'" DW, accessed August 1, 2016, http://www.dw.com/en/chicago-ill-the-german-newspaper-amerika-woche/a-297825.

12. "Brief History of Northwest Turners," American Turners Northwest Chicago, accessed August 1, 2016, http://www.northwestturners.org/aboutus/briefhistory.

13. "About the Verein," Schwaben Verein of Chicago, accessed August 1, 2016, http://www.schwabenverein.org/about.htm; "Resources and Helpful Links," DANK Chicago South and Suburbs, accessed August 1, 2016, http://www.dankchicagosouth.org/links.asp.

14. American Aid Society of German Descendants, accessed August 1, 2016, http://www.americanaidsocietyofgd.org/; Donauschwaben Society of Chicago, accessed August 11, 2016, http://www.donauchicago.com/.

15. "History of DANK," Deutsch Amerikanischer National Kongress, accessed August 11, 2016, http://www.dank.org/history/; DANK Haus German American Cultural Center, accessed August 11, 2016, http://dankhaus.com/.

16. "Goethe-Institut Chicago," Goethe-Institut USA, accessed August 11, 2016, https://www.goethe.de/ins/us/en/sta/chi.html?wt_sc=chicago.

17. "Maifest Celebrates Spring with German Traditions," *Peoria Journal Star*, May 12, 2011, accessed August 11, 2016, http://www.pjstar.com/x730839122/German-tradition; "About Us," German Society of Rockford, accessed August 11, 2016, http://germansocietyofrockford.org/.

18. "Meetings and Events," Schwaben Verein, accessed August 12, 2016, http://www.schwabenverein.org/events.htm; "About Maifest," Maifest Chicago, accessed August 12, 2016, http://www.mayfestchicago.com/; Oktoberfest Chicago, accessed August 12, 2016, http://oktoberfestchicago.org/.

19. Christkindlmarket Chicago, accessed August 12, 2016, http://www.christkindlmarket.com/; Belleville Christkindlmarkt, accessed August 12, 2016, http://www.bellevillechristkindlmarkt.com/; "Christkindlmarkt," The District, Quincy Illinois, accessed August 12, 2016, http://thedistrictquincy.com/promotion/christkindl-market/;

Christkindlmarket Naperville, accessed August 12, 2016, http://www.christkindlmarket.com/naperville/.

20. For more on the Bavarianization of German American culture, see Brent Peterson, "From *Kultur* to Cliché: German Americans and Ethnicity," Max Kade Institute, 1998, accessed August 13, 2016, https://mki.wisc.edu/sites/mki.wisc.edu/files/graphics/Peterson-From_Kultur_to_Clich%C3%A9.pdf. Also by Brent Peterson, *Popular Narratives and Ethnic Identity Literature and Community in Die Abendschule* (Ithaca, NY: Cornell University Press, 1992).

21. Michael K. Brinkman, *Quincy, Illinois, Immigrants from Münsterland, Westphalia, Germany* (Westminster, MD: Heritage Books, 2010), 173–74.

22. Coggeshall, "One of Those Intangibles," 185–86.

23. On the notion of symbolic ethnicity, the best starting points are Herbert J. Gans, "Symbolic Ethnicity: The Future of Ethnic Groups and Cultures in America," *Ethnic and Racial Studies* 2, no. 1 (1979): 1–20; Richard D. Albe, *Ethnic Identity: The Transformation of White America* (New Haven, CT: Yale University Press, 1990); and Mary C. Waters, *Ethnic Options: Choosing Identities in America* (Berkeley: University of California Press, 1990).

24. Gans, "Symbolic Ethnicity," 9.

25. The scholarship on ethnicity and identity is wide and varied. Good examples are Kathleen Neils Conzen et al., "The Invention of Ethnicity: A Perspective from the U.S.A.," *Journal of American Ethnic History* 12, no. 1 (Fall 1992): 3–41. Also by Conzen: "Mainstreams and Side Channels: The Localization of Immigrant Cultures," *Journal of American Ethnic History* 11, no. 1 (1991): 5–20; and "Phantom Landscapes of Colonization: Germans in the Making of a Pluralist America," in *The German-American Encounter: Conflict and Cooperation between Two Cultures, 1800–2000*, ed. Frank Trommler and Elliott Shore (New York: Berghahn Books, 2001), 7–21.

26. Nineteenth-century German immigrants had experience with the usefulness of ethnic group solidarity and nationalism as a means of fighting back against authoritarianism, both during the Napoleonic era and during the Revolution of 1848. Conzen et al., "The Invention of Ethnicity," 9, accessed April 7, 2016, http://www.jstor.org/stable/27501011.

27. James M. Berquist, "German-America in the 1890s: Illusions and Realities," in *Germans in America: Aspects of German-American Relations in the Nineteenth Century*, ed. E. Allen McCormick (New York: Columbia University Press, 1983): 3–4, 10.

28. In the case of Quincy and its sister city, Herford, many of Quincy's residents can trace their ancestry back to Herford, a source of chain migration in the mid-nineteenth century. Eighinger, "German Roots Run Deep."

29. The *Amerika-Woche* was published out of Chicago for decades, but it is now published in Pennsylvania. United States, Library of Congress, "Amerika-Woche," Chronicling America, accessed November 3, 2018, https://chroniclingamerica.loc.gov/lccn/sn83007175/; "Kontakt," *Amerika-Woche*, accessed November 3, 2018, https://amerikawoche.com/kontakformular/.

30. U.S. Census Bureau, American Community Survey 2009–2013, five-year estimates, table B04001, "First Ancestry Reported."

31. As late as the 1980s, Belleville's residents of German descent still butchered their own hogs for making sausage (to be eaten on special occasions) and made their own sauerkraut, potato pancakes, and traditional desserts. The grocery stores throughout the region even reflected the culture and traditions of its people by carrying plenty of sausage, for example, and stocking up on herring around New Year's, during which many families continued the custom of eating herring for good luck. Other German cultural habits included the predominance of beer and the tendency to eat the same meal on the same day of the week. Coggeshall, "One of Those Intangibles," 192–95. For the study, he interviewed sixty locals, mostly from Belleville, who ranged in age from twenty-five to ninety-three years.

32. Ibid., 183, 187. Indeed, postvernacular German has played a role in Illinois' language and culture. Building off of Jeffrey Shandler's notion of "postvernacular language" (*Adventures in Yiddishland: Postvernacular Language and Culture* [Berkeley: University of California Press, 2006]), Reershemius notes in her work (on formerly Low German–speaking communities in northern Germany) that some languages can "serve the purpose of identity building within a community even after they have ceased to be used as a vernacular for daily communication." Gertrud Reershemius, "Post-Vernacular Language Use in a Low German Linguistic Community," *Journal of Germanic Linguistics* 21, no. 2 (2009): 131.

33. Steve Bense, email communication, July 21, 2016.

34. The 1900 figure is based on the number of individuals either born in Germany or with at least one parent born in Germany. Christiane Harzig, "Germans," *Electronic Encyclopedia of Chicago*, Chicago Historical Society, 2005, accessed August 12, 2016, http://www.encyclopedia.chicagohistory.org/pages/512.html.

35. Hofmeister, *Germans of Chicago*, 10. The Poles surpassed Germans in terms of immigration to Chicago in the post–World War I years, though it wasn't until 1940 that they surpassed Germans for the state of Illinois overall. Jens Manuel Krogstad and Michael Keegan, "From Germany to Mexico: How America's Source of Immigrants Has Changed over a Century," *Fact Tank*, Pew Research Center, October 7, 2015, accessed August 12, 2016, http://www.pewresearch.org/fact-tank/2015/10/07/a-shift-from-germany-to-mexico-for-americas-immigrants/.

36. U.S. Census Bureau, "Table 63. Nativity and Language: 1980," *1980 Census of the Population*, vol. 1: *Characteristics of the Population: Illinois*, Ch. C.

37. U.S. Census Bureau, American Community Survey 2011–2015, five-year estimates, table B16001, "Language Spoken at Home by Ability to Speak English for the Population 5 Years and Over."

GERMAN EFFECTS ON ENGLISH IN THE MIDWEST

1. Many of these can be found in the *Dictionary of American Regional English* (*DARE*, 1985–2017), a collection of folk and regional terms used in American English. Also

of interest may be Luanne von Schneidemesser's article "Settlement History in the United States as Reflected in *DARE*: The Example of German," *American Speech* 77, no. 4 (2002): 398–418.

2. Take a look at this vowel chart to learn more: http://www.internationalphonetical phabet.org/ipa-sounds/ipa-chart-with-sounds/. The back-vowel English pronunciation can be heard by clicking on the "u" symbol (top right corner) whereas the front-vowel native pronunciation can be heard by clicking on the "y" symbol (top left corner). Even so, had this prefix been integrated orally, English speakers would have unrounded the umlaut, resulting in the pronunciation corresponding to the "i" symbol (which is next to the "y" symbol)—like what we've seen with surnames going from Müller to Miller.

3. Linguists have long ago revised the notion that regional dialects are vanishing. For readers interested in learning more about Midwestern dialects, including their areas and linguistic features, the go-to authority is the *Dictionary of American Regional English* (*DARE* 1985–2017). Frederic G. Cassidy and Joan Houston Hall, eds., *Dictionary of American Regional English*, 2013, accessed July 5, 2016, http://www.daredictionary.com.

4. Immigrant languages are only one of many potential sources of influence on local or regional speech patterns.

5. See "Bill Swerski's Super Fans: Da Bears in the Indy 500," *Saturday Night Live*, season 16, episode 20, May 18, 1991, NBC.com, accessed July 5, 2016, http://www.nbc .com/saturday-night-live/video/bill-swerskis-super-fans/n10085.

6. These examples are not strictly German either; other immigrant languages common to the Midwest, such as Polish and Dutch, have "stopping" and "devoicing" properties as well. For a nontechnical description of the Chicago dialect, consult Richard Cameron, "Words of the Windy City (Chicago, IL)," in *American Voices: How Dialects Differ from Coast to Coast,* ed. Walt Wolfram and Ben Ward (Oxford: Blackwell, 2006), 112–17.

7. See Joseph Salmons and Thomas Purnell, "Language Contact and the Development of American English," in *The Handbook of Language Contact,* ed. Raymond Hickey (Oxford: Blackwell, 2010), 454–77, for information on and references for "stopping" (4.1 interdental fricative stopping) and "devoicing" (4.2 final fortition) as it relates to regional varieties.

8. Jesse W. Harris, "German Language Influences in St. Clair County, Illinois," *American Speech* 23 (1948), 106–10. In stark contrast to what we know today about imposition, Harris ties these "peculiarities" to "people of limited education in the area" (108).

9. John M. Coggeshall, "'One of Those Intangibles': The Manifestation of Ethnic Identity in Southwestern Illinois," *Journal of American Folklore* 99, no. 392 (1986): 177–207.

10. Ibid., 189.

11. Those found in Harris's article are 3a, 4, and 5a, whereas those found in Coggeshall's are 1, 2, 3b, and 5b. One study in particular to consult on German imposition is Robert B. Howell, "German Immigration and the Development of Regional Variants in American English: Using Contact Theory to Discover Our Roots," in *The German*

Language in America, 1683–1991, ed. Joseph C. Salmons (Madison, WI: Max Kade Institute for German-American Studies, UW-Madison, 1993), 190–212. More literature on this topic can be found in Salmons and Purnell's, "Language Contact," 454–77.

12. There appear to be correlations, however, between the imposed features and the features contemporary Germans learning English as a second or foreign language find particularly challenging or difficult to acquire.

SELECT ANNOTATED BIBLIOGRAPHY

Abendpost. 1889–1950. Chicago: F. Glogauer & Co.

This successful Chicago-area German-language newspaper strived to be politically independent and eventually became one of the largest foreign-language papers in the Midwest. It lasted beyond World War II, making it a good source of information for the early and mid-twentieth centuries.

Adams, Willi Paul, La Vern J. Rippley, and Eberhard Reichmann. *The German-Americans: An Ethnic Experience*. Indianapolis: Max Kade German-American Center, Indiana University–Purdue University at Indianapolis, 1993.

Originally written in German for German audiences, this brief textbook-style overview of the history of Germans in America was translated and adapted for American audiences by the Max Kade Institute. It is divided into clear chapters and provides a chronology and bibliography at the end.

Anzeiger des Westens. 1835–98. St. Louis, MO: Carl Dänzer.

An important source of news for Germans in southwestern Illinois, the *Anzeiger des Westens* was the earliest German-language newspaper in St. Louis and enjoyed wide circulation during its heyday in the pre–Civil War period.

Baron, Frank. *Abraham Lincoln and the German Immigrants: Turners and Forty-Eighters*. Yearbook of German-American Studies, Supplemental Issue, vol. 4. Lawrence, KS: Society for German-American Studies, 2012.

This book examines the relationships of the Forty-Eighters and Turners with Abraham Lincoln as well as their wider involvement in American politics, with an eye toward answering the question of whether the German vote was responsible for electing Lincoln in 1860.

Biles, Roger. *Illinois: A History of the Land and Its People*. DeKalb: Northern Illinois University Press, 2005.

This excellent history of the state of Illinois contextualizes Germans' role in the settlement of the state as well as some of their more significant moments in state history, such as that of the Haymarket incident.

Bodnar, John. *The Transplanted: A History of Immigrants in Urban America*. Bloomington: Indiana University Press, 1987.

This general history of immigration provides a point of comparison between German immigrants and other immigrant groups. It includes information on the German labor movement in Chicago as well as German American religions.

Brakebill, Tina Stewart. "From 'German Days' to '100 Percent Americanism': McLean County, Illinois 1913–1918; German Americans, World War One, and One Community's Reaction." *Journal of the Illinois State Historical Society (1998–)* 95, no. 2 (2002): 148–71.

This article goes into some detail regarding the anti-German hysteria and its impact on the German American community during World War I, focusing on Bloomington and the surrounding area but also providing some larger geographic context. Written in the wake of the 9/11 attacks, it makes a direct comparison between the experience of German Americans during World War I and Muslim Americans after 9/11.

Brinkman, Michael K. *Quincy, Illinois, Immigrants from Münsterland, Westphalia, Germany*. Westminster, MD: Heritage Books, 2010.

This book is a first-rate source for genealogists with ancestors from the Quincy area. It provides detailed historical information regarding this substantially German town up through the present day.

Bruncken, Ernest. "German Political Refugees in the United States during the Period from 1815–1860." *Deutsch-Amerikanische Geschichtsblätter* 3, no. 3 (1903): 33–48.

This piece is no exception to the nationalistic rhetoric of many early historical accounts about German immigrants, but it is nonetheless useful as a primary source documenting German American ethnic consciousness at the turn of the twentieth century.

Bungert, Heike. "Regional Diversity in Celebrating Regional Origin: German-American Volksfeste, 1870–1920." In *Regionalism in the Age of Globalism*. Vol. 2, *Forms of Regionalism*, edited by Lothar Hönnighausen, Anke Ortlepp, James Peacock, and Niklaus Steiner, 93–115. Madison, WI: Center for the Study of Upper Midwestern Cultures, 2005.

This chapter is a good source on German American regional festivals or *Volksfeste*, which helped solidify German identity in America.

Carrier, Lois A. *Illinois: Crossroads of a Continent*. Urbana: University of Illinois Press, 1998.

Though not as strong in German-specific history as Biles's *Illinois*, Carrier's work treats contextual history on subjects such as settlement and industrialization.

Chicago, Illinois, Department of Development and Planning. *Historic City: The Settlement of Chicago*. Chicago: Department of Development and Planning, 1976.

This book is primarily valuable for its detailed maps showing German (and other group) settlement patterns in Chicago over time.

Chicagoer Arbeiter-Zeitung. 1877–1931. Chicago: Socialistic Pub. Society.

A publication of the Socialist Labor party, this radical newspaper was widely read in its time and provides perspective on German involvement in the labor movement.

Coggeshall, John M. "'One of Those Intangibles': The Manifestation of Ethnic Identity in Southwestern Illinois." *Journal of American Folklore* 99, no. 392 (1986): 177–207.

A folklorist, Coggeshall interviewed sixty German Americans in St. Clair County in the mid-1980s and detailed their responses in this article. His study reveals much about surviving cultural practices at the time as well as how German Americans identified themselves and each other.

Conzen, Kathleen N. "Ethnicity as Festive Culture: Nineteenth-Century German America on Parade." In *The Invention of Ethnicity*, edited by Werner Sollors, 44–76. New York: Oxford University Press, 1989.

A renowned scholar in immigration and ethnicity, Conzen provides here a useful introduction to the centrality of German American celebrations in the formation of German ethnic identity in the United States.

Crawford, James. *At War with Diversity: US Language Policy in an Age of Anxiety.* Clevedon: Multilingual Matters, 2000.

In this collection of essays, Crawford provides an excellent introduction to language policy and its historical connection to xenophobia and anti-immigrant sentiment. The first essay, "Anatomy of the English-Only Movement," was of particular interest in writing this book. Readers are encouraged to check out Crawford's language policy website: http://www.languagepolicy.net/index.html.

Cutler, Irving. *Chicago: Metropolis of the Mid-continent*. Carbondale: Southern Illinois University Press, 2006.

Published "under the auspices of the Geographic Society of Chicago," this book explores Chicago through a geographical lens. The chapter on Europeans and their settlement patterns includes a concise history of the Germans of Chicago as well as Chicago's Jewish population, including German Jewish history.

Duden, Gottfried. *Report of a Journey to the Western States of North America, and a Stay of Several Years along the Missouri (During the Years 1824, 1825, 1826, and 1827)*, general editor James W. Goodrich; edited and translated by George H. Kellner, Elsa Nagel, Adolf E. Schroeder, and W. M. Senner. Columbia: University of Missouri Press, 1980.

This seminal 1829 publication by Duden inspired Germans to immigrate to the Midwest in droves. The 1980 edition by the University of Missouri Press includes an introduction describing the book's background and significance.

Faust, Albert B. *The German Element in the United States: With Special Reference to Its Political, Moral, Social, and Educational Influence*. 2 vols. Boston: Houghton Mifflin, 1909. Accessed October 31, 2016, https://archive.org/details/germanelementin07fausgoog.

The first volume of this early work traces the history of Germans in America, while the second one documents their "favorable" influence on American society. Faust's filiopietistic interpretation of German American history is significant in that it influenced ethnic identity and pride at the time of its writing.

Freitag, Sabine. *Friedrich Hecker: Two Lives for Liberty*. Edited and translated by Steven W. Rowan. St. Louis, MO: St. Louis Mercantile Library, 2006.

Freitag's biography is perhaps the best work documenting the life of Friedrich Hecker, arguably the most famous Forty-Eighter to settle in Illinois. It also provides a useful discussion of the antebellum and postbellum periods in the state.

Frizzell, Robert W. "Migration Chains to Illinois: The Evidence from German-American Church Records." *Journal of American Ethnic History* 7, no. 1 (University of Illinois Press, 1987): 59–73, http://www.jstor.org/stable/27500562.

Focusing on church records in the central Illinois cities of Bloomington, Peoria, and Quincy, this article explores the phenomenon of "chain migration" and settlement patterns. Frizzell compares his findings with that of Walter D. Kamphoefner's chain migration research in Missouri (see pp. 70–105 of his *Westfalians*).

Fulbrook, Mary. *A Concise History of Germany*. 2nd ed. Cambridge: Cambridge University Press, 2004.

This overview of German history aids the reader in understanding the political, economic, and religious "push" factors that inspired Germans to immigrate to America. It also clarifies the country's shifting geographies over time.

Furer, Howard B. *The Germans in America, 1607–1970: A Chronology & Fact Book*. Dobbs Ferry, NY: Oceana Publications, 1973.

This book offers a detailed timeline of German American history up to the 1970s.

Gates, Paul W. *The Illinois Central Railroad and Its Colonization Work*. Cambridge, MA: Harvard University Press, 1934.

Based on the Illinois Central Railroad's extensive archives now in the holdings of the Newberry library in Chicago, this book is still the most detailed secondary source on the Illinois Central's role in settling Illinois, providing information on its very successful efforts to attract German immigrants to Illinois.

Gems, Gerald. "The German Turners and the Taming of Radicalism in Chicago." *International Journal of the History of Sport* 26 (2009): 1926–45.

This history of the Chicago Turners focuses on the group's political history, starting with their early connection to radical and labor movements and tracing it through a period of assimilation and political moderation in the early twentieth century.

Gross, Jacob. "A German Family in Chicago: 1856." *Chicago History* 4, no. 10 (1956): 309–17.

This letter, written by Jacob Gross in 1856 and published in 1956, describes a German family's experience immigrating to Chicago, including the journey to America, economic circumstances and employment, and impressions of Chicago.

Güney, Ülkü. "German Ethnic Identity in Chicago before and during the First World War." ***Journal of Faculty of Letters*** **32, no. 1 (Ankara: Hacettepe University, 2015): 151–62.**

This history of Chicago Germans in the late nineteenth and early twentieth centuries uses German-language newspapers to analyze changes in German ethnic identity in the early twentieth century. The article focuses on the rise of German nationalism in the late nineteenth century as well as the negative impacts of the anti-anarchist hysteria (the Red Scare) and World War I on Chicago's German community.

Harris, Jesse W. "German Language Influences in St. Clair County, Illinois." ***American Speech*** **23 (April 1948): 106–10.**

This article documents the persistence of the German language and German speech patterns in southwestern Illinois in the years following World War II. Harris discusses German place names and lists specific German words still commonly used by the population at the time, and also gives examples of speech patterns and phrases derived from German.

Harzig, Christiane. "Creating a Community: German-American Women in Chicago." In ***Peasant Maids—City Women: From the European Countryside to Urban America*****, edited by Christiane Harzig. Ithaca, NY: Cornell University Press, 1997.**

This chapter examines the experiences of women from rural Mecklenburg who immigrated to Chicago in the 1800s. In addition to providing essential information on German American women and families, the chapter also describes neighborhood life in German American Chicago more broadly.

———. "Germans." Electronic Encyclopedia of Chicago. Chicago Historical Society, 2005. Accessed July 1, 2016, http://www.encyclopedia.chicagohistory.org/pages/512.html.

A very brief overview of the history of Germans in Chicago, this well-written synopsis hits all of the salient points and serves as a nice introduction to the topic.

Hoelscher, Steve. ***Heritage on Stage: The Invention of Ethnic Place in America's Little Switzerland.*** **Madison: University of Wisconsin Press, 1998.**

For discussion on tourism and its role in the construction of ethnic identity and place in the twentieth century, this book offers a splendid analysis. While the focus is on New Glarus, Wisconsin (a former Swiss colony), Hoelscher's insights are nevertheless generalizable to ethnic communities in Illinois and beyond.

Hofmann, Annette R. "The American Turners: Their Past and Present." ***Revista Brasileira De Ciências Do Esporte*** **37, no. 2 (2015): 119–23.**

This is a good summary of Turner history in America. Though not focused particularly on Illinois, it provides a good background for those interested in the organization and how it helped German Americans maintain their culture for a significant portion of their history.

Hofmeister, Rudolf A. *The Germans of Chicago*. Champaign, IL: Stipes Pub. Co., 1976.

This much-cited book provides a traditional history of Chicago's German population. While emphasizing description over analysis, it includes a good deal of relevant information and is one of the only books entirely dedicated to the history of Illinois Germans.

Holli, Melvin G. "German-American Ethnic Identity from 1890 Onward." In *Ethnic Chicago: A Multicultural Portrait*, edited by Peter d'Alroy Jones and Melvin G. Holli, 93–109. Grand Rapids, MI: W. B. Eerdmans Pub. Co., 1995.

Holli, who has written other articles on the German experience in Chicago, here provides a traditional narrative of the decline of German culture in Chicago in the twentieth century, focusing on the rise of a strong German American middle class and the subsequent decline of Germans' involvement in labor politics. He also describes Germans' strong influence on Chicago culture prior to World War I and the effect of the war on German American culture. Most significantly, he provides information about Chicago's German American community during the post–World War I years, a subject missing from much of the literature.

Howell, Robert B. "German Immigration and the Development of Regional Variants of American English: Using Contact Theory to Discover Our Roots." In *The German Language in America, 1683–1991*, edited by Joseph C. Salmons, 190–212. Madison, WI: Max Kade Institute for German-American Studies, UW-Madison, 1993.

Though not focused solely on Illinois, this paper has relevance to areas such as Chicago and central and southwestern Illinois. It explores the influence of German on regional American English dialects in areas such as these with historically large German American populations.

Illinois Staats-Zeitung. 1862–1922. Chicago: IL. Brentano.

This German-language newspaper from Chicago enjoys a prominent place in the history of Germans not just in Illinois but in the Midwest overall. Politically moderate, it was often at odds with the Socialist *Chicagoer Arbeiter-Zeitung* during the labor conflicts of the late-nineteenth century.

Jentz, John B., and Richard Schneirov. *Chicago in the Age of Capital: Class, Politics, and Democracy during the Civil War and Reconstruction*. Urbana: University of Illinois Press, 2015.

This in-depth look at Chicago from the 1850s through the 1870s provides valuable insight into the experiences of German industrial workers in Chicago during that period.

Kamphoefner, Walter D. "At the Crossroads of Economic Development: Background Factors Affecting Emigration from Nineteenth-Century Germany." In *Migration across Time and Nations: Population Mobility in Historical Contexts*, edited by Ira A. Glazier, Luigi De Rosa, and the International Economic History Congress, 174–201. New York: Holmes & Meier, 1986.

This chapter, as the title bears out, provides an analysis of the economic factors "pushing" Germans to emigrate.

———. "The German-American Experience in World War I: A Centennial Assessment," *Yearbook of German-American Studies* 49 (2014): 3–30.

Here Kamphoefner examines German American opinions and attitudes during World War I. He presents the German American World War I experience as more nuanced than is often portrayed, and he examines their experiences as enlisted men as well as on the home front. His focus is mainly on Germans in Middle America, including some discussion of Illinois.

———. "German Americans: Paradoxes of a 'Model Minority.'" in *Origins and Destinies: Immigration, Race, and Ethnicity in America,* edited by Pedraza, Silvia, and Rubén G. Rumbaut, 152–60. Belmont, CA: Wadsworth, 1996.

Kamphoefner explodes the prevailing "model minority" myth that Germans were assimilationists. Their actions, as this chapter makes empirically clear, supported linguistic and cultural preservation. Particularly helpful in the writing of this book was the section on geographic concentration, which debunks the image of the German American as primarily agrarian.

———. "German-Americans and Civil War Politics: A Reconsideration of the Ethnocultural Thesis." *Civil War History* 37, no. 3 (1991): 232–46.

Kamphoefner's article discusses the successes and failures of the so-called "ethnocultural" theory of nineteenth-century politics, which asserts that religious background was closely tied to political affiliation. Though he mainly offers praise for the theory, his major criticism is with the failure of its proponents to account for variations between the states. He specifically discusses Illinois as one of the states in which Germans did in fact vote overwhelmingly for Lincoln in 1860. See also: Luebke, Frederick C., ed. *Ethnic Voters and the Election of Lincoln.* Lincoln: University of Nebraska Press, 1971.

———. *The Westfalians: From Germany to Missouri.* Princeton, NJ: Princeton University Press, 1987.

A major reason for German emigration in the nineteenth century was socioeconomic, particularly as cottage industries (e.g., linen-weaving) in northern regions like East Westphalia were drying up. Kamphoefner pulls together extensive data on this, and the explanations given apply equally well to those immigrants who chose to settle in Illinois.

Kamphoefner, Walter D., and Wolfgang Johannes Helbich. *Germans in the Civil War: The Letters They Wrote Home.* Chapel Hill: University of North Carolina Press, 2006.

This collection of letters from the Bochum Immigrant Letter Collection at Ruhr University-Bochum documents the experiences and attitudes of ordinary German Americans during the Civil War era. It explores the differences between the Forty-Eighters and more recent immigrants who often participated in the war for economic rather than ideological reasons. The introduction here provides context and nuance to an often-simplified subject, and several of the letters included are written by Illinois Germans.

Kamphoefner, Walter D., Wolfgang Helbich, and Ulrike Sommer. *News from the Land of Freedom: German Immigrants Write Home*. Documents in American Social History. Translated by Susan Carter Vogel. Ithaca, NY: Cornell University Press, 1991.

This excellent book of published primary-source material draws from the Bochum Immigrant Letter Collection at Ruhr University-Bochum. The background introduction provides a fine overview of the German immigrant experience in America, and a number of letters in the collection were written by immigrants either settling in or passing through Illinois.

Kaufmann, Wilhelm. *The Germans in the American Civil War*. Edited by Don Heinrich Tolzmann, Werner D. Mueller, and Robert E. Ward. Translated by Steven Rowan. Carlisle, PA: John Kallmann Publishers, 1999.

This is an important study of historical significance written in German for a central European audience on German ethnic participation in the war. Thanks to the editors and keen translation by Steven Rowan, it is now accessible to a wide range of readers.

Kazal, Russell A. *Becoming Old Stock: The Paradox of German-American Identity*. Princeton, NJ: Princeton University Press, 2004.

Though focused on Philadelphia Germans, this book is an important contribution to the discussion on cultural pluralism, ethnic assimilation, and racial identity in the first half of the twentieth century.

Keil, Hartmut, and John B. Jentz, eds. *German Workers in Chicago: A Documentary History of Working-Class Culture from 1850 to World War I*. Urbana: University of Illinois Press, 1988.

This book of published primary-source material includes letters, newspaper articles, images, organizational records, and more. Also included are strong analytic introductions to each source, describing the day-to-day lives of Chicago's working-class Germans during the industrial revolution as well as events such as the Haymarket incident. The significant role that Chicago's German immigrants played in the labor movement and the reasons behind this are also addressed.

———. *German Workers in Industrial Chicago, 1850–1910: A Comparative Perspective*. DeKalb: Northern Illinois University Press, 1983.

This is an essential resource on working-class Germans in Chicago as compared with other cities elsewhere in the United States. Arising out of the "Chicago Project" based at the American Institute of the University of Munich, it provides a wealth of data and information regarding occupations, working-class neighborhoods, industrialization, and political activity among a group that, prior to this initiative, had been largely overlooked.

Keller, Christian B. *Chancellorsville and the Germans: Nativism, Ethnicity, and Civil War Memory*. New York: Fordham University Press, 2007.

This book offers a detailed description and astute analysis of the Battle of Chancellorsville and its effect on the German American troops of the Eleventh Corps and beyond.

Körner, Gustav Philipp. *Memoirs of Gustave Koerner, 1809–1896: Life-Sketches Written at the Suggestion of His Children*. 2 vols. Edited by Thomas J. McCormack. Cedar Rapids, IA: Torch Press, 1909. Accessed August 1, 2017, https://archive.org/details/mcmoirsofgustave01inkr, https://archive.org/details/memgustave02khorrich.

Gustav Körner's memoir, originally written for his descendants and later published in two volumes, is available online in its entirety. It covers every aspect of his life, public and private, and includes accounts of his journey to America, his time in Missouri, and settling in Illinois.

Krogstad, Jens Manuel, and Michael Keegan. "From Germany to Mexico: How America's Source of Immigrants Has Changed over a Century." Fact Tank. Pew Research Center, October 7, 2015. Accessed August 12, 2016, http://www.pewresearch.org/fact-tank/2015/10/07/a-shift-from-germany-to-mexico-for-americas-immigrants/.

Here the Pew Research Center illustrates through a set of compelling dynamic maps the changes in immigration to the United States over time.

Levine, Bruce. *The Spirit of 1848: German Immigrants, Labor Conflict, and the Coming of the Civil War*. Urbana: University of Illinois Press, 1992.

This study interweaves central themes during the Civil War period: immigration, industrialization, class formation, and antebellum politics. Particularly noteworthy is Levine's treatment of the free-soil movement of the 1850s, the founding of the Republican Party, and the onset of the Civil War.

Luebke, Frederick C. *Bonds of Loyalty: German-Americans and World War I*. DeKalb: Northern Illinois University Press, 1974.

This major source on the impact of World War I on German Americans begins with a detailed account of the hanging of Robert Prager and goes on to describe German American culture leading up to the war (1870–1914). Then, month by month, Luebke analyzes the escalating anti-German sentiment that accompanied World War I and how the German community reacted to it.

———. *Germans in the New World: Essays in the History of Immigration*. Statue of Liberty–Ellis Island Centennial Series. Urbana: University of Illinois Press, 1990.

Several of these essays help flesh out the history of Germans in the United States, including information on World War I and the twentieth century, politics, settlement, and the Turner society.

Max Kade Institute for German-American Studies. Accessed October 31, 2016, http://mki.wisc.edu/.

An interdisciplinary unit in the College of Letters and Science at the University of Wisconsin-Madison, the institute supports research and outreach on German American history, language, and culture. Their website is commendable for providing a network of free and credible resources on German immigrants and their descendants in the Midwest.

Meyer, Douglas K. *Making the Heartland Quilt: A Geographical History of Settlement and Migration in Early Nineteenth-Century Illinois*. Carbondale: Southern Illinois University Press, 2000.

This book concerns itself with the processes and patterns of early migration to Illinois. Relying almost entirely on 1850 census data, Meyer maps the settlement of four migrant groups (Upland Southerners, New Englanders, Midland-Midwesterners, and foreigners). The geographical configuration and related discussion of German immigrants in early Illinois are of particular interest (pp. 232–41).

Modern Language Association. "The Modern Language Association Language Map." Accessed August 20, 2017, https://apps.mla.org/map_main.

Using data from the U.S. Census and the American Community Survey, the MLA Language Map is a nifty and easy-to-use tool for learning more about the linguistic and cultural composition of the United States (or any specific state selected).

The Newberry. "Chicago Foreign Language Press Survey." Accessed October 16, 2016, http://flps.newberry.org/.

Originally a project of the U.S. Federal Works Progress Administration in the 1930s, this collection of translated newspaper articles from Chicago's ethnic press is available through the website of the Newberry library. It covers the 1860s through the 1930s and includes selected articles from the *Illinois Staats-Zeitung*, the *Abendpost*, and the *Chicagoer Arbeiter-Zeitung*, as well as several other newspapers relevant to this book.

Pickle, Linda Schelbitzki. *Contented among Strangers: Rural German-Speaking Women and Their Families in the Nineteenth-Century Midwest*. Urbana: University of Illinois Press, 1996.

This book is a must-read for those interested in learning more about the roles and actions of rural German-speaking women in the Midwest during the nineteenth century.

Reinhart, Joseph R. *Yankee Dutchmen under Fire: Civil War Letters from the 82nd Illinois Infantry*. Kent, OH: The Kent State University Press, 2013.

This book is a collection of sixty-one letters written over a period of three years by immigrants—mostly native Germans—serving in the Eighty-Second Illinois Volunteer Infantry Regiment under the command of Friedrich Hecker.

Rowan, Steven W. "Gustav Koerner Attacks Gottfried Duden in 1834: Illinois against Missouri?" Presented at the 33rd Annual Symposium of the Society for

German-American Studies, New Ulm, MN, April 17, 2009. Accessed May 24, 2014, http://www.gustavekoerner.org/FINAL%20Rowan%20New%20Ulm%20paper%20.pdf.

This brief paper describes a pamphlet written by Gustav Körner in 1834, five years after Duden's famous *Report of a Journey* was published. Körner, after a disappointing trip to Missouri, refuted Duden's portrayal of the state as an ideal location to settle and criticized its climate, agriculture, and the fact that it was a slave state. Körner, who lived in Belleville, urged Germans to settle instead in Illinois.

Salamon, Sonya. *Prairie Patrimony: Family, Farming, and Community in the Midwest.* Chapel Hill: University of North Carolina Press: 1995.

In her extensive analysis of contemporary Illinois farm families of German and Anglo-American descent, Salamon deepens our understanding of the intersection of agriculture, culture, and ethnicity in the shaping of farming practices, family patterns, and land tenure.

Salmons, Joseph. "Community, Region, and Language Shift in German-Speaking Wisconsin." In *Regionalism in the Age of Globalism.* Vol. 2, *Forms of Regionalism.* Edited by Lothar Hönnighausen, Anke Ortlepp, James Peacock, and Niklaus Steiner, 133–44. Madison, WI: Center for the Study of Upper Midwestern Cultures, 2005.

World War I has long been made the scapegoat for the deterioration of German language and culture in America, but in this and related work (see also Joseph Salmons, "The Shift from German to English, World War I and the German-Language Press in Wisconsin," in *Menschen zwischen zwei Welten: Auswanderung, Ansiedlung, Akkulturation*, ed. Walter G. Rödel and Helmut Schmahl [Trier: Wissenschaftlicher Verlag Trier, 2002], 179–93), Salmons sets the record straight. Using various social, economic, and educational indicators, he presents a model of shift to English in German American communities that ties in with Roland Warren's theory of "Great Change."

Savage, James P. "Do-It-Yourself Books for Illinois Immigrants." *Journal of the Illinois State Historical Society (1908–1984)* 57, no. 1 (1964): 30–48. http://www.jstor.org/stable/40190077.

This article describes mid-nineteenth-century books advising immigrants on the process of settling in Illinois. It also examines the considerable role of the Illinois Central Railroad in the settlement of the state.

Schneider, Dorothee. *Trade Unions and Community: The German Working Class in New York City, 1870–1900.* Urbana: University of Illinois Press, 1994.

Though focused on New York rather than Illinois, Schneider's book gives broad context to German American working-class culture, particularly the role of the *Vereine* in working-class political life.

Schubert, Cornelius. "The Diary of Cornelius Schubert." Translated from the German by Mrs. Henry Klump Sr. and Miss Mary Klump, 1937. Folder 6,

Schubert Family papers, C3005, the State Historical Society of Missouri Manuscript Collection.

Schubert's account of his immigration journey from Dessau to Belleville is both engaging and enjoyable to read. In the space of thirty-five typed pages, he brings to life many of the efforts and challenges described in chapter 3 of this book. Both the original and the translation are available at the State Historical Society of Missouri.

Shaw, Stephen Joseph. *The Catholic Parish as a Way-Station of Ethnicity and Americanization: Chicago's Germans and Italians, 1903–1939*. Brooklyn, NY: Carlson Pub., 1991.

For those interested specifically in Chicago's German Catholic population, this book provides extensive information on German Catholic culture in that city from the mid-nineteenth century onward. The book describes Catholic Church leaders and their relationship with German immigrants, the culture of various parishes in the city, and the church's role in cultural preservation and assimilation.

Skilnik, Bob. *Beer: A History of Brewing in Chicago*. Fort Lee, NJ: Barricade Books, 2006.

Skilnik serves up a colorful book-length treatment of Chicago's brewing industry, including its bearing on social history.

Smith, Carl. "Dramas of the Haymarket." Chicago Historical Society and Northwestern University, 2000. Accessed February 3, 2016, http://www.chicagohistoryresources.org/dramas/overview/over.htm.

The Chicago Historical Society has created an extensive website on the Haymarket Affair, using primary sources and numerous essays to provide context and narrative for understanding this important episode in the history of Chicago.

Spahn, Raymond Jürgen. *German Accounts of Early Nineteenth Century Life in Illinois*. Edwardsville: Southern Illinois University at Edwardsville, 1978.

This article explores in depth the early nineteenth-century literature that played a role in attracting German immigrants to Illinois.

Tolzmann, Don Heinrich. *Illinois' German Heritage*. Milford, OH: Little Miami Pub. Co., 2005.

Tolzman, who is prominent in Illinois' German heritage community, provides here a brief overview of German American history in Illinois along with some descriptions of significant settlement areas (southern Illinois, central Illinois, and Chicago) and biographies of some renowned German Americans in Illinois history. The focus throughout is on significant German American family names, making this book useful to genealogists.

Trommler, Frank, and Elliott Shore, eds. *The German-American Encounter: Conflict and Cooperation between Two Cultures, 1800–2000*. New York: Berghahn Books, 2001.

Part 1 of this edited volume explores "The German Part of American History" and includes chapters by numerous scholars important to the study of German American history, including Kathleen Neils Conzen, Hartmut Keil, and James M. Bergquist. Topics explored include education, German American identity, politics, and religion.

Trommler, Frank, and Joseph McVeigh, eds. *America and the Germans: An Assessment of a Three-Hundred-Year History*. 2 vols. Philadelphia: University of Pennsylvania Press, 1985.

This two-volume anthology of forty-nine essays focuses on the broader German American experience rather than that of specific regions. It also describes the relationship between America and Germany over time.

U.S. Census Bureau. "American Factfinder." Accessed August 1, 2016, http://factfinder2.census.gov.

The Census Bureau's website provides opportunities for investigation of countless social and demographic phenomena in the United States over time, including information on immigration, language, and ancestry. American Factfinder allows for the creation of data sets, graphs, maps, and more from modern census and American Communities Survey data.

"U.S. Newspaper Directory." Chronicling America. Library of Congress. Accessed October 16, 2016, http://chroniclingamerica.loc.gov/search/titles/.

A search in the Library of Congress's Newspaper Directory reveals numerous German-language newspapers throughout the state of Illinois beginning in the mid-nineteenth century. This is the most comprehensive directory of library newspaper holdings, and it provides not only information about which towns had German-language papers and when but also which libraries hold the microfilm of these papers.

Voss-Hubbard, Mark. *Illinois's War: The Civil War in Documents*. Athens: Ohio University Press, 2013.

This book of published primary source documents not only provides the reader with a good overview of Illinois' role in the Civil War but also includes some materials relevant to Illinois Germans.

Walker, Mack. *Germany and the Emigration: 1816–1885*. Cambridge, MA: Harvard University Press, 1964.

This book offers readers and historians a thorough consolidation of the factors influencing nineteenth-century German emigration. While the narrative interweaves American history only somewhat, the value of Walker's work is that it situates the causes for and reactions to emigration within the broader scope of German history. For a concise discussion of the German emigration streams, see also the first chapter ("Germany, German States, and Germans") of Stanley Nadel's *Little Germany: Ethnicity, Religion, and Class in New York City, 1845–80* (Urbana: University of Illinois Press, 1990).

Wilkerson, Miranda E. and Joseph Salmons. "'Good Old Immigrants of Yesteryear' Who Didn't Learn English: Germans in Wisconsin." *American Speech* 83, no. 3 (2008): 259–83.

Wilkerson and Salmons show in their analysis of quantitative data from the 1910 census, supplemented by qualitative evidence from a range of sources, that German immigrants to Wisconsin were not quick to abandon German and learn English. These findings can be generalized to other Midwestern states where German immigrants put down roots during the mid- to late nineteenth century. For further discussion of historical patterns of English learning among immigrants, see work by Teresa Labov, "English Acquisition by Immigrants to the United States at the Beginning of the Twentieth Century," *American Speech* 73 (1998): 368–98; and Walter D. Kamphoefner, "German American Bilingualism: Cui Malo? Mother Tongue and Socioeconomic Status among the Second Generation in 1940," *International Migration Review* 28, no. 4 (1994): 846–64.

Wittke, Carl Frederick. *German-Americans and the World War (with Special Emphasis on Ohio's German-Language Press)*. Columbus: Ohio State Archaeological and Historical Society, 1936.

This book, written between the world wars, was influential in its telling of the anti-German hysteria during World War I. Though later research shows the changes in German American culture in the early twentieth century to be more complex than Wittke portrays, this book is nevertheless an excellent narrative of the experiences of the German American community written at a time when the war was still recent memory.

———. *The German-Language Press in America*. Lexington: University of Kentucky Press, 1957.

This book has long been the standard reference on the subject of America's German-language press. While modern historians may find it dated, Wittke's commentary on the press in relation to historical events and within the context of German immigration was very helpful in writing this book.

Wyman, Mark. *Immigrants in the Valley: Irish, Germans, and Americans in the Upper Mississippi Country, 1830–1860*. Chicago: Nelson-Hall, 1984.

This book provides a useful analysis of the early German immigration and settlement experience, including push and pull factors for immigration, travel literature, chain migration, settlement patterns, and the clashes between American Protestant culture and German religious traditions.

INDEX

Page references with *f* or *n* indicate figures or notes, respectively.

Achtundvierziger. *See* Forty-Eighters
Adams County, 26
Adler, Dankmar, 135
Adler des Westens, 100
agriculture, 160n18. *See also* farmers; farms
alcohol, 65, 75. *See also* beer; prohibition; temperance
ales, Chicago, 72
Allgemeine Auswanderungszeitung, 21, 152n20
Als Arbiter in Amerika (Kolb): on bicycle factory work, 63–66, 163n2; on brewery working conditions, 66–71, 163nn3–5
Altgeld, John P., 94, 108, 125
Altlutheraner (Old Lutherans), 13
Alton, Illinois, 24*f*, 26
American Aid Society of German Descendants, 136–37
American Bottom settlers, 1, 23, 24*f*, 149n1
American Community Survey, 139*f*, 140
American Defense Society, 118
American Federation of Labor, 91
American Party, 75. *See also* nativists and nativism
Amerika-Woche, 139, 186n29
Amish, German language among, 113, 175n1 ("Shift")
anarchists and anarchist organizations, 83, 84, 117
Anglo-Americans: cultural relationship to the land, 52, 160n20; German culture compared with culture of, 3; German immigrant marriages compared with marriages among, 160n13; on Germans as "clannish," 160n23; in Illinois, inconsistent slavery views among, 165n16; taverns and, 164n6; use of term, 149n8
Antwerp, Belgium, as port of departure, 33
Anzeiger des Westens (St. Louis newspaper), 32
apprenticeships, 13
architecture, German imprint on, 134–36, 135*f*, 184n5
Argentina, Germans settling in, 150n1
art, Chicago's German culture and, 107
Austria or Austrian Empire, 6, 8, 14, 16
"Auszug aus den Gesetzen des Staats Illinois" (Körner), 100

Baden, Germany, 12, 86, 88
Baetz, Michael, Franziska, and Joseph, 6*f*, 9
Bairisch dialect, 9
Baltimore, 35, 36*f*, 37, 42

Baptists, German immigrant, 95
Bauer, Johann, 22, 97
Bavaria: artisans and skilled workers from, 57; census page for Baetz family from, 6*f*; cultural traditions, 137; German Jews settling in Chicago from, 27
beer: bicycle factory work and, 65; as big business in Chicago, 73; brewery work and, 68; Chicago Beer Riot and, 76; German immigrant soldiers and, 81; German imprint on, 136; National German-American Alliance and, 115; nativist bigotry and, 75–76. *See also* brewers and brewing industry
Beer: A History of Brewing in Chicago (Skilnik), 73
beer halls, 106–7, 172n57
Belleville, Illinois: German cultural habits in, 187n29; German press in, 100; historic architecture in, 135f, 184n5; industries, 56; Körner home in, 32; Schubert's journey to, 38–42. *See also* American Bottom settlers
Belleviller Beobachter, 100
Belleviller Zeitung, 32
Belleville Teachers' Institute, 106
Bennett Act, Wisconsin, 112
Bense, Steve, 126–27
Better Speech Week, 129–30, 130f
bicycle factory work, 63–66
biological superiority theories, 109–10, 174nn73–75
"Black Tom Island" munitions depot explosion (1916), 116–17
Bloomington, Illinois, German press in, 100
Bonfield, John, 91
Boone, Levi, 76
Bornhold, H. F., 43, 45, 46
Bottomlands, settlers in, 1, 23, 24*f*, 149n1
Brazil, Germans settling in, 150n1
Bremen, as port of departure, 33
brewers and brewing industry: in Chicago, 72–74; in Chicago, work in, 66–71; on Chicago's Northwest Side, 59; German domination of, 53, 58, 61; Prohibition and, 124; workday for, 68. *See also* beer
Bunsen, Georg, 29, 106, 152n11
Bunsen, Gustav, 152n11
Bunsen School (Nichols Community Center), 106
Burleson, Albert, 119
Burschenschaft (German student organization), 30
Busch & Brand (brewery), 72
businesses, German: in Chicago, 61–62, 62*f*; small, on Chicago's North Side, 58. *See also specific types of businesses*
Busse, Fred, 108

Call (Münch and Follenius publication), 28–29
Canada, Germans settling in, 150n1
canals, 35, 36*f*. *See also* Erie Canal; Illinois and Michigan Canal; Ohio & Erie Canal
Carlsbad Decrees, 12, 14
Carriage of Passengers Act (1855), 157n6
Castle Garden, New York, 158n12
Catholics: chain migration by, 9; disputes on language of services for, 111; German, insularity of, 96; German, World War I and, 121; German American, identifying as American, 85; German immigrants, 25, 95; nativism and, 75; Protestant takeover of Rhineland and, 13; Republican Party, 1860 election and, 77; schools, Diversey and, 74
census, 6, 6*f*, 8–9, 10, 149n3
chain migration, 9, 186n28
Chancellorsville, Battle of, 81–82, 88
Chicago: bicycle factory, 63–66; brewing industry, 72–74; brewing industry work,

66–71; de-Germanized street names in, 122–23; demographic changes, 141, 143; eight-hour workday movement in, 91; German American industries in, 54–56; German Catholics in, 25, 28, 95; German ethnic neighborhoods in, 58–60, 59*f*; German immigrants (1860–1900) and population of, 56, 161–62n37; German Jews in, 26–27, 60; German place names in, 134; German press, 100; Haymarket Affair, 84–85; immigrant voters mobilized in (1856), 76–77; industry dispersal in, 66; literacy of German immigrants to, 97; National German-American Alliance, 115, 116; nativism in, 75; North American Turner Bund Festival, 105*f*; rail travel and, 37; Revolution of 1848 and immigration to, 26; settling in, 26–28, 27*f*; skilled and unskilled German workers in, 57; Turner society, 103; winter temperatures, 70, 163n4; World War I anti-German sentiment in, 121–22, 122*f*. *See also specific neighborhoods*
Chicago Abendpost, 116
Chicago Arbeiterverein (workers' organization), 84
Chicago Beer Riot, 76
Chicagoer Arbeiter-Zeitung (Workers' Newspaper), 84, 91, 94, 108
Chicago Fire (1871), 26, 55, 61, 73, 135–36
Chicago Heights industries, 56
Chicago Symphony Orchestra, 107, 122
Chicago Volksfreund, 100
Chicago Women's Club, 129
children, working, 52, 58
cholera, shipboard, 34, 43–44, 47
church records, as historical sources, 10
Cincinnati, Ohio, 54–55, 89, 103
citizenship requirements, nativists on, 75
civil service reform, 88
Civil War, U.S.: agricultural productivity during, 56–57; Eleventh Corps defeat and, 81–82; German immigrant regiments in, 78–79, 166n22; Hecker joins, 87–88; immigration decline during, 17; Körner's support of Union during, 32; letters home from, 80–81. *See also* Forty-Eighters; Hecker, Friedrich; Union Army
clothing, Chicago unskilled manual labor and, 70–71
clubs and societies (*Vereine*), 101–3, 121, 125
Coggeshall, John M., 145
Columbia, Illinois, 25
Committee on Public Information (CPI), 118
Compulsory School Attendance Law (1883), 112
Congress, American passenger laws of, 157n6
Conrad Seipp Brewing Co., 74
consonants, German pronunciation of, 10
Contented among Strangers (letters), 50–51
Cook County, 141–42, 155n59
county histories, as historical sources, 10
craft occupations, 12, 13, 17, 53, 58. *See also* industrialization
Creel, George, 118
crop failures (1840s), 14–15
cultural and institutional life: clubs, festivals, and the arts, 101–7; education, 97–99; ethnic privilege and pride, 108–10; language, 107–8; the press, 100–101; religion, 95–96; shift from German to English, 111–13
Czech Republic, German territory (1800s) now in, 6

Declaration of Independence, Lincoln on, 89, 90
Democratic Party, 31, 77, 125, 164n9, 168n3 ("Lincoln")

Deutsch Amerikanischer National Kongress (DANK), 137
Der Deutsche Auswanderer, 21
Das deutsche Element in den Vereinigten Staaten von Nordamerika 1818–1848 (Körner), 32
Deutsche Gesellschaft von Chicago, 38
Devon, Illinois, 27
diary, Schubert's, 38–42, 158n1
Dillingham Commission, 174n74
Displaced Persons Act, 126*f*, 127, 182–83nn82–83
Diversey, Michael, 72, 74
division of labor, 60, 63–64
Donauschwaben Society of Chicago, 136
Downer, Bemis & Company (brewery), 72
"Dreißiger," 14. *See also* Thirtiers
Duden, Gottfried, 20–21, 23, 25, 28, 154n40
"Dutchy" accent, 145–46

eastern European immigrants. *See* Europe
economic depression, as push factor, 13
Edelweiss (meatpacking plant), 61
Edict of 1812, 151n2
education, 19, 97, 106, 170nn19–20. *See also* schools
Edwards Law (1889), 112
eight-hour workday, 83, 84, 91, 94
Eighty-Second Illinois Volunteers, 79, 79*f*, 80–82, 88, 166n30
Einstein, Albert, 102
elections: 1860, 11, 77–78, 164n9, 168n6 ("Lincoln"); 1873, 166n35; Chicago, 1856, 77
Eleventh Corps (the "German Corps"), defeat of, 81, 88
Emancipation Proclamation, 88
Emigrant Guides, 38
emigration applications, 9–10, 33
Engel, George, 91, 92
Engelmann, Theodore, 30, 152n11
English language: avoided as school subject, 98; Better Speech Week, 129–30, 130*f*; classes, Turners offering, 105; German effects in Midwest on, 143–46, 188nn3–4; German immigrants in isolated areas and, 52–53, 108–9, 160nn22–23; replacing German, 114; shift from German to, 111–13, 175n1 ("Shift"), 176nn4, 6–7, 181n78
Erie Canal, 18, 31, 36*f*, 37, 157n5, 158n4
Ernst, Ferdinand, 154n39
Espionage Act (1917), 118–19
ethnic privilege and pride, 108–10, 172n54. *See also* Turner societies
Europe: eastern, Yiddish-speaking Jews from, 150n12; geographical boundary shifts in, 6; southern and eastern, emigrants from, 18, 114; southern and eastern, immigrants in Chicago, 60–61
Everhart, 39

Die Fackel (The Torch), 84
families, German, 51, 58. *See also* farmers; women
famine, as push factor, 12
farmers: encouraged to emigrate, German population and, 14–15; German, outnumbering other immigrant groups as, 51; German land policies as impetus to emigrate by, 13, 151n3; Hecker's start in U.S. as, 87; in Illinois (1890), 155n61; pre–World War I years and, 114; rich soil of Illinois attracting, 20; second wave of emigration and, 17
farms: already established, German preferences for, 48; Illinois, descriptions of, 49–50, 159n8; life on, 50–53; machinery, 50, 159n10; productivity factors, 160n17; starting costs, 49; urban industrialization and, 56–57

fatigue, Chicago unskilled manual labor and, 70–71
Faust, Albert, 74
Feehan, Patrick A., 111
Felsenthal, Bernhard, 85, 167n46
festivals, 106, 137, 143
Fielden, Samuel, 91–92
Fischer, Adolph, 91, 92
Follenius, Paul, 28–29
food, Germans and, 122, 136, 144, 185n9
Fornero, James, 131
Forty-Eighters (Achtundvierziger): after the Civil War, 82–85; Civil War and, 79, 166n22; German newspapers launched by, 100; as "the Grays" or "the Greens," 19, 156n1; Lincoln's election and, 77; opposition to the South by, 88; political organizing by, 84; Republican Party and, 164n9; Revolution of 1848 and, 172n50; seeking political refuge in the U.S., 16–17; in St. Clair County, 25; Turner clubs and, 103, 104. *See also* Hecker, Friedrich
Forty-Third Illinois Volunteers, 79
Four Minute Men, 118, 120
Fraktur (printed Gothic type), 98–99, 99*f*, 171n28
France: political and socioeconomic upheaval (1848), 16; revolution (1830), 14; settlers in Illinois from, 1, 149n1
Franco-Prussian War, 18
Frankfurter Wachensturm (1833), 14, 30
Franklin, Benjamin, 174n76
freedom of association, 19
Freeport, Illinois, industry in, 56
Free School Idea, 106
Free Society of Teutonia, 128
Free Thinkers, 95, 169n4
Der Freiheitsbote für Illinois, 100
Freitag, Sabine, 87–88
Frizzell, Robert, 25
Fullerton, Illinois, 27
Galena, Illinois, 26, 35
Gans, Herbert, 138
Garden State of the West, Illinois as, 20
Gem City. *See* Quincy, Illinois
Gemütlichkeit, spirit of, in beer halls, 106–7
genealogy, 138
General Land Office, 48
German Aid Society, 38, 107
German American Bund, 128
German-American Citizens League (*Deutsch-Amerikanische Burgerbund*), 125
German American Historical Society, 102, 110
German Americans: after World War I, 125–26; fear of conspiracy against America by, 118–20; National German-American Alliance and, 115; on Nazis, 128; symbolic ethnicity and, 138, 186n26; treatment of other U.S. ethnic groups vs., 183n89. *See also* Catholics; German emigration; German immigrants; German Jews; Germans
German-American Summerfest, 136
German Columbia Club, 136
German Confederation, 5–6, 7*f*, 12, 16, 25–26, 86. *See also* Germany
German culture: after World War I, 125–26, 180n75; celebration of, 107, 125, 136–37; Illinois State Council of Defense and, 119–21; nativist fears and, 3, 4–5; pre–World War I years and, 114. *See also* cultural and institutional life
The German Element in the United States (Faust), 74
German emigration: attitudes about and governmental response to emigration, 152n13; first wave (1845–60), 14–15, 14*f*, 17; newspapers and, 17, 152n20; nineteenth-century sources of, 14–16, 16*f*, 17, 153n23; options for, 157n1; pull factors, 18–26; push factors, 12–18;

German emigration (*continued*)
Schubert's diary of, 38–42; second wave (1861–79), 14*f*, 17; start and end date variations for, 152n12; third wave (1880–99), 14*f*, 17–18, 61, 153n25; transatlantic ship conditions, 33–35, 34*f*
Germania Club, 101–2, 117, 124; Women's, 136
German immigrants: abuse and exploitation of, 37–38, 44–46; after World War I, 125; on American women, 50–51; Chicago election of 1856 and, 77; denying their heritage, census and, 124; eighteenth-century, assimilation and, 183n92; ethnic privilege and pride of, 109–10, 172n54; farm or town selection preferences, 48; German regional antagonisms and, 69; identifying as American, 85; Illinois settlement patterns, 23, 24*f*; labor unions and, 84; letters home on benefits for, 22–23; Lincoln's election and, 77–78; nativism and, 75–76, 164n2; Nazis' rise and, 126*f*, 127, 182n82; positive perceptions of, 150n9; registration with U.S. government requirements, 119; urban industry and, 56; voting and, 164n7; World War I and, 181n79. *See also* Catholics; German Americans; German Jews
German Jews: assimilation fears in U.S., 175n77; in Chicago, 26–27, 60; in Eighty-Second Illinois Volunteers, 79; emigration patterns, 15, 151n7; German Confederation discrimination against, 12, 151n2; German immigration patterns and, 8, 150n13; Germany's Imperial Constitution and, 153n28; identifying as American, 85; as minority of immigrants, 95, 169n4; Nazis' rise and, 127, 182nn82–83; political refuge sought by, 152n18. *See also* Reform Jews
German language: after World War I, 124, 125; *Bairisch* dialect of, 9; codeswitching and lexical borrowing with, 127; dialects, teaching Standard German and, 98; English in the Midwest and, 143–46; German education standards and, 97–98, 170nn21–22; imposition of, 144–45, 188n8, 189n12; Lincoln campaign materials in, 90; nativist fears and, 3, 4–5; postvernacular, in Illinois, 187n32; pride in, 108–9; as primary language in Midwestern communities, 52–53, 160nn22–23; pronunciation, 10; religious institutions and, 96; schools and, 96, 169–70n14, 170–71nn25–26; shift to English from, 111–13, 175n1 ("Shift"), 176nn4, 6–7, 181n78; spoken at home (2015), 142*f*, 143; variations, German heritage and, 140–41; World War I and, 120–21, 179n49
German-language literature: Germania Club's collection of, 102; on organized German state in upper Mississippi Valley, 28–29; on U.S. and the Midwest, 20–21, 154n39, 154n42. *See also* newspapers, German-language
The German-Language Press in America (Wittke), 100
Germans: census records on demographic characteristics of, 8–9; geographic distribution and population density (1870), 2*f*; German speakers referred to as, 8; nineteenth-century migration patterns in U.S., 1–2, 3; push and pull factors in migration of, 2–3. *See also* Illinois Germans
German Settlement Society of Philadelphia, 29
German taverns, Anglo-American taverns compared with, 76, 164n6
Germantown, Illinois, 13

Germany: cultural reputation of, 110, 174–75nn73–6, 175n81; education standards in, 97; National German-American Alliance and, 116; political unification (1866–71), 7*f*; Reformed Church and Lutherans in, 96; unification (1871), 18, 89; unification wars (1864, 1866, and 1870), 17
Giessen Emigration Society, 28–29, 39
Gilded Age, 82–85
Goethe Institute of Chicago, 137
Goldbeck, Fritz, poem by, 102
Gothic type, of German texts, 98–99, 99*f*
Grays, 19, 156n1. *See also* Thirtiers
Great Change theory, 111
Great Depression, 101, 130
Greens, 19, 156n1. *See also* Forty-Eighters
Gregory, Thomas, 133
Griffith, Captain, of the *Medora*, 39, 40, 41
Gross, Jacob, 15–16, 54
gymnasiums (*Turnhalle*), 104

Haas, William, 61, 72
Haas & Sulzer Brewery, 72
Hambacher Fest (1832), 14
Hamburg, as port of departure, 33, 34
Harriersand (island), in Weser River, Germany, 38–39
Harris, Jesse W., 145
Haymarket Affair: advertisement for, 93*f*; anti-labor perspective on, 167n44; events of, 91–94; harassment of German radicals and, 84–85; "revenge" flyer for, 92*f*
Hecker, Arthur, 88
Hecker, Friedrich: carte-de-visite of, 86*f*; Civil War and, 87–88, 168n3 ("Hecker"); emigration from German Confederation, 17, 87; as Lincoln and Republican Party supporter, 77; political activism of, 86; post–Civil War American politics and, 88–89; Republican Party and, 87–88; Union Army regiments formed in name of, 79, 88. *See also* Forty-Eighters
Hecker Rifles Regiment, 79, 88
heritage tourism, German ancestry and, 138, 143
Hermann, Missouri, 29
Hesing, Anton, 166n35
Hildebrand, Frederick, 46
History of St. Clair County, 48
Hoffmann, Francis A., 20, 77–78
Holli, Melvin G., 124
Holy Roman Empire, 6*f*
Homestead Act, 48
Hooker, Joseph, 81
Howard, 34
Huck, John, 72
Hudson River, 36*f*, 157n5
Hungarians, Civil War and, 166n23
Hungary, German territory (1800s) now in, 6
"hungry forties," food shortages during, 14–15
Hyde Park, Chicago, 60
hygiene, Chicago unskilled manual labor and, 70–71
hyphenism, criticism of, 116

Illinois: constitution of, 106, 175n1 ("Bunsen"); as free state, 19; German ancestry in, 138–40, 139*f*; German place names in, 134; German voters in, 164n7; immigrants to, population growth and, 14–15, 14*f*; immigrants to, top five countries of birth among, 140*f*; nineteenth-century migrants to, 1–2, 2*f*, 4; nineteenth-century population increases in, 18; overland migration routes to, 36*f*; percentage Germany immigrants living in (1870), 55*f*, 56; population and demographics (1850), 1, 149n3; postvernacular

Illinois (*continued*)
German in, 187n32; sister cities in Germany and, 138, 186n28; water migration routes to, 36*f*
Illinois and Michigan Canal, 24*f*, 26, 54
Illinois Central Railroad (ICR), 20, 24*f*, 48–49, 50, 154n38
Illinois Constitutional Committee, 106
Illinois Germans, 77, 117, 124, 164n9, 165n19
Illinois Republican State Convention, 31
Illinois Staats-Zeitung: defending Germany's Kaiser (1914), 116; demise of, 124; German immigrant on Union Army service, 78–79; on Haymarket Affair, 94; launching of, 100; Lincoln financing of, 78, 165n15
Illinois State Board of Education, 106
Illinois State Council of Defense (SCD), 119–21
Illinois State Normal School, 106
immigrant-authored accounts, issues with, 10–11
Immigrants in the Valley, 23
imposition, in languages, 144–45, 188n8, 189n12
indentured servants, 13
industrialization: bicycle factory work and, 63–66; brewery work and, 66–71; in Chicago by 1890, 26; division of labor, devaluation of skills and, 60; German emigration and, 12; Gilded Age and, 82; hand production decline and, 13; second wave of emigration and, 17; spread of, 151n5. *See also* Chicago; craft occupations; working class
Industrial Revolution, 56, 73
inflation, as push factor, 12
inheritance system, partible, German emigration and, 12
International Workers' Day, 94
Irish immigrants, 62, 75, 77, 111, 164n2

Jacob Rehm & Company (brewery), 72
Jahn, Friedrich L., 103
Jahn, Helmut, 136
Japanese Americans, 183n87
Jentz, John B., 58
Jews. *See* German Jews
Jo Daviess County, 26, 140
John A. Huck Brewing, 72, 73
Johnson, Moses, 131
Joliet, Illinois, 56
Joseph Schlitz Brewing, 73

Kandern, Battle of, 86–87
Kansas-Nebraska Act (1854), 31, 87, 89
Kaskaskia, Illinois, 1, 149n1, 153n31
Kassner, Frederick, 44
Keil, Hartmut, 58
Know Nothings, 75–76, 78, 89–90
Kolb, Alfred: on bicycle factory work, 63–66; on brewery work, 66–71
Körner, Gustav, 30*f*; "Auszug aus den Gesetzen des Staats Illinois," 100; Hecker and, 87; immigration to U.S., 14, 29–31, 157n4 ("Körner"); as Lincoln supporter, 77; name spelling variations, 156n2; surname pronunciation, 10
Körner, Sophie Englemann, 30–31
Körner Regiment, 79
Kruetgen, Ernest J., 117
Kurrent (cursive English type), 99, 99*f*, 171n28

labor inequities, 82, 91–94, 166–67n35
labor unions, 83–84, 101
La Follette, Robert, 125
lager beer, Chicago, 72, 73, 74
Lager Beer War, 76
lakes, migration by, 35, 36*f*, 37
landownership: eighteenth century challenges with, 1, 149n2; by German immigrants, 62; and stewardship, German immigrants and, 51–52, 160nn18, 20–21

land policies, German, as push factor, 13, 151n3
languages other than English spoken at home, 141*f*, 188nn6–7. *See also* German language
"Latin" settlements, 25, 155n49
Lee, Robert E., 81
Le Havre, France, as port of departure, 33
Leibnitz, New York Immigration Commission on, 43–47
Leo XIII, Pope, 111
Liberal Republican movement, 82
Liberty bonds, 120, 123
Lill, William, 72
Lill & Diversey Brewery, 72, 73
Lincoln, Abraham, 11, 31–32, 77–78, 89–90
Lincoln Club, 117, 124
liquor licenses for taverns, Know Nothings and, 76, 164n5
literacy rates, immigrants and, 97, 170n17
literature: Chicago's German culture and, 107. *See also* German-language literature
loanwords, 144, 187–88nn1–2
Louis Philippe, King of France, 16, 86
Lowden, Frank O., 132–33
lower class, 12, 58
lower-middle class, 12, 15–16, 58
Luebke, Frederick, 5, 110, 125
Lutherans: anti-German incidents against, 123–24; chain migration by, 9; Evangelical Synod of North America, 96; German, insularity of, 96; German immigrants as, 95; language used in services by, 112, 176n4; Missouri Synod, 13, 85, 96; World War I and, 121

Madison County, 25
Main River, migration by, 13
marriage issues, 13, 151n6, 160n13
Massachusetts Two Years' Amendment, 90
McCormick, Cyrus, 55
McCormick Reaper Works, 91
McKinley, William, 65
meals, boardinghouse, 68
meatpacking industry, 61
Mecklenburg, Germany, 17–18, 43
Medora, Schubert's journey aboard, 39–42
Mennonites, 85, 96, 113, 121, 175n1 ("Shift")
Methodists, 95, 96
Metzler, J. D., 123–24
Meyer, Oscar F., 61
middle class: as anti-labor and anti-radical, 85; Chicago neighborhoods of, 58; desire for reform and change among, 19; German immigrants and, 62; Grey Forty-Eighters and, 155n1 ("Grays vs. Greens"); Hecker on expansion of, 87; National German-American Alliance and, 115; second-generation Germans among, 62; Turner societies and, 103. See also *Illinois Staats-Zeitung*
Military Tract, 24*f*, 26
Milwaukee brewers, 73
minimum wage, 69–70
Minnesota, Germans in, 1860 election and, 77
missionaries, in Illinois, 25
Mississippi River, 35, 36*f*, 157n5
Missouri: German group settlement ideals and, 28, 29; German regiments, Illinois Germans joining, 165n19; Germans in, 1860 election and, 77; Körner correcting Duden's view of, 32; Körner on slavery and not settling in, 31; as land of opportunity, Duden on, 20–21; as slave state, Illinois as alternative to, 23, 25
Missouri Compromise (1820), 31, 89
Missouri–Southern Illinois Division, National German-American Alliance, 115

Moline, Illinois, 56
Monroe County, 25
Morris, Nelson, 61, 163nn59–60
Münch, Friedrich, 28–29, 39
Mundelein, George William, 111–12
music, 99, 107, 121–22, 125, 179n49. *See also* singer societies

Napoleon, Jewish emancipation under, 151n2
National German-American Alliance, 115–16
National Grammar Day, 130
National Guard, labor unrest and, 83
National Register of Historic Places, 32
National Road, migration by, 24*f*, 35, 36*f*
National Security League, 118
nativists and nativism, 3, 4–5, 31, 75–77, 104, 115. *See also* political parties
Nazis, 126*f*, 127, 128
Neckar River, migration by, 13
Neely, Charles, 125–26, 127
New Orleans, 35, 36*f*, 37
newspapers, German, emigration trade and, 17, 152n20
newspapers, German-language: ceasing publication before World War I, 114; in Chicago, 139; Diversey and, 74; Englemann and, 152n11; English adopted for, 121, 124; German culture and, 100, 108; as historical sources, 10, 11; Körner and, 32; leftist movements and, 85, 171n35; shift from German to English and, 112–13; socialist, 84; Trading with the Enemy Act and, 119; on World War I, 117. *See also specific newspapers*
New York, as port of entry, 35, 36*f*, 158n12
New York Immigration Commission, *Leibnitz* report by, 43–47
Nichols Community Center (Bunsen School), 106
Nordamerikansicher Turnerbund (North American Gymnastic Union), 104
North Side neighborhood, Chicago, 27, 58, 61, 76, 164n5
Northwest Ordinance (1787), 153n31
Northwest Side (Ward 14), Chicago, 28, 59

occupations, of German immigrants, 53, 161n24
Ogden, William, 72
Oglesby, Richard, 93
Ohio, slavery and formation of, 153n31
Ohio & Erie Canal, 36*f*, 157n5
Ohio River, 31, 36*f*, 37, 157n5
Order of the Star-Spangled Banner, 75
organizational records, as historical sources, 10
overalls, for brewery work, 67–68
overtime, Chicago unskilled manual labor and, 70

Palatinate, famine and inflation in, 12
Panic of 1873, 17, 57, 83
Parsons, Albert, 93
passenger lists, as historical sources, 10
Pennsylvania, Germans settling in, 29
People's Party, 166–67n35
Peoria, Illinois: German American clubs in, 137; German press in, 100; liquor industry in, 56; migration to, 24*f*; Revolution of 1848 and immigration to, 26; Turner society in, 103
personal letters and diaries, as historical sources, 10, 38–42
Peru, Illinois, 26
Pestalozzi, Johann Heinrich, 106
Philadelphia, as port of entry, 35, 36*f*, 37
Phil Best & Company (brewery), 73
physical education, as academic subject, German promotion of, 99

physical fitness, American Turners on, 104
Pickle, Linda Schelbitzki, 159n11
picnics, 106, 107
"Der Pilot," of *Allgemeine Auswanderungszeitung*, 152n20
Poland, German territory (1800s) now in, 6
police, Chicago, nativists on appointments to, 76
Polish immigrants, 6, 109, 187n35
Polish language, 188n6
political news, German press on, 100
political parties: German-led, after the Civil War, 83, 166–67n35; Germans and, 108; in Germany, *Vereine* and, 101. *See also* Democratic Party; Republican Party; Whig Party
Pomerania, 17–18
Pope, Dr. (St. Louis), 98
population increases: in Chicago and Illinois 1845–1900, 1–2, 18, 26, 56, 161–62n37; in Germany, farmers encouraged to emigrate and, 14–15; in Germany, marriage law restrictions and, 13, 151n6
potato blight (1840s), 14–15
Prager, Robert Paul, 131*f*; hanging of, 131–33, 184nn1, 4 ("Prager")
professional work, German immigrants and, 60
prohibition, 76, 77, 101, 115, 124. *See also* temperance
propaganda, World War I, 117–18
Protestant churches, 25, 75, 95, 164n2, 169n2
Prussia, 16, 17–18, 96, 151n3
public office, nativists on requirements for, 75
pull factors, 3, 18–26
Pullman, George, 55
push factors, 2–3, 12–18
Quigley, James, 111
Quincy, Illinois: anti-German sentiment in, 123; German Americans in World War I from, 117; German press in, 100; Herford as chain migration source for, 186n28; marriages within heritage groups in, 23; migration route to, 35; occupations of German immigrants to, 161n24; Revolution of 1848 and immigration to, 26; Saint James Lutheran Church, 25; Wagner's farm near, 49*f*
Quincy Journal, 108

race-based superiority theories, 110, 174–75nn73–6
railroads: general strike against (1877), 83, 83*f*; in Illinois, 161n31; immigrants to Illinois and, 18–19; industrialization and, 56, 57; land sales by, 20, 154n38; migration by, 24*f*, 35, 36*f*, 37
Randolph County, 25, 125–26, 140
Raster, Hermann, 100
reading Gothic type vs. roman type, 98–99, 99*f*
Reformed Church, German Lutherans and, 96
Reform Jews, 96, 150n12. *See also* German Jews
Reisen im Nordwesten der Vereinigten Staaten, 20
religion: as academic subject, German opposition to, 99; English adopted for, 121; freedom of, as push factor, 13; German immigrants and, 95–96; identifying as American and, 85
Report on a Journey to the Western States of North America (Duden), 20–21, 28, 32, 154n40
Republican Party: Germans voting for, 82, 125, 164n9, 168n6 ("Lincoln"); Hecker and, 87–88; Illinois, Schneider

Republican Party (*continued*) and, 78; Körner joins, 31; Lincoln and, 89–90; nativist attitudes and anti-Catholic rhetoric of, 77
Revolution of 1848, 16, 25–26, 152n17
Rhine River, migration by, 13
Riegel, Joseph, 131, 133, 184n3 ("Prager")
rifle shooting societies (*Schützenvereine*), 102
rivers: migration by, 18, 24*f*, 36*f*
roads: migration by, 24*f*
Rockford, Illinois, 56, 137
Roeder, John Leonard, 108
roman type of American texts, 98–99, 99*f*
Rotterdam, Netherlands, as port of departure, 33
rural communities, 123, 125. *See also* American Bottom settlers; farmers; farms
Russia, 6, 151n4
Rynders, John, 123

safety equipment, brewery lack of, 69
Saint James Lutheran Church, Quincy, 25
Sand's Ale Brewing Company, 72
Sängerbunde, 102. *See also* singer societies
Saturday Night Live, "Bill Swerski's Superfans" skit, 144–45
Scandinavians, Civil War and, 166n23
Schaack, Michael, 167n44
Schlitz, Joseph, 73
Schmieding, August Heinrich, 25
Schneider, George, 77, 78
Schneider, John, 72
schools: Catholic, Diversey and, 74; English adopted for, 121; German, in Chicago, 98; public, Germans and, 97, 98, 99; shift from German to English and, 112, 176nn6–7, 181n78
Schroeder, Adolf E., 29
Schubert, Cornelius, diary, 38–42, 158n1
Schützenvereine (rifle shooting societies), 102
Schwaben Verein, 136
scientific racism, 110, 174nn74–75
screw propeller, steamships and, 157n4 (chap. 3)
Second Hecker Regiment, 79, 88
Sedition Act (1918), 119
Seipp, Conrad, 74
Seipp & Lehman (brewery), 72, 73
Shawnee Hills, 1. *See also* American Bottom settlers
Siebel, John E., 73–74
Siebel Institute of Technology (Zymotechnic Institute), 73–74
Siegel, John H., 131
Sieveking, Carl, 34–35
Sigel, Franz, 88
singer societies (*Sängerbunde*) or singing clubs, 102, 107, 138, 172n43
Sinnhuber, Karl A., 6
Skilnik, Bob, 73
slaves and slavery: German press on abolition of, 100; Hecker's opposition to, 87; in Illinois, 19, 153n31; Körner's observations of, 31, 157n5; Lincoln on, 90; Midwestern states' formation and, 153n31; Turner society opposition to, 104
Sloman, Robert M., 43, 47
Socialistischer Turnerbund von Nordamerika (Socialist Gymnastic Union of North America), 104
Socialist Labor Party, 167n41
socialist organizations, 83, 117, 131, 133
Socialist Party, German membership in, 84
Sokol, among Czechs, 171n45
southern European immigrants. *See* Europe
South Side (Ward 5) , Chicago, 28, 60, 76, 164n5

Southwest Side, Chicago, German neighborhoods, 59
Spanish speakers, in Illinois, 141*f*, 143
speech islands, in Europe, 6
Spies, August, 91, 92
Springfield, Illinois, 26, 56, 100
St. Clair County: after World War I, 125–26; Bunsen as superintendent of public schools in, 106; farm description (1889), 50, 159n8; German ancestry in, 140; German immigrants to, 25; German language influences in, 145
steamboats or steamships, 13, 33, 35, 36, 157n4 (chap. 3)
Stein-Hardenberg reforms, 151n3
Stern des Westens, 100
Steuben Society of America, 125
St. Louis, Missouri, 54–55, 89, 98
St. Marie, Illinois, 25
Stock, Frederick, 122
strikes, 83, 83*f*, 91, 131
Struve, Gustav, 86
suburbs, Chicago, transportation improvements and, 60–61
suffrage laws, 19, 89, 90, 101, 153n32. *See also* voting
Sulzer, Konrad, 61, 72
Sundays, beer drinking on, 76, 81
Switzerland, 6, 14
symbolic ethnicity, 138

taxes, in Illinois vs. German states, 20
temperance, 76, 77, 101, 104. *See also* prohibition
Teutopolis, Illinois, 25
Texas, Germans settling in, 153n32
theater, 107, 125
Third Missouri Volunteer Regiment, 88
Thirtiers ("Dreißiger"): German newspapers launched by, 100; as "the Grays" (1848), 19; Hecker as irritation to, 87; Lincoln's election (1860) and, 77; opposition to the South by, 88; seeking political refuge, 14; in St. Clair County, 25
Thomas, Theodor, 107
Tonk Manufacturing Company workers (1893), 62*f*
trades. *See* craft occupations
Trading with the Enemy Act (1917), 119
trains. *See* railroads
transportation, 18–19, 56, 60–61. *See also* canals; railroads; rivers; roads
True, Captain, 44, 46
Truman, Harry S., 182–83n83
Turner societies (*Turnverein*): Bund Festival in Chicago (1869), 105*f*; emphasizing patriotism of, 124; German, split in, 172n50; on German customs and traditions, 102–4; mid-1880s class of, 103*f*; Northwest club, 136; political agendas, 104; on public school reform and change, 99; reforming select American institutions and, 105
Twenty-Fourth Illinois Volunteers, 79, 88, 166n23
typhus, shipboard, 47

Umlaut, German letters with, 10
unemployment, as push factor, 13
Union Army, 78–79, 81, 104
Union Stock Yards, Chicago, 56–57, 60
United States Immigration Commission, 109
upper class, 58, 85, 107
urbanization and urban centers: city life, 57–62, 62*f*; community verticalization and, 111; German immigrants to, 54; Gilded Age and, 82. *See also* Chicago; industrialization

Val Blatz Brewing Company, 73
van der Rohe, Ludwig Mies, 135–36

verticalization theory, shift from German to English and, 111
Der Vorbote (The Harbinger), 84
voting, 76–77, 82, 125, 164n9, 168n6 ("Lincoln"). *See also* suffrage laws
vowels, German pronunciation of, 10

Wacker, Charles, 136
Wagner, Jacob, farm owned by, 49*f*
Walker, Mack, 15
War of 1812, Military Tract for veterans of, 26
Warren, Roland, 111
"Watch Your Speech Pledge," 129–30, 130*f*
Waukegan, Illinois, industries in, 56
Western Brewer, 74
Western Wheel Works, 63–66
Westphalia, Saxony, 25, 96
West Side (Wards 6 and 7), Chicago, 28, 59, 60
Whig Party, 31, 168n3 ("Lincoln")
Wilhelm II, Kaiser, 115, 118
Wilson, Woodrow, 116, 118, 133, 177n10
Wisconsin, German effects on English in, 145–46, 188nn3–4
Wittke, Carl, 100
women: American, German immigrants on, 50–51; famine and inflation (1816–1817) in, 21; German, census on roles and jobs for, 53; in German farm families, 52, 159n11; small businesses of North Side, Chicago and, 58; voting rights for, 89, 101. *See also* families, German
working class: beer halls and, 172n57; "Bill Swerski's Superfans" skit and, 145; Chicago neighborhoods of, 58–59; Chicago's industrialization and, 26; community picnics and, 107; German capitalist class and, 61; German culture and, 107–8; German immigrants' rise from, 62; labor unions and, 83; left-wing radicalism and, 82; socialist newspapers read by, 84; Turner societies and, 103, 104; as unskilled laborers or farmers, 57. See also *Als Arbiter in Amerika*
working conditions: bicycle factory, 63–66, 163nn3–5; brewery, 66–71; German press on, 101. *See also* industrialization
Workingmen's Party, 166–67n35
World War I: anti-German fervor and, 111; German agents sabotaging arms supplies for Allies, 116–17; German immigrants to U.S. and, 126*f*; German press and, 101; integration and Americanization efforts and, 5; Prager hanging, 131–33; tension for German Americans before, 114
World War II, 11, 183n87
writing, old German script vs. English cursive, 99
Württemberg, famine and inflation, 12
Wyman, Mark, 25

Yankee Dutchmen under Fire: Civil War Letters from the 82nd Illinois Infantry, 80–81
Yankees. *See* Anglo-Americans
yeoman farmer tradition, 160nn20–21
Yiddish language, Hasidic Jews and, 113

Miranda E. Wilkerson is an associate professor at Columbia College in Columbia, Missouri. She has published articles in the *Journal of English Linguistics*, *Journal of Transnational American Studies*, *Die Unterrichtspraxis/Teaching German*, and *American Speech*, among other outlets.

Heather Richmond is a certified archivist at the State Historical Society of Missouri in Columbia, where she catalogs manuscript collections and provides opportunities for the public to interact with historical sources in person and online.